An
Unmastered
Past

Edited with
an Introduction
by Martin Jay

An
Unmastered
Past

The Autobiographical
Reflections of
Leo Lowenthal

University of California Press

Berkeley   Los Angeles   London

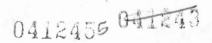

University of California Press
Berkeley and Los Angeles, California

University of California Press, Ltd.
London, England

© 1987 by
The Regents of the University of California

Library of Congress Cataloging-in-Publication Data

An unmastered past.
    Includes bibliographical references and index.
    1. Lowenthal, Leo.   2. Sociologists—United States—
Biography.   I. Jay, Martin, 1944–
HM22.U6L698   1987   301′.092′4   86–24942
ISBN 0–520–05638–8 (alk. paper)

Printed in the United States of America

1   2   3   4   5   6   7   8   9

For Susanne

Contents

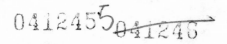

    Illustrations follow page 150

Acknowledgments

Of all of the chronically undersung heroes of intellectual production, two deserve special mention for making this volume possible: the interviewers and the translators. Posing evocative questions is almost as challenging a task as answering them, and so it is gratifying to acknowledge how well served Leo Lowenthal has been by his several interlocutors: Peter Glotz, W. Martin Lüdke, Emilio Galli Zugaro, and, most notably, Helmut Dubiel. The translators who worked hard to retain the spark of Lowenthal's conversation as well as the grace of his written prose merit no less praise: David Berger, Benjamin Gregg, David J. Parent, David J. Ward, Sabine Wilke, and especially Ted R. Weeks.

It is a genuine pleasure to acknowledge the enthusiasm and cooperation of the publishing houses that allowed this venture to succeed. James Clark of the University of California Press has been a strong supporter from its inception and has placed it in the capable editorial hands of Naomi Schneider, Laird Easton, Mary Renaud, and Anne Geissman Canright. The publishers of Lowenthal's collected works, the Suhrkamp Verlag in Germany, led by Siegfried Unseld, and Transaction Books in America, directed by Irving Louis Horowitz, have also been generously helpful. The journals in which several of Lowenthal's interviews and essays first appeared or were first translated also deserve a word of thanks: *Frankfurter Rundschau, New German Critique, Die Neue Gesellschaft/Frankfurter*

Hefte, The Philosophical Forum, and *Telos.* I would also like to express my appreciation to Jürgen Habermas for kindly permitting the republication of his birthday felicitation and to Donald Reneau for preparing the index.

Finally, two people deserve special recognition. Catherine Gallagher, my wife, has been involved in the project from the beginning; her contribution reflects not only her constant support of my work but also her deep affection for its subject. It is, however, Susanne Hoppmann-Lowenthal, to whom *An Unmastered Past* has been dedicated, who deserves the most gratitude. Deeply engaged in virtually all aspects of the project, from checking the translations to selecting the pictures, she has sustained this book with the same animating vigor that has enlivened its hero during their decade together. Like Figaro in Mozart's opera, Leo had to hold off until the last act to win his Susanne; in both cases, it was well worth the wait.

Martin Jay
Berkeley, October 1986

Introduction

BY MARTIN JAY

To anyone familiar with the history of postwar Germany, the phrase "unmastered past" (*unbewältigte Vergangenheit*) will have an ominous ring, for it has been widely used to signify the unwillingness of German society to confront head-on the full implications of the terrible events of the period 1933–1945. Not only does this refusal imply a failure to acknowledge the real extent of the horror, but it also, and even more disturbingly, reflects a reluctance to probe the still-potent links between the Nazi regime and the two inheritor states that succeeded it.[1] By positing the end of the war as a *Stunde Null* or *Nullpunkt,* a moment of absolute beginning, German society displayed a blindness to the subterranean continuities in its recent history. In contrast, another concept, drawn primarily from psychoanalysis, has often been used to indicate a healthier alternative: the *Aufarbeitung der Vergangenheit,* or "working through of the past." Only a kind of collective anamnesis combined with a

---

1. The precise nature of the continuities is, of course, different in the two cases. Broadly speaking, the Federal Republic has changed its political system more than its social or economic one, whereas the German Democratic Republic did the reverse. In both countries, self-congratulation about the changes that did occur has often been used to forestall discussion about those that did not.

ruthless emotional self-examination could provide a partial release from the trauma, whose effects, to be sure, will never be entirely undone.

In recent years, it has at times seemed as though Germany, at least the Federal Republic, was moving in this second direction—for example, in the wake of the extraordinary national debate sparked by the television series on the Holocaust in 1979.[2] But as the sordid fiasco of Bitburg six years later sadly demonstrates, the yearning to turn the page on Nazism rather than really work it through is still strong. It is thus difficult to gainsay the sober judgment of the historian Hans Mommsen, made even before Kohl and Reagan placed fallen SS men on the same plane with their victims, that "the burden of the Nazi past has not been lightened . . . the historical consequences of the 'Thousand Year Reich' have not been resolved."[3]

To anyone conversant with the role of the Frankfurt School after its postwar return to Germany, the phrase "unmastered past" will resonate with special meaning, for Max Horkheimer, Friedrich Pollock, Theodor Adorno, and new colleagues such as Alexander Mitscherlich were among the most outspoken critics of the Federal Republic's failure to work through its recent past. As early as Horkheimer's 1950 essay on the debacle of denazification,[4] through Adorno's widely discussed ruminations in "What Does 'Working Through the Past' Mean" and "Education After Auschwitz" in the

2. See the discussion of the reception of the series in Anson Rabinbach and Jack Zipes, eds., *Germans and Jews Since the Holocaust: The Changing Situation in West Germany* (New York, 1986).

3. Hans Mommsen, "The Burden of the Past," in *Observations on "The Spiritual Situation of the Age,"* ed. Jürgen Habermas, trans. Andrew Buchwalter (Cambridge, Mass., 1984), p. 263.

4. Max Horkheimer, "Lehren aus dem Faschismus," in *Gesammelte Schriften,* vol. 8, ed. Gunzelin Schmid Noerr (Frankfurt am Main, 1985).

1960s,[5] and up to Jürgen Habermas's angry evaluation of Bitburg and denunciation of historical revisionism,[6] these critics resolutely challenged Germany to confront rather than repress its unhappy history.

Ironically, there is another sense in which the Frankfurt School can be linked to the concept of an "unmastered past." When Horkheimer and his colleagues returned to Frankfurt to reestablish their Institute of Social Research, they were deeply ambivalent about the more explicitly Marxist aspects of their earlier work. Their journal, the *Zeitschrift für Sozialforschung,* in which many of their most explosive writings first appeared, was kept, so Habermas later revealed, "in a crate in the Institute's cellar, nailed shut and out of our grasp."[7] Horkheimer stubbornly refused to allow the republication of many of his earlier works, several of which were already fueling the radical student movements of the 1960s in pirated editions. When he finally agreed to the appearance of a limited selection,[8] it was only with a warning added to forestall the improper use of

5. Theodor W. Adorno, "Was bedeutet: Aufarbeitung der Vergangenheit" and "Erziehung nach Auschwitz," in *Gesammelte Schriften,* vol. 10, pt. 2 (Frankfurt am Main, 1977).

6. Jürgen Habermas, "Entsorgung der Vergangenheit," in *Die Neue Unübersichtlichkeit* (Frankfurt am Main, 1985). Habermas's title is taken from Helmut Dubiel and G. Frankenberg, who coined the phrase to refer to a widely discussed talk by Hermann Lübbe designed to "remove concern" (*entsorgen*) about the past. His critique of recent historical revisionism appears in "Eine Art Schadensabwicklung: Die apologetischen Tendenzen in der deutschen Zeitgeschichtsschreibung," *Die Zeit,* July 11, 1986.

7. Jürgen Habermas, "The Inimitable *Zeitschrift für Sozialforschung*: How Horkheimer Took Advantage of a Historically Oppressive Hour," *Telos,* no. 45 (Fall 1980), p. 116.

8. Max Horkheimer, *Kritische Theorie,* 2 vols. (Frankfurt am Main, 1968).

obsolete ideas for contemporary purposes. However one may judge the reasons for this timidity—certain aspects of the Institute's earlier work were in fact outdated—it struck many observers as an embarrassment that the Institute should be so secretive about its own roots at a time when it was loudly urging Germany to be forthright in dealing with the recent past.

With all of this baggage attached to the term "unmastered past," it may seem curious to adopt it as the title of a collection of autobiographical reflections by a leading figure of the Frankfurt School. And yet, in the case of Leo Lowenthal, the choice is appropriate for a number of compelling reasons. First, Lowenthal's own personal history as an exile hounded out of Germany in 1933 needs no compensatory "working through." The traumas he suffered—the loss of friends and family, the disruption of one career and the uncertain beginning of another—require no long overdue day of reckoning; contrary to the undiscriminating spirit of Bitburg, there are still differences between the ways in which victims and victimizers should confront the past. Second, of all the members of the Frankfurt School's original inner circle, with the salient exception of Herbert Marcuse, Lowenthal has remained defiantly and proudly committed to the initial impulses of Critical Theory. Although he by no means slavishly defends every nuance of the school's earliest positions, he has nonetheless kept faith with its radical, even utopian, spirit. And yet, he has done so with a remarkably sober dose of realism, which has given all of his work a balance and measure sometimes absent from that of his erstwhile colleagues. As Habermas noted in an appreciation of the *Zeitschrift* and Lowenthal's role in its publication, he can be seen as offering an alternative to the alarmist reactions of Adorno and Marcuse to the disillusioning implications of the "dialectic of enlightenment":

> While Marcuse relegated reason's historically darkened claim below the threshold of culture by a theory of instincts,

Adorno set his empty hope on the solitary exercise of a self-negating philosophy. Lowenthal, who was overshadowed by the other two, represented a third possibility: one can object to the accusatory thesis of the end of reason without having to choose between metaphysics on the one hand and one of the fashionable or scientifically promoted forms of the liquidation of reason on the other.[9]

That Habermas himself identifies more closely with this third position is evident in the warm praise he bestowed on Lowenthal in the eightieth-birthday tribute included in the expanded German edition of his *Philosophical-Political Profiles,* which is translated here as a fitting preface to Lowenthal's own autobiographical recollections.

Leo Lowenthal's past remains unmastered in one other sense as well. As is readily apparent in the remarkable intellectual, emotional, and even physical vigor he still displays well past his eighty-sixth birthday, Lowenthal remains very much an active participant in the world of today. Symptomatically, his most recent interview, given while at the Wissenschaftskolleg in Berlin in 1985, reveals his current preoccupation with no less a phenomenon of our time than postmodernism. In other words, Lowenthal has resolutely resisted turning himself into a Jungian "wise old man" who totalizes his past into a harmonious pattern. Refusing to arrive at Erikson's eighth stage, where one must choose between ego integrity or despair, wisdom or renunciation, he manages instead to move playfully through virtually all the other seven stages. In this sense, his past is not mastered but rather remains a potent force in his present, very active life.

As the last surviving member of the original Institute circle, Lowenthal has, to be sure, been compelled to serve as a representative of its past, both as its spokesman and as the recipient of the

9. Habermas, "The Inimitable *Zeitschrift für Sozialforschung,*" p. 121.

honors it has increasingly accumulated. Indeed, whenever he has been the object of personal tributes, Lowenthal, at once flattered and embarrassed by the attention, has made it a point to acknowledge the collaborative contributions of his former colleagues. In 1980 *Telos* published a festschrift to commemorate his eightieth birthday, and the publishing house Suhrkamp began to reissue his works in a collected edition.[10] In 1982 in the Paulskirche in Frankfurt, Lowenthal delivered the main address at the celebration honoring the 150th anniversary of Goethe's death;[11] he was then awarded the State of Hesse's Goethe Medal. In 1984 the University of California gave him the Berkeley Citation, that campus's highest honor, and the translation into English of his collected works was launched by Transaction Press. In 1985 he received an honorary degree from the University of Siegen, only the second in that young institution's history. Shortly thereafter, the president of the Federal Republic, Richard von Weizsäcker, bestowed on him the Distinguished Service Cross (Großes Bundesverdienstkreuz), and Stanford University dedicated a conference entitled "Literature, Culture, and Social Theory" to him. And in 1986 the Free University of Berlin granted him a second honorary degree.

Of even greater significance than these honors has been Lowenthal's willingness to give interviews about his career and to comment on those of other Institute figures. In 1979 he spoke at the Adorno conference at the University of Southern California;[12] three years later he addressed the Frankfurt colloquium on Walter

10. Appearing in *Telos,* no. 45 (Fall 1980), the festschrift included essays by David Gross, W. Martin Lüdke, Robert Sayre, and Ferenc Fehér and Agnes Heller, as well as the piece by Habermas cited above and my short introduction.

11. The talk has appeared as "Goethe und die falsche Subjektivität," in Leo Lowenthal, *Schriften,* vol. 4 (Frankfurt am Main, 1984).

12. Most of the talks, including Lowenthal's, are published in *Humanities in Society* 2, no. 4 (Fall 1979).

Benjamin, and in the following year he returned to that city to give an informal presentation at the massive conference honoring Adorno on what would have been Adorno's eightieth birthday.[13] And in 1985 Lowenthal spoke in Paris at the international conference on the centenaries of Ernst Bloch and Georg Lukács, both of whom played important roles as stimuli and foils for the development of Critical Theory.

In addition, Lowenthal has willingly served as a resource for many younger students of the history of the Frankfurt School. My own forays into this territory have been helped immeasurably by his guidance and critical judgment. When German scholars began in the mid-1970s to interest themselves in the origins of Critical Theory, Lowenthal was no less generous with his time and materials. Interviews conducted by W. Martin Lüdke, Matthias Greffrath, Rainer Erd, Peter Glotz, and, most notably, Helmut Dubiel soon made available in German a broad spectrum of Lowenthal's autobiographical reflections,[14] which no future history of the Frankfurt School, indeed of the intellectual migration to America as a whole, can afford to ignore.

It is therefore especially gratifying to be able now to present the most important of these reflections to an English-speaking audi-

13. Ludwig von Friedeburg and Jürgen Habermas, eds., *Adorno-Konferenz 1983* (Frankfurt am Main, 1983). Lowenthal's talk was given to the reception hosted by Suhrkamp Verlag after the official conference proceedings were concluded.

14. The interviews not included in this volume, essentially because they repeat material covered elsewhere, can be found in Lowenthal's *Schriften,* vol. 4 (Matthias Greffrath's "Wir haben nie im Leben diesen Ruhm erwartet" is also available in his collection *Die Zerstörung einer Zukunft; Gespräche mit emigrierten Sozialwissenschaftlern* [Hamburg, 1979]). See also the recent full-length study of Lowenthal's career by Michael Kausch, *Erziehung und Unterhaltung: Leo Löwenthals Theorie der Massenkommunikation* (Göttingen, 1985).

ence. Those who have been personally touched by Leo Lowenthal during his more than fifty years in America will recognize the remarkable personality revealed in these pages, a personality made especially vivid by the conversational form of the interviews. Those who have known him only through his publications or his reputation as a leading Frankfurt School figure will have a unique opportunity to glimpse the extraordinary man behind the texts. Here a life well lived has been transformed into a story well told. Here an unmastered past demonstrates how much it has to tell the present and future.

Leo Lowenthal—A Felicitation

BY JÜRGEN HABERMAS

A few days ago, Leo Lowenthal delivered a lecture at our Starnberg Institute, a sovereign retrospect of his own work in the sociology of literature. Listening to him, I realized that in the broad body of writings on the Frankfurt theory, only the most general aspects of this imposing lifework have been addressed, that the spotlight of public attention has neglected the details of an oeuvre that easily compares with the art-sociological studies of Lukács, Kracauer, and Adorno. Yet it is precisely these details that reveal the uniqueness of their author, a man who decoded the literary testimony of the bourgeois era as "obituaries of the socialization patterns of past centuries."

The first volume of Leo Lowenthal's collected works appears today. They offer the occasion and the incentive to raise his intellectual physiognomy into greater relief against the background of the Horkheimer circle, to which, in his productivity, he selflessly subordinated himself. Of course, such a goal cannot properly be the task of a short felicitation; it would require more serious efforts. I

Originally published as "Leo Löwenthal—Ein Glückwunsch," in Jürgen Habermas, *Philosophisch-politische Profile,* rev. ed. (Frankfurt am Main, 1981), pp. 426–31. Translated by Benjamin Gregg.

should merely like to express my hope that a qualified person will be found as soon as possible, someone able to assume, with the appropriate judgment, a task as provocative as it is laudable.

For my part, dear Leo, I would like to address myself to a characteristic you share with your friends, a mentality that distinguishes you and your friends not only from most American intellectuals but also from those in postwar Germany. I mean that characteristic imperturbability that enables you and your friends to make value judgments from a theoretical stance. Social scientists and philosophers today lack the courage to do this—and the good conscience as well. Does this make you dogmatists, or the others defeatists?

Recently in Starnberg you encountered something you've experienced time and again. In your lecture you claimed—as always, with great self-confidence—the scholar's right, and ability, to distinguish between literature as art with a cognitive content and the kind of trivial literature that can only be a consumer good, a commodity, a means of ideological manipulation. During the discussion, someone accused you of elitism; in pretended innocence, of course, you responded, "What, I ask you, is so wrong with elites when they possess a trained faculty of judgment?" In one respect, however, I would say that your innocence is real: you would, if you knew of them, find the most recent West German efforts to regenerate the ideologically exhausted concept of the elite to be indefensible. Indeed, something else is the issue here.

The attitude you so impressively embody reveals a problem beyond the cognitive status of considered, theoretically significant value judgments, a problem that can be dismissed only with positivistic naïveté. With all due respect to methodological fallibility, isn't the trustworthiness of the valuating judgment also a function of the well-founded self-assurance of those who make it?

One finds incidentally many examples of this self-assured mentality in your conversations with Helmut Dubiel: "We had not abandoned praxis, rather, praxis had abandoned us";[1] "If I may put it arrogantly, I never abandoned politics and the revolution; rather, the revolution abandoned me."[2] This was also the orientation of Horkheimer, Marcuse, and Adorno, who always disputed the claim that theory is immediately falsifiable by a bad reality to which theory always wants to hold up a mirror. While this contention sounds outrageous to respectable scholars, it is self-evident for a theory that has both descriptive and normative concerns. The question is really one of the *kind* of normative certitudes, of the *manner* in which they are ascertained. The following profession inimitably expresses this attitude: "My first years [at the Institute] were a sort of anticipated utopia; *we were different, and we knew the world better.*"[3]

I can already see the critics pouncing on this declaration with glee, dismissing it as dogmatic self-conceit, as the attitude typical of German mandarins. Although I, too, have imputed such an attitude to this bearing, so serious a matter cannot be that swiftly reduced to the merely psychological.

Of course, it is not entirely misguided to presume that the venerable German *Gymnasium* was responsible for such value judgments, which today are no longer self-evident. The eighty-year-old Lowenthal apparently recognizes only *one* authority unconditionally, that of his teachers at the Goethe Gymnasium in Frankfurt in 1918: "They were so good that some of them became honorary professors at the university."[4] And to this day Lowenthal is haunted by the lingering suspicion that he sustained, even into old age, lasting injuries to his educational formation when, before complet-

---

1. Leo Löwenthal, *Mitmachen wollte ich nie: Ein autobiographisches Gespräch mit Helmut Dubiel* (Frankfurt am Main, 1980), p. 79.
2. Ibid., p. 226.
3. Ibid., p. 75.
4. Ibid., p. 51.

ing secondary school, he had to move to Hanau to start military service. Nonetheless, such reminiscences do not capture the attitude of "we were different, we knew it better."

Somewhat more instructive is the situation in New York in the 1930s, when the Horkheimer group decided to continue the *Zeitschrift für Sozialforschung* in German in the conviction that the "German language is better preserved within the small circle of the Institute than in the Third Reich."[5] Such a decision was not self-evident: it meant that these scholars had to cut themselves off from American scholarship, from the culture of their immediate environment. Indeed, it was possible only thanks to an economic independence unique for emigrants. Thus, this reaffirmation of an identity bound up exclusively with German traditions must have required an already deep certitude in fundamental values.

However, value judgments made from a theoretical stance eventually become ruptured and turn into rigid dogmatism if their validity is not also confirmed by the very critique those judgments guide. But this confirmation was realized. Did not Horkheimer, Pollock, and Lowenthal see coming, as early as 1930, the catastrophe of 1933? Did not Lowenthal already in 1937 decipher in Hamsun's work the character Hamsun was to confirm through his actions in 1940? Anyone familiar with the difficulties of social-scientific prognoses will be scarcely inclined to gainsay the analytical power of a theory that can pride itself on such achievements.

But now we have left behind the contingent circumstances of that certain characteristic of the Frankfurt circle's mentality that is open to the charge of dogmatism. Instead, a new question poses itself: might not the older school, with its value judgments, be right after all? Let me briefly return to the example with which I started.

When Lowenthal believes himself capable of distinguishing be-

5. Max Horkheimer, *Kritische Theorie,* 2 vols. (Frankfurt am Main, 1968), 1:xvi.

tween literature as art and literature as mass culture—and this despite all the homogenizing tendencies of the surrealist and postsur-
realist movements, and in the face of the fashionable revalorization
of the trivial and the kitschy—he is not traveling the usual trajecto-
ries of *Kulturkritik;* rather, he is allowing himself to be guided by a
precise intuition. Lowenthal seeks in art the message of the socially
unredeemed: "Art is in fact the great reservoir of creative protest
against social misery, which allows the prospect of social happiness
dimly to shine through."[6] Yet when the tenacious protest of the
losers, of the marginalized, of those passed over by world history,
announces itself in a work of art, then it becomes possible to identify what does *not* belong to art. Mass culture is everything that does
not belong to art. Mass culture is the preservation of the status quo:
"In Hamsun even the minor characters are scoundrels; there is absolutely no redemptive phenomenon, no assertion anywhere that
things could and should be different. And that was a touchstone for
me to use in distinguishing between what is and what is not genuine
art."[7]

Your interest in the case of the loser, dear Leo, expresses a partisanship that you recognize with great objectivity. A value judgment owes its analytically illuminating power to its objectivity.
That's why I've always been impressed by your remarks about
Franz von Baader, about whom you wrote your dissertation: that
Baader, too, was a loser, since in Germany there was never a true
restoration philosophy, any more than there was ever a politically
emancipated enlightenment.

I've dwelt on a characteristic trait of the older Frankfurt generation's way of thinking only because Leo combines this sometimes
irritating imperturbability with a completely different trait, one
that distinguishes him from his friends. So great is Leo's charm in

6. Löwenthal, *Mitmachen wollte ich nie,* p. 175.
7. Ibid., p. 176.

being always ready to place himself in question, so great, so natural is his humility, that within his circle of friends he is in fact the only one who can allow himself to display that methodologically motivated judgmental arrogance without being misunderstood. This infinitely charming trait may also explain why Leo Lowenthal has, more than the others, opened himself to his American environment, to empirical research and the analytical style of thought; why he alone of the older Frankfurt group, without being a pragmatist, has not denied his respect to America's great philosophy, from Peirce to George Herbert Mead; why he has occupied for a quarter of a century, and with extraordinary success, a professorship in one of America's leading sociology departments; why he was the one who in the decisive years managed the affairs of the Institute of Social Research, who not only edited the *Zeitschrift für Sozialforschung* but, even more important, assumed the management of a review section that subsequently attained historical significance. As recently as a few days ago, however, Hans Mayer characterized and misconstrued these achievements of a managing editor of the *Zeitschrift für Sozialforschung* as those of an "editorial secretary"— perhaps this actually says more about the unobtrusive style of the man we celebrate today.[8]

8. *Die Zeit,* November 1, 1980.

Part I

I Never Wanted to Play Along: Interviews with Helmut Dubiel

1

The Weimar Republic

Dubiel: There's a conventional method of interpreting the biographies of left-wing intellectuals. The resistance to the *Weltanschauung* transmitted by paternal authority is explained psychoanalytically by the Oedipus complex. Does this fit in your case?

Lowenthal: Actually, my complicated relationship with Judaism is a classic illustration of the Oedipus complex. My grandfather on my father's side was a strict orthodox Jew who taught at a Jewish school in Frankfurt. This school, the Samson Raphael Hirsch Schule, was named after the founder of German-Jewish Orthodoxy. He also ran a boarding school where orthodox families from all over Germany sent their sons. Here the parents could be sure that the kosher laws would be strictly observed and that the boys would lead the life of pious Jews in accordance with the religious precepts. But my father took exception, and this really did have an oedipal significance.

Dubiel: So your father rebelled against your orthodox grandfather?

Lowenthal: My father wanted to be a lawyer. But my grand-

This chapter and the four that follow, collectively entitled *I Never Wanted to Play Along,* were originally published as Leo Löwenthal, *Mitmachen wollte ich nie: Ein autobiographisches Gespräch mit Helmut Dubiel* (Frankfurt am Main, 1980). Chapter 1 translated by Ted R. Weeks.

father—according to my father, at least—refused to grant him permission because he thought this would mean that my father would have to work and write on the Sabbath. Consequently, he prevailed on my father to study medicine, which my father did, though his heart wasn't in it at all. But then he took his revenge—either consciously or unconsciously—when he later became totally "free": not just irreligious, but decidedly antireligious. He was a convinced adherent of the nineteenth century in the sense of a mechanistic-materialistic, positivist way of thinking. My first "serious" readings were from Darwin, Haeckel, and a popular philosopher of the Darwinist school, Carneri. My father encouraged me to read Schopenhauer. In short, the whole atmosphere at home was secular, enlightened, and antireligious. I hardly knew anything about Judaism, for example about Jewish holidays—with the exception of Yom Kippur, when we had a particularly good dinner at home because a cousin of my father's, who didn't "live religiously" but lived in a kosher-run boarding house, did not get anything to eat on that day. I still remember when they divided us up for religious instruction in sixth grade. When the teacher told the Protestants to gather in one part of the classroom, the Catholics in another, and the Jews in a third, I remained seated—I really didn't know what religion I belonged to!

Dubiel: Later in your life that changed considerably for a time, in the form of an "about-face," a return to Judaism. Not in the sense of a religious renewal, but rather as a political identity mediated through Jewish tradition. Can it be put this way?

Lowenthal: Well, it didn't happen quite so quickly. At first the Jewish element was introduced very indirectly. Through the influence of Luise Habricht, an older educator and close friend of Walter Kinkel, a professor of philosophy at the University of Giessen, I became involved with the Marburg neo-Kantian school and consequently with Hermann Cohen. Although Hermann Cohen was a

liberal Jew, he nonetheless had a very intense relation to Judaism
and to Jewish religious philosophy, which was imparted to me
through exchanges with various intellectual friends I had at that
time. But at first that was still very abstract. This changed when I
began my studies at Heidelberg in 1920 and joined certain groups of
Zionist and socialist students. At that time, Zionist students were
politically on the left. They stood in direct opposition to the KC
[Kartell-Convent der Verbindungen Deutscher Studenten Jüdi-
schen Glaubens; Syndicate of Organizations of German Students
of the Jewish Faith], the assimilationist student organization,
which was an offshoot of the Central Association of German Citizens of Jewish Faith [Zentralverein Deutscher Staatsbürger Jüd-
ischen Glaubens]. I hated the latter because I saw them as fellow
travelers of German nationalism.

   Dubiel: The term "assimilationist," then, refers to those Jews
who believed in total integration into the German nation?

   Lowenthal: Yes, but only now do I realize what I hated about
that assimilationist group. Not that they as Jews wanted to be human beings like everyone else, but that their convictions were essentially capitalist. It was most likely the socialist-revolutionary
factor that caused me to cast my lot with the Zionist students,
whom I generally liked as individuals. It's also characteristic that in
1923 I married a woman from Königsberg who came from a relatively orthodox Jewish family. A sort of Jewish cult was forming
around the charismatic Rabbi N. A. Nobel in the circles I was involved with in Frankfurt and Heidelberg. He wasn't technically
orthodox, but conservative and well-educated in philosophy. He
attracted a following of many young—but not only young—talented Jews. Under the influence of this Jewish atmosphere, which
also contained some philosophy, socialism, and even a little mysticism, there developed in my young wife and me the desire to live a
conscious Jewish life. She was already a Zionist (as was the rest of

her family); I myself was amiably disposed toward Zionism, but only half-heartedly. I can come back to that later. We decided to keep a kosher Jewish household, to go to synagogue, and to observe Jewish holidays. Of course, this had a catastrophic effect on my father, who took an immediate dislike to my wife because she came from Königsberg (for him, that was Russia!)—he automatically considered any Jews who lived east of the Elbe *Ostjuden,* which was quite absurd, of course. But he didn't like any of this Jewish atmosphere, and when we began to keep a kosher house—I still remember it very well—he broke out in tears of anger. It was a terrible disappointment for him that his son, whom he, the father, the true scion of the enlightenment, had raised so "progressively," was now being pulled into the "nonsensical," "obscure," and "deceitful" clutches of a positive religion. Well, the kosher household didn't last very long, but the relationship to Judaism and to Jewish questions and issues remained central in my life for quite some time. You know that my first publications were essentially concerned with Jewish problems. The very first is an essay, published in a Jewish student journal, on Jakob Wassermann's book *My Life as German and Jew*.

Dubiel: In the early twenties you engaged in political, pedagogical, and organizational activities that illuminate your relationship to Judaism at that time. I'm thinking first of all about the circle around Rabbi Nobel, then about your work on the Advisory Board for Jewish Refugees from Eastern Europe [Beratungsstelle für Ostjüdische Flüchtlinge], and finally about your work together with Ernst Simon on a Jewish weekly. Who actually belonged to the Nobel circle?

Lowenthal: A few names: Martin Buber, Franz Rosenzweig, Siegfried Kracauer, Erich Fromm, Ernst Simon, and several others. The names of the most important members of this circle can be found among the contributors to a festschrift for Rabbi Nobel that appeared in 1921. These names convey a good impression of the sort of Jewish renaissance that developed around Nobel and that later found its institutional continuation in the Jüdische Lehrhaus.

Dubiel: There is always mention of "the circle around Rabbi Nobel." What was this actually, in more precise terms? In our sociological jargon, was it a loosely organized group of intellectuals [*Intellektuellenbund*], or was it some sort of cult or sect?

Lowenthal: In a certain sense it was a cult. This man was a rabbi, originally from Hungary, who had also studied philosophy. He knew Hermann Cohen and represented a curious mixture of mystical religiosity, philosophical rigor, and quite likely also a more or less repressed homosexual love for young men. It really was a kind of "cult community." He was a fascinating speaker. People flocked to hear his sermons. He kept his house open to all, and people would come and go as they pleased. Of course, that was a godsend, especially in the chaotic times after World War I. If I were to place this whole story about the Nobel circle in a broader context, namely that of my somehow politically motivated return to Jewish tradition, I would say that it was the Zionist, anti-assimilationist impulse that first motivated this new identification. Then came, encouraged by these groups, the acceptance of a Jewish style of life, and very soon thereafter, professional activity in Jewish organizations.

Dubiel: Before you talk about your work with the Advisory Board for Jewish Refugees from Eastern Europe, can you explain what the Jüdische Lehrhaus was?

Lowenthal: Well, the Jüdische Lehrhaus in Frankfurt was a kind of Jewish center for adult education [*Volkshochschule*]: its spiritual fathers were Franz Rosenzweig and Martin Buber. The Lehrhaus also saw itself as a secularized form of Jewish-Talmudic doctrine. Today I can't even say whether all the lectures there concerned Jewish themes. I myself can remember having given a few lectures on Buddhism. Martin Buber lectured there, Ernst Simon, and others. Franz Rosenzweig was already too ill to actually take part in the lectures. The Jüdische Lehrhaus in Frankfurt remained in operation until the Nazis came to power in 1933.[1] My association with it became progressively looser in the late twenties. For that reason I can't give any reliable information about its later development.

Dubiel: Perhaps you could talk about your work with the Jewish social welfare agency.

Lowenthal: Yes, my job with the Advisory Board for Jewish Refugees from Eastern Europe—I got this job through my friend Ernst Simon, who was very influential in Jewish circles in Frankfurt. I had the pompous title of *Syndikus* [trustee] of this advisory board. It was also a quasi-juridical position. The board's main purpose was the following: as a consequence of the upheavals of the war and the postwar period, progressively more Jews were coming to the West—not just from Russia but also from Poland and from the Polish areas of Upper Silesia. Most likely they left partly because of manifestations of anti-Semitism there and partly because they hoped for a better life in the West. So, there was a great exodus of mostly illegal emigrants. These people—often naïve to the point of simplicity—generally arrived without papers, without a passport or identity documents. They wanted to settle in Germany and work there, which was in most cases impossible, although we did manage, a number of times, to find them—especially the younger people—jobs as apprentices to merchants or artisans. Mainly, however, we had to try to get these people to France, a country that, as you know, was traditionally more open to refugees than Germany. But we often had to try to obtain at least temporary residency permits in Frankfurt for our clients. On the one hand, I had to see that money was at our disposal; on the other, I had to deal with local authorities, especially with police headquarters and the head official in the alien registration office. That was very interesting. I remember this gen-

---

1. The Lehrhaus was revived in November 1933 and remained open until 1938.

tleman perfectly. His name was Polizeirat Schmidt, and he looked like Hindenburg. For some reason he took a great liking to me. We always had the best of relations. In general, whatever I requested, he approved. But I'm sure that good old Herr Polizeirat Schmidt didn't always act only out of goodwill, but also because he was obsessed with the anti-Semitic legend of the vast power of Jews, especially at that time in Frankfurt. This attitude, nourished by a deep-seated misconception, but very advantageous for us, functioned so well that I often had to make concessions; that is, I had to take less than he wanted to give, because otherwise his subordinates would certainly have created insurmountable difficulties.

Dubiel: Was this organization a local phenomenon limited to Frankfurt or a part of a wider net?

Lowenthal: It was part of a broad system. Its organizational support was the Jewish Workers' Welfare Office [Jüdisches Arbeiterfürsorgeamt] in Berlin. But the name—"Workers' Welfare"—shouldn't be taken too seriously for this Jewish organization. After all, there weren't many Jewish workers in Germany. Essentially we dealt with immigrant Jews from the East, and this had the effect, of course, that the Workers' Welfare Office wasn't a popular organization because nobody wanted to identify with Eastern Jews. The Jews who had lived in Germany for generations preferred to identify with the Germans. An especially characteristic phenomenon for this Jewish type of social help is the following: imagine that for some reason we wanted to send an individual or a family to Berlin, Hamburg, or Paris. The most obvious thing to do would have been to buy a train ticket for the destination, say, Berlin. Of course, this would have been possible only if there were a national Jewish parent organization that administered the monies of the individual Jewish communities in a national fund. But precisely this kind of fund didn't exist because all the small Jewish communities on the road wanted to contribute their own empirically identifiable bit of compassion. So, if I wanted to send the man to Berlin, I gave him a

ticket for, say, Kassel. The community in Kassel gave him another
ticket that got him to Hanover, in the welfare jurisdiction, so to
speak, of another Jewish community, and so on.

Dubiel: An interest in palpable, concrete charity to one's neigh-
bor, as it were, not in an abstract principle of charity that would be
paid into the central fund of a national organization.

Lowenthal: Yes, that is an expression of the Jewish tradition of
mitzvah, the duty to do good deeds. And they wanted to do these
good deeds in a concrete and palpable way. All my organizational
attempts with the Berlin branch to make funds centrally available
failed. But in spite of that, in many cases we did some good and
interesting work. As I said, sometimes we managed, especially for
the young Jewish emigrants from the East, to provide training and
occasionally a job as well. Many of them later emigrated to Palestine.

Dubiel: Before we go into the fundamental problematic of the
relationship between Jews and Germans, I'd like to hear something
about your work as editor at the *Jüdische Wochenzeitung* [Jewish
Weekly] with Ernst Simon. When was that, actually?

Lowenthal: Around 1925. Ernst is now a highly respected professor emeritus of pedagogy in Jerusalem.

Dubiel: Can it be said that this was a Zionist newspaper?

Lowenthal: Yes, I suppose it was a Zionist newspaper, but with
the quite naïve ambition of being an internationally known publication, which we of course weren't. We published our own and
others' articles about the international situation, especially on international problems and Jewish politics, a lot on cultural politics,
book and theater reviews. Above all, the newspaper was concerned
with specifically Jewish matters. It was a modest enterprise; financially it was never a success. I finally left because I increasingly
disagreed with its Zionist tendency. That is, inasmuch as I came to
see Zionism no longer as an oppositional movement but rather as a
short-sighted political reality, stripped of all messianic ideas and

robbed of its utopian elements—through this policy of settlements in Palestine. . . .

Dubiel: What was your stand on this policy?

Lowenthal: Negative, negative. It was my impression that the settlement policy carried out by the Zionist central organization was very inconsiderate toward the Arab population. At that time I wrote an article in our newspaper entitled, "The Lessons of China." I referred to contemporary events in China and wrote that dealings of these Jewish organizations with the rich Arab landowners would result in the creation of a great mass of discontented, landless Palestinian peasants and rural poor, a development that sooner or later would have negative consequences for the entire Zionist movement. As it turns out, I wasn't all wrong. After that I broke with the movement and stopped writing for the newspaper, particularly since I was by then starting with my own Marxist-oriented literary-sociological studies and on the verge of working for the Institute of Social Research.

Dubiel: If we were to draw up a kind of balance sheet for this period, could one say that this turn to Jewish tradition, aimed against your father, was less religiously motivated than . . . what should I call it . . . politically? Or is that putting it too narrowly?

Lowenthal: "Political" isn't the right word for it. I would simply say oppositional. I was a rebel, and everything that was then oppositional, that is, to quote Benjamin, on the side of the losers in world history, attracted me as if by magic. I was a socialist, a supporter of psychoanalysis and of phenomenology in neo-Kantian circles. I took a job that brought me in contact with Eastern European Jews, something that, for example, was extremely embarrassing for my father and for Adorno's. . . . It was nothing short of a syncretic accumulation in my brain and heart of aspirations, tendencies, and philosophies that stood in opposition to the status quo. I still vividly remember reading Lukács's *Theory of the Novel* and his indictment of "the infamy of the status quo." This formulation summed up my fundamental feelings—namely, to hate and reject as "infamous" all elements of the status quo. This was deeply rooted in me.

Dubiel: I'd like to shift from this group of questions to the problem of anti-Semitism.

Lowenthal: Perhaps I should quickly add one story that is very characteristic of this entanglement of intellectual and Jewish traditions, namely, the development of psychoanalysis during the Weimar Republic. Throughout Europe, but especially in Germany, Austria, and Switzerland, psychoanalysis was extraordinarily esoteric. I don't want to elaborate on that here. I first came into contact with psychoanalysis through Erich Fromm, a friend from student days. My then-marginal contact with the psychoanalytic movement was mediated through the relationship that developed between Erich Fromm and the woman who was later to become his wife, Frieda Reichmann. Frieda was a psychiatrist in a sanatorium near Dresden. In 1924, or maybe 1925, Frieda moved to Heidelberg, where she started a psychoanalytic treatment center. My wife Golde and I joined her and Erich Fromm there. The sanatorium was a kind of Jewish-psychoanalytic boarding school and hotel. An almost cultlike atmosphere prevailed there. Everyone, including me, was psychoanalyzed by Frieda Reichmann. The sanatorium adhered to Jewish religious laws: the meals were kosher, and all religious holidays were observed. The Judeo-religious atmosphere intermingled with the interest in psychoanalysis. Somehow, in my recollection I sometimes link this syncretic coupling of the Jewish and the psychoanalytic traditions with our later "marriage" of Marxist theory and psychoanalysis in the Institute, which was to play such a great role in my intellectual life.

Dubiel: Do you mean in particular Fromm's studies and essays on an analytic and materialistic social psychology?

Lowenthal: Yes.

Dubiel: Leo, I'd like to ask you a little about your own personal everyday experiences of anti-Semitism during this time. I'm reminded of two contradictory impressions. In conversations I've had with Marcuse, with Horkheimer, and with you, everyone emphasizes, even with a certain pride, that your group around the Institute of Social Research was able to foresee the disaster of 1933 because of an alert historical-political sense and relevant research. Both you and Marcuse have frequently told me that although you knew about the phenomenon of anti-Semitism, you were seldom directly victimized by it. You probably know Franz Neumann's radical thesis, that before Hitler's rise to power in 1933 the German population was the least anti-Semitic in all of Western Europe. How do these two facts fit together: on the one hand, the quite clear presentiment of the rising specter of national socialism, and on the other, this trivialization—I don't know what else to call it—of anti-Semitism in the late Weimar Republic?

Lowenthal: I've probably always overstated or understated this point. Let's just say it was generally very clear to me that I was a Jew. My parents' social circle was limited essentially to Jews. I can scarcely remember a non-Jewish friend of my father's. And later, my closest friends in school and at the university were almost all Jews.

Dubiel: When was the first time that you came physically into contact with anti-Semitism?

Lowenthal: Well, it was well known that in Wilhelmine Germany a Jew couldn't become an officer and that it was difficult to become a professor. But personally, we hardly experienced it at all. To answer your question, though, I remember Kiesstraße in Frankfurt, the street around the corner from where I lived. That was a "proletarian" street; workers lived there. And if you walked along Kiesstraße, you had to be pretty brave, because it could happen that one of those unfriendly young scamps would yell "Yid!" at you. That was actually the extent to which I had personal contact with anti-Semitism. We always noted with a certain amount of humor that there was a tiny hotel in Frankfurt—I've forgotten its name— that had a sign, "Jews not welcome" or "Jews not allowed." And there was a little spa, Borkum-bei-Norderney, that was "reserved" for anti-Semites. But we didn't take all that seriously. That was vulgar anti-Semitism. The people in Borkum or in that hotel in Frankfurt were pathetic repressed, petit-bourgeois nobodies.

Dubiel: At some point later that must have changed. At the end of the twenties, did anti-Semitic attacks become more noticeable in everyday life, commensurate with the growing strength of the National Socialist movement?

Lowenthal: Yes, there were people who acted more shamelessly. But these were isolated incidents. I'll tell you a few such episodes. In 1929, I think it was, I was with my friend Siegfried Kracauer in Oberstdorf in Bavaria. This area was particularly anti-Semitic—you know, it started very early in Bavaria. I remember once going through the dining room of our hotel with a cigarette. I asked someone for a light, and he said no. It was obvious that he didn't want to light a Jew's cigarette. The other episode I'm thinking of occurred at the annual Convention of Germanists; I believe it was 1931 in Munich. I went into one of the halls where a lecture was to take place later. Hardly anyone was there except Hans Naumann, a then well-known specialist in Old High German from Frankfurt. Later he became a leading Nazi in Bonn. At the end of the twenties Hans Naumann and I knew each other well; we were practically friends. He had tested me in my exam for my secondary teaching credential, and I remember him holding me up to his students as the example of a well-trained Germanist because I could translate the first stanza of the *Hildebrandslied* into all Franconian dialects! So, I amiably went up to Hans Naumann to shake his hand. Without offering me his hand he asked me, "Herr Löwenthal, where is the men's room here?" I turned right around and left him standing there. It was completely clear that he no longer wanted to have anything to do with Jews. And I have one more story. This was around the end of 1932, when it was already clear that the Nazis would come to power. I was telephoning the director of the city library about some matter concerning the Institute—I was then the acting head of the Institute, because the others were already in Geneva. I remember that he said on the phone, "Hello, Herr Löwenstein." I hung up immediately. He had known my name for five years, but suddenly all Jewish names were interchangeable. Such little things should perhaps be mentioned. They helped to call into question my notion of an apparently completely successful emancipation. Suddenly these little pinpricks signal that you're an outsider, that you're not accepted. At that time I was teaching at a *Gymnasium* and had some interesting discussions with one of my pupils there, a high school senior. His name was Friedrich, and he was a fervent Nazi. We would discuss politics quite openly together. I asked him once in jest, "Well, Friedrich, you'll see to it that nothing happens to me later, won't you?" For some reason, Friedrich had great respect for me even though he was an ardent anti-Semite. He answered, "No, that's out of the question. We have our principles. You're just as bad as all the others. That has nothing to do with my respect for you."

Dubiel: In view of these kinds of experiences, what do you think about Franz Neumann's statement that before 1933 the German population was the least anti-Semitic in Europe?

Lowenthal: Yes, I always said that, too. I think I even wrote that sentence somewhere. Now, your question regarding the extent of anti-Semitism and the predictability of fascism in the late twenties concerns two different things. We foresaw Hitler's rise to power not because we thought that the German people were becoming more and more anti-Semitic, but because through political analysis and insight we believed very early that the Nazis would come to power and that resistance was so poorly developed, particularly in the Liberal Democratic and the Social Democratic parties, that they wouldn't be capable of any great resistance against victorious fascism. Moreover, we grew increasingly disappointed and pessimistic, first independently from each other, and then in the political

exchange of opinions within our group, about the Soviet Union
and the international Communist movement. And then developments in the Weimar Republic made us more and more worried and
uneasy. Of course there was progressive literature and progressive
theater, but in the final analysis these were only futile fringe-
phenomena. No, precisely in cultural matters one could notice,
from the middle of the twenties on, that Germany was becoming
increasingly conservative, if not reactionary.

But back to anti-Semitism, *la vie quotidienne*. Well, then, in everyday life it really made no difference if one was a Jew or not. One
could go into practically any hotel, join almost any club. We always
laughed about the fact—precisely because it was such a phenomenon of the fringe—that the island Borkum didn't allow any Jews. I
only learned about a kind of anti-Semitism—that which made it
impossible for one to go to certain restaurants, hotels, or clubs—
here in America. To be sure, I had heard about this already in Germany, but I couldn't believe it. So, I came to America in 1934, and in
1935 I wanted to take a vacation with my wife for the first time. We
went for advice to a very elegant travel agency in Rockefeller Center. They gave me the addresses of some twenty hotels and resorts
to which I then wrote, always adding at the end, "Please tell me
whether Jews are welcome." I had been advised to do this by friends
who had already lived some time in America. Of these twenty
letters—and you have to keep in mind that this was 1935, at the high
point of the depression in America—at least half weren't answered
at all. Some of the others wrote that they generally rented to older
people, which was quite ridiculous, since I hadn't mentioned my
age at all. And others wrote that of course they had nothing against
Jews but that we might feel "uncomfortable" with their other
guests. So, in short, we suddenly discovered that something like a
real everyday anti-Semitism did exist here and that as a Jew one
couldn't freely take part in all social spheres. That was a nasty
disappointment. That hotels and clubs, even whole professions,

were simply closed to Jews—that didn't yet exist in Germany to such an extent. German anti-Semitism in relation to other European varieties of anti-Semitism is still an issue. Look, Jews were driven out of England, France, Spain, Portugal, Poland, Turkey, and who knows where else. That sort of thing was quite rare in Germany until Hitler came. To be sure, then he drove the Jews straight into the gas chambers.

Dubiel: As a former German and a Jew you have, so to speak, the moral right to speak about non-German types of anti-Semitism. Any gentile German who did that would expose himself to the suspicion of trying to relativize or to trivialize German anti-Semitism and its apocalyptic consequences. No German has the right to relativize Auschwitz. Do you actually see an essential difference between German anti-Semitism and that in other parts of Europe or in America? Was German anti-Semitism under Hitler just an extremely pronounced and artificially whipped up mass hysteria, used as an instrument by the Nazis?

Lowenthal: Now you're talking about the anti-Semitic atrocities committed under Hitler. Well, there are antecedents to that which reach back to before Hitler. Our friend Paul Massing wrote a good book about that.[2] Yes, there's a great difference, I believe. It's a bit difficult to answer the question conclusively, because my present formulations are based on methodologically different sources. What I have to say about German anti-Semitism is based on what I personally experienced. What I know about American anti-Semitism—I can't say anything verifiable about types of anti-Semitism in other European countries—is something for which I have my own theoretical and empirical experiences, also as a "participant observer." I would say that German anti-Semitism was derived from the feudal estate structure, which excluded certain groups from society. Thus, for example, a professorial career at a university

2. Paul Massing, *Rehearsal for Destruction* (New York, 1949).

was usually unattainable for Jews, as were the ranks in the bureaucracy and the military. Something like a latent institutional anti-Semitism existed there. But, as I've said, it was here in America that I first experienced an anti-Semitism that manifested itself in everyday life.

I have to expound some on this point. After all, it's a fascinating fact that in all known history there exists no single social or ethnic group that became so much the symbol of something perhaps extraordinarily admirable but also, and principally, detestable, as the Jews. It originated in Roman times and has never ended. How is this riddle to be solved? I consider anti-Semitism a perverted and suppressed form of utopia. The Jews represent something that others would like to be. Let's just go through the topoi of anti-Semitic prejudices: First, "clannishness." That can, after all, be interpreted as "community." Then second, the Jews live by exploiting others, that is, they themselves don't really work with their hands and by the sweat of their brow. Now, if you will, this refers to the elimination of heavy physical labor. Third, Jews love luxury, they're lascivious, they like good food, they throw their weight around in spas and summer resorts, they're loud, they're expressive. All of these "characteristically Jewish" modes of behavior can be summed up within the concept of a hedonistic life-style. Jews do things that are forbidden. Nobody knows exactly what they're really doing. They slaughter Christian children, rape Christian girls, they like to eat dill pickles, they eat kosher food, they have weird holidays during which nobody quite knows what happens, they carry around that strange Torah, they build huts out of tree branches, they play a trumpet. . . . In short, Jews know something about a life that is more than everyday life, and, because of this whole aggregate of unencumbered pleasure, they enjoy their lives fully; they know a freedom for which one doesn't have to pay continually, the obvious lack of a necessity to constantly battle with nature. For example, think about the Jewish joke, "The Jew doesn't belong in nature, the Jew belongs in the coffeehouse." Well then, that also means that one doesn't have to exert oneself so much. So—if Jews aren't heavy manual workers, or in heavy industry, either as workers, as businessmen, or as managers—so what do they do? Supposedly, they control the media, they control the so-called sphere of circulation, banks and so on, they control insurance companies—all areas where manipulation rather than physical labor is most important. The psychology of anti-Semitic reaction, of anti-Semitic rage, of anti-Semitic mass actions and outrages is connected with this. The fact is that all I've pointed out—the entire communications industry, banking, parts of the consumer industry—aren't the sources of actual social power; they don't represent strong political or military power. In short, anti-Semitism sees the Jews ultimately as a colossus of clay. It will suffice to give the Jews a little kick, as one might kick over a vase, and the whole thing will collapse. For that reason I consider the terrorist activities of 1948 in Palestine the worst blow to anti-Semitism: it demonstrated to the world for the first time that Jews, too, could commit violent acts. Of course, I'm exaggerating, but that way it's clearer: I support anything that destroys this anti-Semitic image of the Jew as a weakling, as castrated and effeminate.

Dubiel: Leo, I'd like you to talk about the formation of your political consciousness. Can one say that your father influenced you, either by recommending certain books to you or by his own political positions?

Lowenthal: Oh yes, one can certainly say that. My father was politically committed. He was a liberal democrat, a member of the Liberal People's Party [Freisinnige Volkspartei], later known as the Staatspartei, and was a great admirer of the formation of democratic parties in Germany. I have in mind such names as Eugen Richter, Ludwig Bamberger, and Friedrich Naumann. My father very much encouraged me to think in a politically liberal vein, and not nationalistically. He was such a dyed-in-the-wool democrat that he called me crazy when I told him that I was going to emigrate because of Hitler. He was firmly convinced that there would be new elections that would do away with the Hitler regime.

It was decisive for the development of my own political consciousness that from about the age of fifteen I was strongly influenced by a maternal friend named Luise Habricht. She was a socialist, a feminist, and a pacifist. She was extraordinarily well educated in philosophy and literature, and I'm very indebted to her. And this woman, the private tutor in a wealthy friend's house, "radicalized" me, so to speak. She was a socialist without being revolutionary. She was a pacifist and fought for women's suffrage. I would say that she was a radical reformist. It was quite impressive for a young person like me to be acquainted in the middle of the war with the works of the pacifist movement, which was naturally illegal at that time. The German Pacifist Association [Deutscher Friedensverein] and similar organizations couldn't carry out their work openly at that time. There was a representative in the Reichstag, Ludwig Quidde. He was a very brave man whom I met in Frankfurt through my friend Luise. I was proud when he entrusted me with the illegal and secret task of mailing leaflets.

Dubiel: That was perhaps your first practical political act. . . .

Lowenthal: Yes, I was fifteen or sixteen years old at that time. It was, in fact, my first political and at the same time "illegal" activity. It can't be said that this activity was particularly risky or dangerous. It was much more dangerous later, in 1920 in Frankfurt, to flee over rooftops from the police. Early, in school, my friends and I were predominantly liberal or socialist. I already told you that many of my classmates and most of my friends were Jews. In their parents' homes, too, the war was generally thought of very critically and openly discussed. We greeted the Russian Revolution in 1917 with enthusiasm. In school we secretly read antiwar novels by Henri Barbusse and Leonhard Frank.

Dubiel: Can you elaborate on that, please?

Lowenthal: I saw the Russian Revolution as an act of human liberation, not just politically but also culturally and philosophically. You understand, we saw it as a great democratic revolution, and continued for quite some time to see the Communist movement as a liberating democratic philosophy. I still remember the horrid five months I spent as a soldier in Hanau. I only knew one person there, a cousin of mine, and he was a member of the Spartakusbund.[3] At his place I felt at home.

Dubiel: Was the connection between developments in the Soviet Union and the politics of the Spartakusbund as close then as it was in the late twenties? Was the Spartakusbund already perceived as a sort of German branch of a Russian-dominated international movement?

Lowenthal: Well, not in the sense of being seen as a kind of Soviet envoy, which in the late twenties was more or less the case for the KPD [German Communist Party], which is why I finally lost all sympathy for the party. No, at that time it was a kind of brotherhood; in any case, I saw it that way.

Dubiel: Let's speak for a while about the postwar years.

Lowenthal: I became active in the socialist student movement. In Frankfurt I joined the General Student Parliament [Allgemeiner Studentenausschuß/ASTA] in 1918. While still in Frankfurt, along with people such as Franz Neumann and Ernst Fränkel, among others, I helped found the socialist student group at the University of Frankfurt. That was 1918–1919. When I transferred to the University of Heidelberg in 1920 I became friends with the then president of the German Socialist Student League [Deutscher Sozialistischer Studentenbund]. He was a Greek by the name of Karanikolos. He hired me and granted me the pompous title Secretary General of the German Socialist Student League [General-

3. The Spartacus League, led by Rosa Luxemburg and Karl Liebknecht, was a forerunner of the German Communist Party (KPD).

sekretär des Deutschen Sozialistischen Studentenbundes]. It didn't last long—the money soon ran out.

Dubiel: The name German Socialist Student League suggests that this organization wasn't limited to Frankfurt and Heidelberg. Is it accurate to say that this organization was influential in student politics, or perhaps even in general politics?

Lowenthal: Hardly in national politics, but certainly at the university. We were definitely in the minority when compared to groups on the right, such as those linked with fraternities. At this early stage we had had some vehement discussions with these groups but as yet no violent confrontations. That changed by the time of the Kapp Putsch in March 1920.[4] At that time I was still in Frankfurt; I only started in Heidelberg in the summer semester of 1920. We socialist students were then very active; we not only demonstrated, but a group of about ten or twelve of us one day even searched the houses of the most reactionary fraternities for weapons. We were practically trespassing, and all for nothing, since we didn't find any weapons. These people then—justifiably, I'd have to admit today—brought a complaint against us to the president [Rektor]. A group of four or five ringleaders, including me, was called before him. He was a good-natured man named Kautzsch, an art historian by training. I remember him perfectly: he was a nice, kind, old man. He summoned the so-called ringleaders into his office and informed us of his intention to institute proceedings to have us expelled. Half in a state of shock, half out of impudence, I had a good idea. I said, "Herr Rektor, you can, of course, do as you please. But if you institute expulsion proceedings against us, every streetcar driver in Frankfurt will go on strike tomorrow." We were immediately asked to leave the office, and nothing ever happened to any of us. His behavior was certainly based on the fantasy that there

---

4.   The Kapp Putsch was an unsuccessful attempt by right-wing military elements, the so-called Erhardt brigade, to seize control of Berlin and install Wolfgang Kapp as chancellor. It was defeated by a general strike.

are certain social groups that possess mysterious powers. Somehow that kindly old art historian must have imagined secret links between the socialist students and the Frankfurt labor unions. Unfortunately, such links never existed in reality. I had just made it up. The affair with Kautzsch is similar to my dealings with Polizeirat Schmidt and his fantasies about the powerful influence of Jews in Frankfurt.

Dubiel: So the moral of this story is that the president was foolish? That the socialist student groups of your youth were just as lacking in influence and alienated from the workers as those of my generation?

Lowenthal: No, Helmut, your formulation is too radical for me. After all, the parties and the unions recruited large numbers of cadres from students and young intellectuals. As you know, Franz Neumann and Ernst Fränkel, whom I just mentioned, both later became legal counsels for large labor unions, one for the metal workers' union, the other for the construction workers'. So there were connections, especially in cultural politics. I can mention myself as an example. I mean my later advisory work for the People's Theater [*Volksbühne*]. This is just one example that shows how the Social Democratic Party recruited young academics for their cultural work.

Dubiel: Which grouping in the socialist camp was most open to intellectuals?

Lowenthal: Well, without being able to remember precise data too well, I'd assume that the USPD [Independent Socialists] and, initially, the KPD were more interested in intellectuals, because they had hardly any mass basis, at least not in the early years of the Weimar Republic. It was somewhat more difficult with the Social Democrats, you know, because of the influence of the party bosses. But nonetheless, even there the intellectuals weren't totally ignored.

Dubiel: Could you now describe your political development in the course of the Weimar Republic—not only which parties you actually belonged to, but also your changing preferences for certain political groupings?

Lowenthal: I don't know exactly, any more. I just know that I was a member of the USPD in 1919 and 1920. When the USPD split into a left and a right wing—I think that was around the end of 1920—I remained in the left wing. Already early on I had regarded Social Democracy as something petit-bourgeois or bourgeois, as the betrayer of the revolutionary cause, so to speak.

Dubiel: Betrayer of which revolution, the Russian or the German?

Lowenthal: The two can't be separated. The Russians betrayed the German revolution—at least, that's how we saw it then.

Dubiel: Can you give dates or events after which you saw things that way?

Lowenthal: Actually, it already started in the Hölz revolts, with the government in Saxony-Thuringia, in which Karl Korsch was involved.[5] Already one could see that the Russian support wasn't there. That became extremely obvious.

Dubiel: Of course, there are big differences between how such events are experienced by contemporaries and how they are reconstructed by historians. I'm just recalling the arguments of people who, although not really apologists for Stalinism, hold that the Russians simply lacked any resources in the twenties with which to help revolutions in foreign countries. But I'd like to ask once again, because I'm not really well acquainted with this argument, especially in this clear form and in reference to this early period. First of all, can the estrangement from the Soviet Union felt by this radical intelligentsia, which belonged to neither the Social Democratic nor

5. Max Hölz led an unsuccessful rebellion in the Saxon Vogtland in April 1920. Korsch was a left Communist theoretician and activist, best known for his Hegelian Marxist study *Marxism and Philosophy* (1923; trans. Fred Halliday [New York, 1970]).

the Communist Party, be dated this early; and second, can it be interpreted as a function of the disappointment felt because of the lack of support from the Soviet side for the German revolution?

Lowenthal: There's no doubt at all that we in Germany saw it that way. In America it took another twenty years. Developments in the Soviet Union were really traumatic for large sections of the radical intelligentsia in the Weimar Republic. And the trauma lingered on. The high point and, in a certain sense, the working through of this traumatic experience came with the show trials in the Soviet Union during the thirties, then the Spanish Civil War, and finally, of course, the Hitler-Stalin pact.

Dubiel: Leo, I'd like to formulate an impression of mine and test your reaction to it. Today's perception of the critical and radical intelligentsia during the Weimar Republic always focuses on their relation to the development of the labor movement. This is even true of people like you and many others who were not involved in the practical organization of the labor movement. When I read memoirs of, for example, Wolfgang Abendroth who, so to speak, worked at the heart of the labor movement organizing effort, I get the distinct impression of a strong difference between an intellectual like Abendroth and the type of intellectual you represent. However, one really can't call your sympathy for the labor movement just that of a mere observer. How would you describe your own relation with the labor movement and that of your friends at the Institute?

Lowenthal: I definitely had contact with workers' groups. I remember that I often went into the country on USPD business to give lectures to workers, to hold training courses, and the like. And at the time of the Kapp Putsch we worked together with the workers and organized defense squads against the Kappists. It came as a great shock to us when we came to America and discovered that all these Communist and Trotskyist organizations were nothing but small sectlike groups without any mass support. No, it was quite different for us then. For us there was never any doubt that as a socialist one had to work together with the workers.

Dubiel: It's always struck me how in the twenties and early thirties your circle seemed imbued with a sense of unabashed fellowship with the labor movement, without ever translating it into a concrete organizational form. But nonetheless, there were places between organizations in which you were active, which couldn't be called definitely KPD- or SPD-oriented. I'm thinking, for example, of your work with the People's Theater.

Lowenthal: That was certainly a political activity. And it's probably a bit naïve to take activity within the internal organization of one of the socialist parties of the Weimar Republic as the only criterion for partisanship for the labor movement. What developed in the course of the twenties was a sort of free-floating intelligentsia, not in Mannheim's sense,[6] but in the sense of a generalized revolutionary attitude. I never wanted to conform; I always saw myself as somebody who was in opposition. Already in 1920 at the university, I was forever "against"—that was my fundamental attitude. For that reason I attacked Jaspers, for example, because he was then a positivist and thus perceived by us as fundamentally reactionary. To a large extent we didn't attend lectures, because that seemed like bourgeois fraud and ideology to us. Besides, we were all expecting the great socialist revolution any day. In my memory now, that seems perhaps somewhat exaggerated; when I leaf through my papers I see that in spite of it all I studied quite diligently. Be that as it may, my basic feeling during my university years and the first years at the Institute was: We're outsmarting bourgeois society. They have no idea of our dream of a radical revolution.

6. Karl Mannheim posited a "free-floating," unattached intelligentsia in *Ideology and Utopia* (1929; trans. Louis Wirth and Edward Shils [New York, 1936]).

Dubiel: So you saw yourselves as people who were somehow mimicking bourgeois society?

Lowenthal: We always perceived ourselves in opposition to the status quo; we were radical nonconformists. We didn't want to play along. Probably if we hadn't done that, we wouldn't have survived. Ultimately the thought of the disasters that resulted from "playing along" never left us. Everything we did later in the Institute of Social Research in Frankfurt (already at that time it was known in the academic community as "Café Marx") was tinged with this radical conviction.

Dubiel: Was that really possible? If I compare it with the chances today at West German universities to express Marxist attitudes, there's such a pressure to be labeled as a Spartacist, a Maoist, as the representative of some group or another, that such an independent Marxist attitude—as some malicious people say, "left-bourgeois"—is just not possible any more. Wasn't it similar at that time? Even within your own circle, weren't there people who pursued an orthodox course? After all, there were some committed Social Democrats among them. Didn't this "dissent" function as a barrier against the independent humanistic Marxism you describe?

Lowenthal: Very little. Well, in any case the orthodox didn't belong to the innermost circle of the Institute.

Dubiel: Weren't you attacked by any group at that time? I'm thinking for example of a biographical interview with Wolfgang Abendroth, where in reference to you and your Institute colleagues, he says, more or less, that you were insignificant marginal figures on the Frankfurt political scene. At that time, you played no role for Marxist theory and politics. One could easily back up Abendroth's perception with a comparison between, say, Horkheimer's rhetoric and that of organized party people. What for the former is "struggling humanity" is for the latter the "forward-storming proletariat."

Lowenthal: We've always been accused of that. We retained our independence from all sides, but our sympathies were quite obvious. This political and intellectual independence was made easier by the fact that we had money. Actually, the Institute could do what it wanted.

Dubiel: Leo, a passage from Horkheimer's *Dämmerung*[7] just occurred to me. I can cite it only approximately, but I'd like to know what you think about it. He said that one can't criticize socialist parties and organizations from the outside—you know what I'm referring to . . .

Lowenthal: I think so. I believe the formulation was as follows: One can criticize Communism only if one simultaneously criticizes anti-Communism. It has to be done dialectically. Communism and Social Democracy are bad enough, because they stand in opposition to the principles they once stood for; but those who criticize Communism the most sharply must be criticized sharply themselves, because they are guided by motives that are far worse yet.

Dubiel: Now I don't know which passage you're referring to. I just remember the two last sentences of the passage I was thinking about: a critique of the socialist revolution and its supporting groups on the part of bourgeois intellectuals is a logical impossibility. So anyone—in 1929 Horkheimer apparently thought that way—who criticizes a socialist party ought to apply this criticism within the framework of this same organization. That's quite a strong moral postulate.

Lowenthal: A moral postulate, indeed. But not an organizational one.

Dubiel: Organizational, too: a morally formulated postulate of organized political activity.

7. Published under the pseudonym Heinrich Regius in 1934; translated into English as *Dawn and Decline* (New York, 1978).

Lowenthal: One should, so to speak, keep it in the family. But that doesn't mean that one has to be a member of that party. However, one shouldn't embrace the opposite extreme, as happened so frequently later, when erstwhile radicals came to identify totally with political reaction.

Dubiel: Let's talk about that later. First I'd like to discuss the beginnings of your intellectual development. I'd like to start once again by asking about paternal influences on your intellectual development.

Lowenthal: My father was, so to speak, both a formal and a material influence. As a formal influence he succeeded in making an intellectual out of me. My father, an idealist and an intellectual, stood in contrast to my mother who was materialistically and hedonistically oriented. I readily admit that I myself still haven't completely resolved this conflict.

Dubiel: (laughs)

Lowenthal: Even today I feel very indebted to my father. He was a typical representative of the educated German-Jewish middle class. I was encouraged to read Goethe, Schopenhauer, and Darwin. I was encouraged to go to concerts and to the theater, to prepare myself for operas and the like. Later my father was very dissatisfied with me because I pursued my university studies without a definite goal, changing from one faculty to another. Quite frankly, I studied everything besides medicine. That certainly has to do with the just-mentioned Oedipus complex. Sometimes I'm sorry about that. I think I could have become a quite wealthy psychoanalyst!

Dubiel: (laughs)

Lowenthal: Substantively speaking, I owe my own materialistic orientation to my father. Naturally not Marxist-materialistic, but materialistic in the nineteenth-century sense. Haeckel's *World Riddles,* Darwin's *Origin of Species,* and the standard popular scientific books by Carneri were extraordinarily important for him and then later for me, too. He also urged me to read Schopenhauer intensively. But I've already told you about all this.

Dubiel: How great was the influence of school?

Lowenthal: Very great. Most of the teachers in the higher grades of the Goethe Gymnasium in Frankfurt were excellent. They were so good that some of them became honorary professors at the university in 1918. Particularly strong was the influence in the classical subjects. I'm still proud today that I excelled in Greek, Latin, and German in the *Abitur* [general examination after completion of the *Gymnasium*]. At the same time I regret to this day that I was drafted in the last year of the war and consequently missed part of my senior year. Sometimes I think that this gap in my education still shows. The attitude of these teachers, by the way, was not nationalistic—a "Wilhelmine" tone was hardly in evidence. My teacher for German and history wrote the standard history of the city of Frankfurt. The other influence came from my schoolmates themselves. Many of them came from prosperous Jewish households. There was really an *esprit de corps* among internationally oriented young people who often, encouraged by their parents, got together after school to read and discuss. I still remember reading Dostoevsky. We read Freud, Zola, and Balzac. We would voluntarily meet in the afternoons in school to do this. Many of my classmates later had distinguished careers. I remember, for example, my late friend Otto Kahn-Freund, who later became one of the most distinguished English legal scholars.

Dubiel: And your university studies? When did you actually graduate from the *Gymnasium*?

Lowenthal: I graduated in early 1918 with the *Notabitur* [an emergency examination necessitated by the war effort]; then I was drafted into the army. The boys from middle-class families in Frankfurt would go into either the 63rd Artillery Regiment in Mainz or the 81st Infantry Regiment in Frankfurt. By bribing the corporals, during their training period they could live at home or on their own, have their own uniforms, and eat what they wanted. My naïve father dissuaded me from doing that. One of his patients, who was also a friend, was a captain in the reserve of a railway regiment, which was stationed in Hanau. My father thought that his friend could pull a few strings to make my life in the army more palatable. So I reported there, as a simple recruit, of course. As was to be expected, no one there knew this Captain Schröder, who by then was stationed somewhere in France. So, believe it or not, I ended up in a workers' regiment made up of sons of proletarians and poor peasants. Poor devils, rough, sometimes brutal, uneducated men. We had to live in the barracks and eat the horrible swill there; we weren't allowed to have our own uniforms but were given the sweat-covered uniforms of previous "grunts." Besides drilling and shooting (which I was really not good at—the rifle butt would almost always recoil and hit me on the cheek), we were mainly kept busy loading rails for railroad tracks. Once a rail fell on my fingers; you can still see my crooked fingernail. I was the constant object of mockery. At that time I experienced the potential anti-Semitism and anti-intellectualism of the German proletariat and peasants. It was an awful time. I tried everything to get out of there. I volunteered for the front; I would have preferred to die. I was rejected. I then applied to become a cadet officer so that, as an officer, I could escape those circumstances. Refused. All of this was for me—and I am not exaggerating—a kind of anticipatory concentration-camp experience. It certainly contributed to the strengthening of my alleged elitist arrogance as an intellectual. As you know—we've discussed it often enough—I don't consider the accusation of elitism an insult, but rather praise. We felt that the war was already lost, and that we were thus involved with a fundamentally meaningless business. Sometime I'll show you a couple of pictures of me as a soldier in 1918 along with my company. Looking at these photos, one might say that I should demand a veteran's pension from the American government! I was really the epitome of a "sad sack," a personal representation of the "stab-in-the-back" legend, so to speak. But enough of that.

Dubiel: When did you start your university studies?

Lowenthal: I started at the University of Frankfurt in the winter semester of 1918. In the summer semester of 1919 I went to Giessen, together with my maternal friend Luise Habricht, whom I've already mentioned. She was—as you remember—a friend of the philosopher Walter Kinkel, who taught there. He wasn't a very significant philosopher, but he was a good Social Democrat who appreciated good wine. In Frankfurt I had started out, under paternal pressure, with the study of jurisprudence, and I promptly gave that up in Giessen under the influence of Luise and Kinkel. I had also heard some lectures on philosophy in Frankfurt; I still remember those of Hans Cornelius quite well.[8] I heard the Germanist Peterson's lectures on Goethe, Cornelius's lectures on Kant, Kautzsch's—I've already spoken of him—lectures on medieval art, and Schönflies's introduction to higher mathematics. This interest in mathematics was influenced by my great sympathy with the Marburg philosophical school—for which a certain understanding of infinitesimal calculus was important. I also took part in classical proseminars, and I heard lectures on ancient history, aesthetics, and psychology. My intellectual tastes were very eclectic. I wanted, so to speak, to get everything into my head—a little Faust, if you will.

Dubiel: Could we proceed to your time in Heidelberg? Pardon the feeble metaphor, but Heidelberg at that time must have been an intellectual hothouse. Even for my generation it's still well known. I always think of the Max Weber circle, which was, of course, a prewar phenomenon, but I imagine its offshoots are still present there.

Lowenthal: Well, if you want to call his brother Alfred an "offshoot," then okay. Karl Mannheim didn't come to Heidelberg until

8. Cornelius, a heterodox neo-Kantian, also influenced other members of the Frankfurt School, including Horkheimer, Adorno, and Pollock.

1921, when I was a student. Ernst Bloch was there frequently, and Jaspers was a member of the Weber circle. As for figures of really international stature, there were Heinrich Rickert, Karl Jaspers, and Alfred Weber. Also very significant were the historians, such as Hermann Oncken and Karl Hampe; the economist Emil Lederer, whose lectures on nationalization I attended at that time; and the Germanist and close friend of Stefan George, Friedrich Gundolf. Gundolf was for me a political issue. I didn't attend his lectures regularly because he was too reactionary for me. I attended lectures on philosophy: that was part of the Marxist tradition—it was necessary to be educated philosophically if one wanted to be a young nonconformist, a revolutionary thinker. I should remind you once again that I was fundamentally imbued with the conviction—don't forget, this was 1920, 1921—that the world revolution was around the corner and that this whole bourgeois lecture business would soon be done with.

Dubiel: Can we now turn to your first small publication, "The Demonic,"[9] and give some examples of those intellectual influences that really had an effect on you? How did this text come about, anyway? Perhaps you could begin with the anecdote about the row you had with Jaspers.

Lowenthal: I'd prefer to start with Rickert. In the winter semester of 1920–1921, Rickert held a seminar on Husserl's phenomenology, and in the same semester, Jaspers gave a course on his recently published book *The Psychology of Worldviews.* The Rickert seminar was particularly important for me because, as you know, I was originally committed to the Marburg neo-Kantian school of Hermann Cohen and Paul Natorp, which was what one might call a hostile sibling of the southwest German neo-Kantian school. I be-

9. Leo Löwenthal, "Das Dämonische: Entwurf einer negativen Religionsphilosophie," in *Festgabe für Rabbiner Nobel* (Frankfurt am Main, 1922), pp. 50–62.

lieve that this was the first time that Rickert dealt with Husserl's *Ideas—General Introduction to a Pure Phenomenology*. My impression at the time was that they would destroy each other—Rickert and Husserl were, after all, bourgeois philosophers—and I, as a Marburg neo-Kantian and Marxist, would win the day. To repeat once again, Rickert's intention was the critical destruction of phenomenology. My own attitude was one of ambivalence. On the one hand, profoundly steeped in Kantian philosophy as I was, I found it difficult to understand Husserl's concepts in the first place, let alone accept them; on the other hand, I thought I discerned an intention to go beyond the mere formalism of Kantian philosophy in the direction of a metaphysics that could possibly be of use for the kind of philosophical, revolutionary radicalism to which I was then committed.

Dubiel: Was it for that reason that you finally found yourself closer to phenomenology than to Rickert's neo-Kantianism?

Lowenthal: Yes. I myself realized that for the first time in the course of the Jaspers affair. At that time, Jaspers was exactly the opposite of what he is now famous for. Today, Jaspers is renowned as a metaphysical philosopher; the Jaspers of those days was a psychiatrist-cum-philosopher, essentially a scientistic positivist. The decisive book was *The Psychology of Worldviews*.

Dubiel: I must admit, to my shame, that I've never read the book. But the title sounds rather like a psychologically reductionist theory of *Weltanschauung* systems, some sort of vulgarization of Dilthey.

Lowenthal: On that point I'd defend Dilthey against you, but let's not get into that now. Yes, it was a reductionist book; unfortunately, I no longer own a copy. It was lost like so many other books of mine. At one time I had a library of ten thousand volumes, including an extensive collection of radical works from the German revolution, publications that, as people from the Hoover Institute in Stanford later told me, would be worth thousands of dollars.

Before we left for America, Horkheimer insisted that such works be either burnt or given away. He was afraid that we would be immediately deported if they opened my boxes of books. Nobody ever checked a single box.

Dubiel: Back to Jaspers.

Lowenthal: Right. Helmut, a couple of days ago I showed you suicide notes from 1920. At that time, I was in a mystical, radical, syncretic mood, a mixture of revolutionary radicalism, Jewish messianism, infatuation with an ontologically conceived phenomenology, acquaintance with psychoanalysis. . . . All of that was blended together to form a very missionary-messianic Bloch-like rapturous philosophy, if I look at it today. For instance, I was terribly agitated by Jaspers's book; it was, so to speak, the devil incarnate. Topics for presentation were distributed quite mechanically in the seminar, and I got the chapter on the demonic, which, as you correctly assumed, was essentially reductionist. Wherever the concept of the "demonic" came up in the history of literature or philosophy, it was reduced to merely psychological categories, which I have long since forgotten. In a kind of trance, I wrote as an oral presentation for the seminar this article, which flew in the face of all that Jaspers taught, and I referred to this psychologistic-positivistic method of explanation with obvious contempt. Jaspers became furious, even aggressive and insulting. He showed no pedagogical understanding whatsoever for this young student who had just let these ideas pour out. After Jaspers's outburst, I stood up, bowed to my fellow students, and left the seminar room, slamming the door. The episode became known all around Heidelberg. So that was the business with the "demonic." Later Ernst Bloch read it and was quite enthusiastic about it. It was finally published in the Nobel festschrift, although there were some critical protests from Franz Rosenzweig, who was the editor. There were also criticisms from Siegfried Kracauer, who was then my closest personal and intellectual friend and mentor. The syncretic elements in my essay were typical for that time. I had friends and allies active in various intellectual spheres—psychoanalysis, Marxism, the Kantian school, Zionism, the religious Jewish movement—and I must have been a kind of focal point for all these intellectual currents.

Dubiel: One can see this phenomenon in a general sense, namely, that many of your intellectual fellow travelers at that time were given to syncretic tendencies, albeit to varying degrees. In Benjamin's case there were certainly also very heterogeneous aspects of his orientation as a whole, and that's no less true for Bloch.

Lowenthal: And, to a certain extent, for Lukács. Just look at *Soul and Form* or *The Theory of the Novel*—these works are far from *History and Class Consciousness*.

Dubiel: For Lukács it's quite simple. You just have to take *The Destruction of Reason*. All the people he attacks in that book represent the currents that he had to overcome in himself.

Lowenthal: Yes, an awful book.

Dubiel: Let's now turn to your dealings with psychoanalysis. How did that start?

Lowenthal: Like so many other things in life, quite by chance. I already told you that I fell in love with a woman—it must have been around 1922—who originally came from Königsberg and then lived in Frankfurt, and who was at that time a friend of Erich Fromm's. She later became my wife. Since her youth, she had been good friends with Frieda Fromm-Reichmann. Through my wife, Golde Ginsburg, Erich Fromm got to know Frieda, who later became a physician in a clinic near Dresden. I also became acquainted with Frieda through Golde. Before 1922, I was only somewhat familiar with psychoanalysis; I believe that there are certain allusions to this in the "Demonic" essay. But all of that isn't so important, just as *The Critique of Pure Reason* says: the empirical beginning can be established, but the conceptual origin is elsewhere. The systematic interest that must have spawned this fascination with psychoanalysis for me and many of my intellectual fellow travelers was very likely the idea of "marrying" historical materialism with psychoanalysis. One of the fundamental problems in Marxist theory is, after all, the absence of mediating elements between base and superstructure, which psychological theory might supply. And for us, psychoanalysis came to fill this gap. I probably foresaw this already in the early twenties. It became consciously apparent to me and to all of us starting around 1930, perhaps already in 1927–1928. Intellectually, it was terribly exciting to familiarize oneself with psychoanalysis and to maintain psychoanalytical contacts, because it was so avant-garde. Later, in the circle of my colleagues in the Institute, we often referred in jest to my having brought Fromm to the Institute as one of my major contributions. In those days, he was certainly one of the most important influences. Particularly during the Frankfurt years the connection with Fromm was extraordinarily stimulating, even though at first he wasn't a formal member of the Institute and was usually not in Frankfurt.

Yes, and I might mention my modest role in connection with awarding the Goethe Prize to Sigmund Freud, in 1930, I think. At that time, no one wanted to grant Freud an official prize; psychoanalysis was a despised and scorned science; it was anathema— extreme and avant-garde. For that reason, for the city of Frankfurt to grant Sigmund Freud the Goethe Prize was quite extraordinary. I was indirectly involved, since through the People's Theater movement I was friendly with Gottfried Herzfeld, an important member of the selection committee. Another incident, perhaps less noticed, was the establishment of a psychoanalytical institute in Frankfurt at the end of the twenties. At that time we made it possible for this institute to hold its lectures in the rooms of our Institute of Social Research. That was only possible because from 1930 on Max Horkheimer was the director of the Institute and we owned our own building on the university campus. This situation was optimal in Germany at that early time—the mere fact that a psychoanalytical institute was allowed to use rooms on a university campus was then almost a sensation.

2

The Institute of Social Research

Dubiel: Can you tell me something about the early history of the Institute of Social Research, that is, since the time you worked at the Institute? The earliest history of the Institute, up to its formation in 1924 and then including the first two years of its existence, have been described and documented in Paul Kluke's book *Stiftungsuniversität Frankfurt am Main*.[1] Martin Jay, too, deals with this period, and thus we need not refer to it. So, tell us about the time you were at the Institute.

Lowenthal: I am not familiar with Kluke's book. Leaving aside the matter of the earlier history, the Institute as we know it is clearly Horkheimer's intellectual creation. It became evident as early as, let us say, 1926, and surely by 1928, after Carl Grünberg's illness, that Horkheimer was to become the Institute's director. I joined the Institute in 1926, but only part-time; I was in close intellectual contact with Horkheimer and Pollock, though. First I worked on my essays in the sociology of literature, now collected in *Literature, Popular Culture, and Society*. Our collaboration became more in-

Translated by David Berger.

1. Paul Kluke, *Stiftungsuniversität Frankfurt am Main 1914–1932* (Frankfurt am Main, 1972).

tense in 1928 and 1929, when Grünberg's retirement was expected. There now was the matter of preparing for Horkheimer's directorship, which was not simple. Horkheimer was only a lecturer [*Privatdozent*], and a regular professorship was a precondition for the directorship. He had not yet published much—his only published works so far had been his dissertation and an essay on Mannheim in the *Grünberg Archiv*.

Dubiel: Are you referring to the critical review of Mannheim's *Ideology and Utopia*?

Lowenthal: Yes. One of the things that occupied us at that time was the completion of Horkheimer's *Anfänge der bürgerlichen Geschichtsphilosophie*, which appeared as a book in 1930. I collaborated on that a great deal, at his request. In general, my editorial labors wind like a red thread throughout my connection with the Institute. In 1929 a large part of the activity at the Institute was devoted to strategic planning, as it were. And we were successful: Horkheimer became a professor and director of the Institute. Shall I give you some details?

Dubiel: No, they are contained in Kluke's book.

Lowenthal: So, in 1930 Horkheimer became the Institute's director and I became one of two full-time chief assistants—the other being Henryk Grossmann, who dated back to the Grünberg period. By saying this, I do not mean anything detrimental concerning this wonderful and distinguished man. But in matters of theory we had very little in common.

Dubiel: During this phase were you already planning to emigrate?

Lowenthal: The decision to emigrate, or rather to prepare to do so, took place on September 14, 1930, when 107 National Socialists entered the Reichstag. These elections were crucial. During the previous months we had not paid much attention to the general state of the world, for we were still celebrating our honeymoon at the Institute. However, during 1930–1931 it was becoming clear how the situation was developing. The emotional and political atmosphere was such that emigration had to be seriously considered. The day after the Reichstag elections Felix Weil, Max Horkheimer, Fritz Pollock, and I had a decisive meeting. We asked Felix Weil to provide the funds to establish a branch office in Geneva. The idea of a Geneva branch was Horkheimer's, and it was jointly accepted and immediately executed. In Geneva, Pollock knew Albert Thomas, then the director of the International Labor Office. Pollock told the ILO that we wished to set up an international research office there, and he succeeded in winning Thomas's moral support. This request was quite natural, given the Grünberg tradition of the Frankfurt Institute; Thomas, himself a good socialist, knew and respected Grünberg. We then found a Dutch sociologist, Andries Sternheim, who at first worked alone at the Geneva branch office and cultivated friendly relations with the International Labor Office. That this branch was to be the focal point for our emigration was not to be publicized. Therefore, we followed normal routines: Horkheimer went to Geneva frequently, as did Pollock, and I went occasionally. The university was to get the impression that this branch was a bona fide institute. Also, in 1931 we shifted the foundation's funds from Germany to the Netherlands. At the Deutsche Bank in Frankfurt we kept only a letter of credit that barely covered the Institute's monthly requirements. This is why the Nazis didn't get anything from us. Only one of the employees, who had forgotten to pick up her check early enough, lost any money—we compensated her for it. We donated our library to the London School of Economics, a library that, through Grünberg, had become a choice collection of documents from the history of the labor movement and had been expanded by Horkheimer with innumerable valuable texts on philosophy and cultural history. It was not so easy to transfer ownership to the LSE, though, so the title to the library had to be transferred first to a Swiss foundation whose name I have forgotten. This foundation, made up mainly of a board of Swiss citizens, then transferred title of the library to the London School of Economics, whose director, Sir William Beveridge, accepted the donation. Then, when the Nazis came, the London School of Economics would be able to save the library. You know that this did not work out. Mr. Ribbentrop told the British ambassador that we were a bunch of Communists, and so the British did not make any effort to save the library from the National Socialists' interference. Eventually, during the war, the library went up in flames. It may even have burned, by an irony of history, as the result of a British bombing.

Dubiel: As far as Europe is concerned, the international reputation of your Institute was almost meteoric, judging from the famous names among the *Zeitschrift*'s reviewers.

Lowenthal: Everyone we invited to lecture at the Institute came: Raymond Aron, Edmund Husserl . . .

Dubiel: How do you explain that?

Lowenthal: I'm afraid I can't be very specific about that. Our guests were lavishly received, and the University of Frankfurt had a certain reputation. Through Horkheimer's skill and personality, we had excellent relations with the university's curator, vice-chancellor, and its leading intellectual figures such as Paul Tillich. You must also remember that many talented left-wing students were drawn to the Institute. We organized seminars on Hegel and Marx that drew large crowds—although no university credit was given. Also important were the connections with the Piscator Theater and the Malik and Marx-Engels publishing houses. As you must know, the Institute was dubbed the "Café Marx"—first in friendly fashion, later not so friendly.

Dubiel: Can you tell me more about the emigration?

Lowenthal: As I mentioned before, we, unlike others, realized early on how quickly totalitarian terror would spread in Germany. Many were naïve, and because of their narrow academic interests they refused to recognize the catastrophic situation in Germany.

Later they paid bitterly for it. I was the last one to leave the Institute and Frankfurt—on March 2, 1933. On March 5, the SA [*Sturmabteilung*, or storm troops] occupied the building. Later we read a grotesque article in the local Nazi press, which I showed you, listing the dreadful items they had seized—including an alleged sadistic correspondence with my mistress!

We had made connections with Celestin Bouglé in Paris—he had been one of Durkheim's students. He immediately offered to set up a branch at the Sorbonne. He also facilitated relations with the Félix Alcan Press, which offered to take over our *Zeitschrift*. Then we decided to form another branch in London, at the Institute of Sociology in the Le Play House. This policy of forming branches was part of our tactics. We were like the child who had been burned once—we were not too sure about our situation in Switzerland. We needed our branch in Paris because our publisher was there. The London branch, in turn, was a gathering place in case things didn't work out in Switzerland. You know that the history of Switzerland during the Hitler period was not exactly a glorious one. You have to imagine our situation in Geneva. Only Horkheimer had an unlimited residency permit, so only he could have a home with all his furniture there. Pollock, Marcuse, and I could not do this; we had to keep our libraries and furniture in a bonded warehouse. We remained visitors. We had only tourist visas, and every few weeks or so we had to go across the border to Bellegarde and reenter with a new visa. And there was much more. We often found that Jewish emigrants were scrutinized closely, and in their cases regulations were enforced most strictly. We took this as an indication that fascism would eventually spread to all of Europe; at that time we still did not anticipate a war.

Then there was the matter of the United States. Julian Gumperz, Pollock's assistant, was an American, and Erich Fromm had already been in the United States. And so the idea of emigrating there began to take hold. There were invitations from leading universities such as Chicago and Columbia. We decided in favor of Columbia on the basis of New York's proximity to Europe. We knew very little about the United States. We thought, for instance, that one could not take a walk in Central Park, although at that time one could still do so. Columbia University was quite generous: organizationally and legally they offered us the same conditions we had enjoyed in Frankfurt. We turned into the "Institute of Social Research, affiliated with Columbia University," and obtained a house on University Heights, which we kept into the late 1940s. The move to the United States took place in 1934: Horkheimer and his wife were the first to leave; Marcuse followed, then I, then Pollock, and finally our wives and children. Fromm was already there. One of the complications we ran into in New York was the publishing of the *Zeitschrift*. It was still put out by Alcan in Paris, and it was therefore important to get the material there promptly. I recall how many times, late at night, I rushed by car to the post office so that material would reach the *Ile de France* or another ship in time. There was no airmail service yet.

Dubiel: Did you have someone in the Paris branch arrange for the final editing of the *Zeitschrift* before going to press?

Lowenthal: At first the Paris branch was managed by Paul Honigsheim, a left-wing Catholic who had been a professor in Cologne. When Honigsheim left for the United States, he was succeeded by a Dr. Hans Brill, who did a good job looking after the *Zeitschrift*. The Paris branch stayed in operation until the Nazis marched into the city. Because we hardly knew any English— Horkheimer and Pollock had a smattering of it, Marcuse and I scarcely anything—it was necessary to get help with the language. We were lucky: through academic recommendations we were able to hire two young men who later became important scholars. One of them, M. I. Finley, is today one of the most important classical scholars in Cambridge, England, and a friend of mine.* The second was the late Benjamin Nelson, who became a professor at the New School for Social Research. Part of my activity in New York was devoted to developing the review section of the *Zeitschrift*. Among other things, this section was an important means of getting financial aid to intellectual emigrants. If you leaf through the journal you see many well-known names. We also commissioned and paid for many reviews knowing full well that we could not or would not publish them. Recently, I was looking through some of my old papers and came across an exchange of letters with Kurt Goldstein, an outstanding psychiatrist. In one letter I confirmed that I was sending him an honorarium of nine dollars. Don't be surprised at that—do you know what secretaries were making then? Fourteen dollars a week. That's why we had good secretaries: on Wall Street at that time they would have earned only twelve dollars. That was during the depression, but we weren't very aware of that. We were so concerned with building our own German island that we nearly forgot what terrible times America was going through. Well, we remained an island, no doubt about that.

Dubiel: It seems to me—and this is shared also by Americans who had intellectual contacts with you—that the most important period of your life, and intellectually the most formative, was that which you spent at the Institute. I think that this was true of all members. Would you agree?

Lowenthal: I certainly do. In my case this period extended for almost a quarter of a century; I was associated with the Institute full-time from 1926 to 1949. True, during the first years—I mean in the late 1920s—I was still teaching high school, but my intellectual home was the Institute. And at the end, in the late 1940s, I was the only one of us living alone in New York. But, as you know from the huge correspondence with Horkheimer and Adorno, our close association remained intact.

*Professor Finley died in 1986.

Dubiel: You received so many formative impulses from this group—from the overall perspective, what would you single out? How has the Institute affected your style, intellectual habits, theoretical approaches, ways of evaluating traditions, choices of books?

Lowenthal: Well, that's quite a big question. The whole atmosphere of the Institute, not just the influence of Max Horkheimer, allowed me to further develop my view of the world, of nature, and of life. Of course, the basis for this was already there, characterized essentially by a concern for independence. This is best captured by our slogan of *nicht mitmachen,* not playing the game. The Institute's intellectual tradition made it possible for me to achieve a satisfactory synthesis of my philosophical, literary, sociological, and hedonistic feelings. In a sense, I relived my student years at the Institute. My first years there were a sort of anticipated utopia: we were different, and we knew the world better. Looking at it in retrospect, our history seems quite extraordinary. First of all, Horkheimer's becoming the director and the founding of a new periodical represented something new. The *Zeitschrift für Sozialforschung* was like Karl Kraus's *Die Fackel* [The Torch], although written not by one person but by a group working closely together. Then there was our anticipation of the decline of the Weimar Republic and the preparation of our flight abroad, along with our conviction, at that time, that the spread of fascism was more likely than a world war. We had left for the United States and built there an island of German radical intellectuals. This in itself was rather significant. If I were to elaborate on all of this in detail it would add up to a unique fusion of intellectual talent, worldwide political perspectives, and a far-ranging imagination molded by an upper-class Jewish lifestyle. None of us believed that all this would be confirmed by the reputation earned by the Frankfurt group. Nor could I say with certainty that I am happy about all this, because I am not sure whether this "integration" isn't also part of this society's ability to integrate and thereby defuse everything. But there it is. First of all, it was a miracle we survived and were able to overcome all the obstacles to emigration, to rise eventually from the ashes from the 1950s onward. For we really have become an ineradicable part of Western intellectual life and, in a certain sense, of political life. So, this is my long reply to a complex question.

Dubiel: What has often surprised me is the astounding certainty, the almost instinctual deep-seated self-assurance, in the organization of your theoretical work. In all of you I feel an extraordinarily precise topography, a very detailed theoretical map on the basis of which every theoretical task can be quickly identified as to its immanent quality as well as to its intellectual-political relevance.

Lowenthal: You remind me of my opening statements in the address that I gave in 1974 on the occasion of the fiftieth anniversary of the Institute of Social Research in Frankfurt. At that time I pointed to the *Zeitschrift*'s format to explain the meaning of Critical Theory: that is, it is a perspective, a common, critical, basic attitude toward all cultural phenomena, that never claimed to be a system. The *Zeitschrift* contains the critical programs of the founding fathers, if I may call them such, on philosophy, economics, psychology, music, and literature. Critical Theory, then, must be understood as nothing but such a collective denominator. It was an expression, by the way, that we never used with as much emphasis during the first twenty years as may appear to posterity. This is my reply: it is a perspective. For that reason I'm always a bit baffled when someone requests that I offer a seminar on Critical Theory— I never know how to deal with that. I usually call my friend Martin Jay and ask him to define the main characteristics of the so-called Critical Theory. Now I'll ask you—after all, you wrote a book about it.

Dubiel: It's really impossible to come up with a few general characteristics and say: this is Critical Theory. In the case of so-called traditional theories it is frequently possible, because with the aid of given central premises one can derive one's own hypothesis. For a while, in reaction to this problem, I took an agnostic stance and maintained that Critical Theory was a myth fabricated by self-serving second-rate literati, supported by the commercial interests of publishing houses, having no relation to reality. But, now that I have known you for quite some time, I feel that you represent a specific style of thinking and living. On the one hand I consider myself privileged to be able to partake of it, and on the other I resist reducing a theoretical tradition to a personal physiognomy. I find it difficult to abandon the idea that theoretical theses must also be cognitively transportable and that they must not exhaust themselves in the authenticity of a person. For this reason I reiterate my question: what are the symptomatic characteristics of what is known as Critical Theory?

Lowenthal: Well, something of it is codified, in particular in Horkheimer's great essay "Traditional and Critical Theory," and in Marcuse's supplementary essay.[2] But I should like to say something else. Recently, in one of my seminars, one of my most gifted students attacked our group, saying that our attitude was Olympian, that we had separated ourselves completely from Marxism and had lost sight of reality. I replied that such criticism missed the meaning of Critical Theory: we had not abandoned praxis; rather, praxis had abandoned us. I have often talked about the great trauma represented by the developments in the Soviet Union and the Communist Party. But of far greater significance was the insight that the idea of the proletariat's revolutionary potential was historically dated. This was then especially clear in the United States, and now it is clear throughout the world. Here, as well as in most of Western Europe, the so-called proletariat is now a petit-bourgeois group with a massive interest in the status quo. Yes, in a mediating sense,

2. Max Horkheimer, *Critical Theory: Selected Essays,* trans. Matthew J. O'Connell et al. (New York, 1972); and Herbert Marcuse, "Philosophy and Critical Theory," *Negations: Essays in Critical Theory,* trans. Jeremy J. Shapiro (Boston, 1968).

Critical Theory was always in favor of praxis. The essential difference between Critical and Traditional Theory was this: the problems that concerned us—whether it was the critique of liberalism or of phenomenology, literature, or music—were determined essentially by the given historical situation. Our main interest was not methodology but the hopefully successful attempt to analyze critically those tendencies and movements that stood in the way of reestablishing a possible unity between politics and theory. So, Critical Theory did not in the least regard itself as esoteric; its most crucial feature was a reflection on the relation between theory and praxis.

Dubiel: You—as a group—have answered such a reproach concerning Critical Theory's lack of practical political interests by saying that today's labor movement has itself become confused, that the separation of theory and practice was the fault of praxis.

Lowenthal: I recall having heard in intellectual and personal conversations the reproach that one could not always be critical, that sometimes one should also be constructive. We were always scandalous troublemakers. You are familiar with the famous reproach to Erich Kästner: "Herr Kästner, and what about the positive aspects?" Well, it is exactly the negative that was the positive: this consciousness of not going along, the refusal. The essence of Critical Theory is really the inexorable analysis of what is.

Although I do not agree with Horkheimer's excessively religious symbolism during his last years, when he defined the "completely other" of this society by referring to the name of a God who must not be named, this reticence points to something that unites us. What man can do in freedom should not be anticipated, and one must always say no to what is happening because it is not happening in freedom. We cannot escape from Hegel's antithetical position. How could we really do so? After all, the synthesis is to be made by the subjects themselves. We are the involved collaborators of the negative phase of the dialectical process. It was this belief that held us together and gave us so much strength. It helped us avoid seduction by reality, which is not to say that we do not, on occasion, enjoy the good things life has to offer. Yet none of us has ever succumbed to the Faustian warning: "If ever I say to any moment: Linger, you are so wonderful."

Dubiel: When I now use the word "attitude," I do not mean it negatively. After all, this attitude of critical distance was developed on the basis of historical experiences and was not a departure point. During the early 1930s, when you all defined your theoretical direction still as materialistic, you still considered yourselves, at least morally, part of the labor movement. This definitely changed in 1936 (I mention this date because of Horkheimer's classic essay). Since then you have considered yourselves as, in Adorno's apt description, a *Flaschenpost* [a message in a bottle]—a lonely, marginal group critically examining the course of the world.

Lowenthal: I agree with that.

Dubiel: I want to get back to what the core of Critical Theory is. Clearly, that question cannot be readily answered. There are so many different perspectives from which one can view Critical Theory.

Lowenthal: If it were a dogma, the question could be readily answered. In fact, this question derives from a positivistic way of thinking, even though it may be asked by well-meaning autonomous individuals.

Dubiel: I would like to pursue the notion of "perspectives." Can you compare your group's theoretical orientation with what the Institute stood for in Frankfurt in 1930? How would you describe yourselves in relation to the frequently mechanistic, even historically unreflected, materialism of people such as Grünberg and Wittfogel—and even Henryk Grossmann? Comparing the table of contents of the last issue of Grünberg's *Archiv für die Geschichte des Sozialismus und der Arbeiterbewegung* with the program of the *Zeitschrift für Sozialforschung* reveals a surprising shift toward problems of philosophy and cultural critique and, in general, super-structural problems.

Lowenthal: Yes, there is no doubt about that. The emphasis did shift to superstructural problems, but not entirely. Don't forget the works of Pollock and his collaborators—especially during the 1940s the political-economic works of Pollock and Franz Neumann were crucial to us. I am referring to the theory of state capitalism and *Behemoth*. Even Henryk Grossmann's earlier theoretical conviction that the collapse was imminent is part of this context, which represented a counterweight to the program of a materialistic philosophy of culture. But these studies were not the core. Its character was also determined by personnel contingencies, intellectual qualities, and the ability to be heard within the group.

Dubiel: Let us now turn to the relation to Marxism. In West Germany, and even more here in the United States, Critical Theory is seen as an enlightened version of Marxism.

Lowenthal: That was never abandoned. I would go even further and say that Critical Theory is a progressive form of Marxism that no longer mechanically accepts Marxist categories in changed historical situations. The theory of immiseration, the unmediated reduction of the superstructure to the base, the theory of the crash as deriving from the fall in the rate of profit have all turned out to be untenable. But basic Marxist themes have never been abandoned. The hypothesis that world history can be described as the result of the struggle between outer and inner nature, and the theory of productive forces and class relations, have never been given up. What have been abandoned are certain economistic categories and predictions that have proven to be wrong. That was entirely in Marx's spirit. He always referred to tendencies and countertendencies. You are right: our interest turned toward a cultural area neglected by the Marxist tradition—psychology. Psychology does not exist in classical Marxism and so we have surely added something to that theory. This, of course, does not fit into that petit-bourgeois catechism of Marxism as proposed by Bukharin. Thus, if the Russian tradition is seen as the legitimate successor of Marxism, then we have not been Marxists.

Dubiel: The theoretical development of Marxism cannot be separated from the practical movements that appeal to it. Your Marxism was defined by opposition to the Social Democratic and Bolshevik versions of Marxism. Other perspectives could be chosen to represent Critical Theory, such as its relation to the Enlightenment tradition.

Lowenthal: Indeed! Like the young Marx we have always considered ourselves critical continuers of the radical Enlightenment tradition.

Dubiel: Do you see the theoretical and intellectual development of the Frankfurt circle between 1930 and 1950 as in some way typical of, say, the socialist emigré intelligentsia between the two world wars?

Lowenthal: No. We were completely isolated; ours was a singular story. Please do not consider it presumptuous, but we did not wish to be typical. Of course there were other schools, for example, the logical positivists, but they had no political purpose.

Dubiel: How about comparing you with clearly political groups such as the SPD in exile? I am referring to the New Beginning group.

Lowenthal: We cannot be compared to these groups.

Dubiel: So, the uniqueness of your group then seems defined as "in between" unmistakably political groups on the one hand and scholarly groups on the other.

Lowenthal: Perhaps the psychoanalytical movement can be roughly compared to ours. But this, too, would be inaccurate. Such groups must always be perceived against the background of specific political constellations. Think of the beginning of our interdisciplinary orientation and collaboration within the framework of our political philosophy, to our determination as emigrés to

uphold this tradition, as the only progressive voice of German intellectual life—that was something out of the ordinary. Adorno's
metaphor of the *Flaschenpost* couldn't have been more to the point.
In the 1960s, of course, all of us were surprised at the pop this bottle
made when it was uncorked. But we all reacted differently.

Dubiel: There is another question I want to ask. You were not a
homogeneous group. What subgroups or factions were there, and
what conflicts arose from this?

Lowenthal: In the 1930s the basic conflict involved the Soviet
Union and the trials. There was quite a split about that, and it
frequently resulted in heated conversations and unpleasant scenes.
The defenders of the Soviet Union were Wittfogel, Grossmann, and
Bloch—although the latter was not strictly a member of our group.
It went so far that one of these three called us the "swine on 117th
Street" (that was where our Columbia house was located). I can
still remember one such scene involving Horkheimer, Marcuse,
Wittfogel, and myself. It took place at a luncheon in a New York
restaurant, the Tip-Toe Inn. In the course of our conversation
Horkheimer remarked that it would not surprise him if an alliance
developed between Hitler and Stalin, if Hitler made only the least
overture. At this, Wittfogel leaped up as if bitten by a tarantula,
threw his napkin onto the table in a rage, threw out some insulting
remarks that I shall not repeat, and left the restaurant in a huff. We
even had to pay his bill. We had various scenes like this one at the
Institute itself because he constantly sought to justify the trials—
and he was not the only one.

The disappointment over what took place in the Soviet Union
and in those countries that called themselves Communist is a key to
our political development. For instance, when people say that fascism and Communism are the same, I disagree. Soviet Communism is a perversion of a theory, a moral system, and a style of
thought that are essentially good. Hitler's fascism, in contrast, is
bad for the very reason that its basic conception of man is inhuman.

A Jew can never be saved, while a capitalist can freely declassify himself and convert to a new religion. That this does not happen in practice is not the fault of Marxist philosophy.

Dubiel: Now I should like to touch on a subject that would have been obsolete had it not been raised again in the recently published biography of Benjamin by Werner Fuld.[3] You know better than I the background of the accusation, going back over a decade, that during the late 1930s the Institute in a sense blackmailed Benjamin ideologically, threatening to cut off funds in order to make him give up his allegedly strict Marxist course. There are certain forms of malice against which even the most honest arguments are powerless. That's why this legend is still alive today. Can you comment on this?

Lowenthal: I feel extremely sad about this matter. On the basis of our conversations, the documents and the correspondence that you have seen, you could have convinced yourself that, within the constraints of its relatively limited funds, the Institute did indeed spend large sums in helping emigré intellectuals. Walter Benjamin was one of those who from the very outset, and uninterruptedly, benefited from this solidarity on the part of the Institute. It is true that Benjamin was not a formal member of the Institute, but he was a close friend of Adorno and his wife, and we all knew him well. Since the Frankfurt days and since his aborted attempt to earn a university lectureship, we were in almost constant contact with him personally and, later, through letters. As you know, Benjamin always remained a seeker, a doubter, and a lone wolf; he had strong moral and intellectual ties to Zionism, to Communism, to aesthetic theory, to Jewish mysticism, and to literature. He had an extraordinarily complex relation to art in modern society and to the role of popular culture and the mass media. It was unavoidable that the intellectual motifs of such a many-sided and brilliant person

3. Werner Fuld, *Walter Benjamin: Zwischen den Stühlen* (Munich, 1979).

were frequently contradictory, and this sometimes brought him into conflict with those close to him. All this is well documented in his correspondence with Adorno. I myself had an argument with him over Knut Hamsun, although he later admitted I was right. We were glad that Benjamin regularly wrote articles for the *Zeitschrift*. He was in no way a merely pro forma colleague, but someone who intellectually, if not physically, belonged to our group even though he lived on the other side of the Atlantic. Of course, it was easier—after all, you know how the *Zeitschrift* was edited—to deal with a co-worker in the New York office in making changes and adjustments relating to differences of opinion. Unfortunately, Benjamin was far from the scene. It was Adorno's main task to look over Benjamin's essays and to correspond with him about them. All of us, of course, also read them and discussed them directly with Benjamin or through Adorno. Correspondence may at times have a more irreversible and quarrelsome effect than conversation, in which misunderstandings can be immediately removed. The charge that we blackmailed Benjamin has been raised by the journal *Alternative*. Certain sources in East Germany have added to it, as, unfortunately, did Gershom Scholem and Hannah Arendt—both of whom I greatly respect.

This matter is especially painful for me because now I am the only survivor who, from an intimate knowledge of the entire staff, can say that an infamous distortion took place here. The Institute never politically censored its co-workers. Of course, we discussed editorial changes and proposed them to the authors. As far as Benjamin was concerned, we always secured his approval. You will look in vain for a letter from Benjamin in which he protests against any alleged deletion by us. By the way, at the request of Rolf Tiedemann, the editor of Benjamin's works, I wrote a letter that is reprinted in the second part of the first volume of Benjamin's collected works. In that letter I described how we handled editorial matters and stated that the imputation of political censorship was downright grotesque. It was true—as the managing editor of the *Zeitschrift* I plead guilty—that at times we stylistically reformulated certain expressions that might have been misunderstood politically; but this was always with the approval of the authors in question. This involved all of us—Horkheimer, Adorno, Pollock, Marcuse, and myself; none of us was spared. We proceeded this way only because our *Zeitschrift* was essentially the platform for Critical Theory and we were pursuing a clear, philosophical, scientific, and political line. At any rate, the charge that we were making arbitrary changes behind an author's back or that we financially blackmailed a man like Benjamin is an insult to the members of the Institute, not least to Benjamin himself. To claim that he had to accept changes in his essays to secure modest financial assistance is a posthumous insult to Benjamin. I hope that I have contributed something to burying this legend at last.

Dubiel: Now I wish to touch on another complex matter. As you know, I have a clearly defined picture of the pioneering theoretical work of your group during the Frankfurt period before Hitler—I mean the project of an interdisciplinary social science. Generally speaking, when one engages in theory one always seeks to transpose particular theoretical efforts into an overall framework. What has fascinated me in some texts—especially in Horkheimer's inaugural address at Frankfurt University, in the preface to the *Zeitschrift für Sozialforschung,* and in various passages he wrote on dialectics—was this project, which Horkheimer called the "theory of the historical process." This reveals an intention to provide a theory of the present historical process by social scientific methods, in the best sense of that term. Was that really the case?

Lowenthal: Quite correct so far. At the end of the 1920s and the beginning of the 1930s a metaphysical and basically antihistorical reaction occurred in Germany: Husserl and his followers, the materialist metaphysics of Nicolai Hartmann, Max Scheler, Jung's psychology, Ludwig Klages, and a whole configuration of new "perennial philosophies." Early Nazi ideology was also an ahistor-ical, pseudo-metaphysical play with history and society. Our group attempted to trace the historical self-consciousness that had been achieved; to heighten critical historical consciousness was our theo-retical agenda. Is this what you are after?

Dubiel: Exactly! But is there something else?

Lowenthal: Well, that's what we did, we carried out the inten-tion.

Dubiel: How?

Lowenthal: In a broad study of Rhineland workers and em-ployees, which was an attempt to investigate the question of what holds a society together in a postfeudal period, in other words, to determine what the social-psychological cement of that society is.[4] The operational plan was to carry out research on authority. It was unorthodox in the history of organized intellectual and academic life to bring together philosophy, technical, and scientific reflec-tions and then translate them into research. After all, we had learned from Marx that the theoretical requires the empirical, as well as the reverse. So, the unity of theory and empirical research was something we assumed from the outset. Although we were no longer able to do much about changing society, our interpretation of events enabled us to save our lives.

Dubiel: You have now touched on it yourself. There was the attempt to unite general theoretical perspectives with detailed em-pirical work. So, there was the goal of integrating philosophy with various particular scientific approaches. Well, that's fine. But to what extent was this methodology made explicit? Did you discuss this epistemology together, or were these exclusively Horkheimer's private views?

4. Erich Fromm, *The Working Class in Weimar Germany: A Psychological and Sociological Study,* ed. Wolfgang Bonss, trans. Barbara Weinberger (Leamington Spa, 1984).

Lowenthal: That's difficult for me to answer. All of that tends toward an organizational form. . . .

Dubiel: Which is exactly what you and Marcuse have always argued against.

Lowenthal: All of this took place rather informally; it was not organized.

Dubiel: If there was indeed such a methodology, as part of the basic principles you all shared, then it must have been somewhere.

Lowenthal: Well, if you really want to know, it came through more in the preliminary editorial work and in the conferences over the studies to be published in the *Zeitschrift*.

Dubiel: That's what I thought.

Lowenthal: There you would hear such phrases as, "you cannot put it that way," or "we mean this in a different sense," or "we do not use such an expression," or "this expression we employ differently," and so forth. This is how the language of Critical Theory began. In common theoretical work a collective opinion emerged within our group.

Dubiel: All right. Was there in this rhetoric an awareness of the project, which I call the fusion of philosophy and scientific disciplines and the integration of the scientific disciplines themselves? Perhaps it was really through organized research by way of various personally assigned roles, so that Marcuse's task was in technical philosophy, Lowenthal's in literature, Adorno's in music, Pollock's in economics, while Horkheimer worked out the synthesis in his programmatic essays. Could your editorial sessions be pictured as having that formal structure?

Lowenthal: It did not take place that formally. There was no such planning of our work, such that Marcuse, for instance, would write an essay on political philosophy, Adorno on music, and I on literature. Each of us worked in a definite field on the assumption that something would eventually come out of it for the *Zeitschrift* and for our common theoretical perspectives. What you are imputing as the special competence of each one of us was valid only for music. There Adorno was indeed the "specialist" whom none of us could match. But in other areas the situation was different, because none of us was entirely ignorant of what everyone else was doing. Horkheimer was very knowledgeable in philosophy, but also in political sociology, literature, psychology, and history. The same was true of Marcuse, Teddie, and myself. Although specialists in the narrower sense, Pollock and Fromm were also highly cultured. None of us had chosen narrow fields of study at the university. This was a good basis for our collaboration.

Dubiel: Well, I get the feeling that I'm insisting on a personal *idée fixe.*

Lowenthal: In many cases our conversations stimulated future works. I think I have already told you how I came to write my essay on Hamsun. In conversation with Horkheimer and Marcuse, the latter claimed that Hamsun was the greatest living novelist. At that point I became very agitated and took issue with him, stating categorically that Hamsun was a fascist. Horkheimer then proposed that I explain this in an essay.[5] Until then, in 1934, there were still no leads on that subject. And so this study came about, as did many others, through conversations. When Mortimer Adler wrote his history of culture from Aristotle to the movies, Horkheimer thought this was a good opportunity to clarify our theory of popular culture. That's how the essay "Art and Popular Culture" came into being.[6] Again, in my essay on Hamsun there is a long footnote signed by Hektor Rottweiler—Adorno's pseudonym. In it he

---

5. Originally published in *Zeitschrift für Sozialforschung* 6, no. 2, in 1938; English version appears as Leo Lowenthal, "Knut Hamsun (1860–1952)," in Lowenthal, *Literature and the Image of Man,* vol. 2 of *Communication and Society* (New Brunswick, N.J., 1986).

6. Horkheimer, *Critical Theory,* pp. 273–90.

brings out that in Sibelius's music the same motifs reappear as in Hamsun's works. You can see from this how careful we were in reading one another's essays.

Dubiel: Now I want to ask you about *Autorität und Familie.* Basically, this was the first major collective project.

Lowenthal: Yes, *Studien über Autorität und Familie* [Studies on Authority and the Family], published in Paris in 1936, is a beautiful example of this type of collaboration. The idea was to study authority as the cement of society, that is, the idea missing in Marx: a theory of the mediating psychic links between base and superstructure. We asked ourselves whether there were mechanisms other than the pure use of force to explain conformity. A theory of the family as an agency of society was formulated by Fromm on the basis of Freudian theory. It appeared theoretically and empirically promising to investigate the family as a matrix of what authority meant in modern society. The very title expresses the unity of our interests.

Dubiel: Would this project's result have been different if history had followed a different course and if you had not been forced to emigrate, if you had had sufficient time and resources to carry the studies through according to plan?

Lowenthal: I think so.

Dubiel: Would you agree that the published volume was, after all, only a sort of report on work in progress?

Lowenthal: Yes. The work was uneven. Yet the first part, containing the theory of authority in modern society—a survey of the treatment of authority in philosophy from the Renaissance to the present time and a social-psychological discussion of authority with special reference to the family—would presumably have remained unchanged in a more developed version of the project. I myself would probably have written more on how this program was reflected in literature. And were it not for Hitler, the empirical research would have included additional sections and would not have restricted itself to the study of workers and employees in the Rhineland; it would have extended to other regions, such as Bavaria or areas east of the Elbe River. Had we had the means and the personnel, we would have undertaken comparative studies in other European countries. In a more refined version, we would have either omitted the third part of the study or structured it differently. That part contains a wealth of reports on scholarly literature written by persons from outside our circle and was devised largely as a means of supporting emigré colleagues in distress. Perhaps all of this might have developed in such a way that the *Zeitschrift für Sozialforschung* would have published research reports on other inquiries. The book was not very successful. But how could it have been otherwise? It was a huge work printed in German in 1936 by Alcan in Paris! It turned out to be a somewhat damaged *Flaschenpost*. I must reiterate: we never believed in fame and never sought it. But we all shared Adorno's urge to publish the work in German in spite of an uncertain future. In a sense, that publication, as well as the *Zeitschrift,* was a body of work by emigrés conceived in sadness and filled with hope.

Dubiel: Your reply to my query as to how the *Studien über Autorität und Familie* would have turned out had history not intervened with fascism strikes me as a little too pragmatic. My question should have been more subtle. I was in fact alluding to Horkheimer's formulation in the preface. In a passage referring to the crude character of the overall undertaking, Horkheimer says that it "would be possible for the issues involved in the investigations to disclose their true significance only in the context of an all-embracing theory of social life." What about this formulation?

Lowenthal: This was the principle for continuing to differentiate our individual works to the point of obtaining a theory of society, but surely it would not have led to the writing of a volume entitled *Theory of Society.*

Dubiel: So, this information was only an option for some sort of theoretical utopia.

Lowenthal: Well, yes; what we meant was a theoretically adequate approach—a successful grasping of the whole mechanism of modern society.

Dubiel: But couldn't Horkheimer's formulation be interpreted differently? Let me just read this formulation my way: "The volume at hand is a preliminary component of a theory of the historical process." When one mentions a part and a whole in a methodology, individual operations and an anticipated overall view, then one must conceive of certain rules that govern their interconnection. There would have to be the formulation of a methodological parameter by which one could gauge the progress of the historical development up to the point of a theory of historical movement.

Lowenthal: I don't think so. You are attributing to all of us foreign theoretical motives. All this would be aimed at a system, whereas Horkheimer's style, and Adorno's as well, were always in the direction of aphorisms.

Dubiel: For the period we are talking about, the 1930s, I would simply question whether the aphoristic form would have been adequate to Horkheimer's way of thinking. Besides, I do not mean to ascribe to your group a systematic approach. What interests me is what a methodology and a research technique would look like, and perhaps also what the literary form would be of a scientific work that attempts to formulate, on the basis of a "concrete totality," a theory of the historical process.

Lowenthal: Now listen. In reality, Horkheimer never wrote such a book. This is not an accident. You may, if you wish, collect essays, as has already been done, choose a title for publication purposes, and call it *Critical Theory*. And yet, this will not provide a systematic theory.

Dubiel: Leo, I'll stop pressing that point. I want to touch on other problems: questions of the continuity and discontinuity in the biography of your theory. When we talked about difficulties in locating constants that might characterize Critical Theory, we established that each theoretical contribution was interwoven in the historical moment. If that is so, then the theory changes with its subject. In that sense, Critical Theory is not a set of tenets that can be applied anytime, but only at a particular historical juncture.

Lowenthal: That's very much in the Marxist tradition! Mankind sets for itself only those tasks that it can solve. The task we set for ourselves at that time was the analysis of the social situation in which we found ourselves, in particular, the situation in Germany and Central Europe.

Dubiel: Good. In the preparatory work for my book on your group,[7] I read the texts in the following order. With regard to fascism, for instance, I excerpted and documented all pertinent passages in letters and all allusions in theoretical texts and entered them on a time scale from 1930 to 1945. It was then that I came upon some interesting points. Although it was the year of your emigration, for you 1933 did not seem to be the break it is commonly perceived as in contemporary accounts. Your group saw a much stronger continuity between the last years of the Weimar Republic, especially those since 1931, and the first years of Hitler's rule than is normally understood. In other words, fascism came gliding in. You did not experience Hitler's chancellorship as a historical watershed. According to your view at that time, fascism developed gradually out of monopoly-capitalist conditions. And this theory of fascism as the adequate political form of highly developed monopoly capitalism also determined your historical perception. I recall a letter Marcuse wrote to Horkheimer in which, on the occasion of Horkheimer's essay in *Studien über Autorität und Familie,* he discussed the question of periodization. There in 1934, alluding by analogy to the

7. Helmut Dubiel, *Theory and Politics: Studies in the Development of Critical Theory,* trans. Benjamin Gregg (Cambridge, Mass., 1985).

National Socialists, Marcuse stated that this fascist bunch of gangsters did not necessarily introduce a qualitatively new epoch. Later on, all of you, especially Marcuse, became much more skeptical. A good document is the 1939 essay "The Jews and Europe."[8] That essay still assumed that fascism was a great force in Europe before the war. I was surprised to learn that in 1939 there were eleven countries in Europe with fascist or quasi-fascist governments. In addition, many of the "still"-democratic states had strong fascist movements. Under these historical circumstances your group must have considered fascism as, indeed, a quasi-universal historical phenomenon—something you shared with many contemporary, exiled historians—and the political-economic interpretation of fascism gradually disappeared. Other explanations then surfaced, either in terms of a philosophy of history as in the *Dialectic of Enlightenment* or in terms of social psychology as in the later *Studies in Prejudice*. What I want to ask is this: would you agree that your view of fascism developed from a political-economic interpretation to one that rested in a global philosophy of history, before evolving into a social-psychological interpretation?

Lowenthal: I'm afraid not. This is the first time in our conversations that my position differs drastically from yours. I have no idea how you have reached this conclusion. It does indeed reflect the view of some people within our circle, but never that of the hard core that determined the Institute's theoretical orientation.

Dubiel: Not so fast. I need hardly tell you that I am alluding to Marcuse's beautiful essay on liberalism and Pollock's first two essays in the *Zeitschrift*.

Lowenthal: Well, Marcuse was not at the Institute in 1930 and 1931. Pollock did have such tendencies but, thank God, we were able to steer him in a different direction. Horkheimer, Fromm, and

8. Max Horkheimer, "Die Juden und Europa," *Zeitschrift für Sozialforschung* 8, no. 1 (1939): 115–37.

I have never believed or stated that fascism was merely—as you put it—a new political strategy of monopoly capitalism. None of us ever said that.

Dubiel: But now I will cite you chapter and verse. Today, what writer has become a classical reference of a most solid and precise formulation in almost all theoretical texts on the interpretation of fascism along capitalist lines? Which writer do you think?

Lowenthal: Franz Neumann?

Dubiel: No, Horkheimer. The most precise thesis I know by heart: "If you do not want to talk about capitalism, then you must also not mention fascism."[9]

Lowenthal: This had a totally different meaning: one should not grovel before the United States.

Dubiel: One should not grovel before a social order that tends likewise to give rise to fascism. As a highly developed capitalist country, the United States is not immune to fascism. This is what Horkheimer meant. You must be familiar with another passage in which he gives a political-economic interpretation of anti-Semitism. There he states, similarly, that fascist anti-Semitism was a sequel to the liquidation of the circulation phase in highly developed capitalism. If this is not an economic interpretation of fascism, then I don't know . . .

Lowenthal: It can also be said differently. After all, fascism is not simply just another manifestation of high finance. Once it comes into the historical arena it represents a qualitatively new social order. It is not necessarily the intention of monopoly capitalism to exterminate the Jews and to execute the gypsies and the insane or to plot a world war. These passages in Horkheimer must be viewed dialectically. National Socialism must not be interpreted as a continuation of the economic strategy of high finance, as Franz Neumann's analysis does; nor must fascism be reduced to an inde-

9. Ibid., p. 115.

pendent petit-bourgeois mythology that accidentally seizes and maintains power. Both tendencies are seen as unequal partners in an overall historical process. It became clear to us all, even before January 31, 1933, that political life had taken on a new quality. This is why we emigrated. This is why we believed that political normalcy would no longer dominate and that high finance would not prevail, that it would eventually cast off small businessmen when it no longer needed them. But this does not mean giving up the theory of a class society organized by finance capital. The logic of events had probably driven both wings, big capital and the Hitler power apparatus, to unleash the world war. Despite the terrible sacrifices, I sometimes say: Thank God! I believe I already told you this story: when I took a walk with Horkheimer in the summer of 1934, he said that fascism in Germany had one positive effect, namely the politicization of society. This had never occurred so extensively, throughout the entire population. People now found that what happened in the political sphere concerned them directly, and this meant an end to public apathy as a characteristic of German political life—a topic about which I have written frequently. Such a politicization of the population is contrary to the interests and ideology of big capital.

Dubiel: This is only a marginal note: Is it not surprising that this apathy should, immediately after 1945, reappear more strongly than ever before in German history?

Lowenthal: This only proves our thesis that fascism creates a new political context characterized by the total mobilization of society, where everyone is a fellow prisoner, fellow culprit, and conscious fellow traveler of the political order. When this authoritarian and totalitarian terror apparatus disappears, the society falls back into public apathy—everywhere, not only in Germany. Fascism has not succeeded in politicizing the American nation; during World War II the population here was as unpolitical and uninvolved as ever. Let me repeat: this economistic interpretation is one-sided. We surely would not have feared to remain in Switzerland merely because big capital was in power. We feared that a specifically fascist political culture would arise in Europe and that the inner and outer realms of one's life would no longer be secure.

Dubiel: So, we could reformulate: Developed capitalist societies produce the socioeconomic conditions under which fascism can develop. But when the political apparatus of the society organized by capital has fallen into fascist hands, that system takes on a new quality no longer compatible with the interests of finance capital.

Lowenthal: This is exactly what I meant. This was our theory.

3

The Voice of America

Dubiel: Today I'd like to talk with you about the time you spent working as a communications specialist for the American government. First of all, could you discuss how and where you worked during the war? Perhaps you could start by naming the institutions where you were employed, either part- or full-time.

Lowenthal: For nearly the entire war period, I held an advisory position in the Domestic Media Department of the Office of War Information. Later, in 1944, I worked for the Bureau of Overseas Intelligence, on German material specifically. This bureau was a part of the Office of War Information. While I was working in Washington, Marcuse was working for the Office of Strategic Services, and we often saw each other there. Several of my colleagues from the Institute worked there: Neumann, Kirchheimer. Pollock was an advisor for the War Production Board. Adorno and Horkheimer didn't hold any government jobs.

Dubiel: It would be hard to imagine that they could have.

Lowenthal: I can't say much about my work for the Domestic Media Department. It wasn't especially exciting—mainly routine. My job after 1944 in the Bureau of Overseas Intelligence was more interesting. There each of us had to evaluate radio programs and press materials in our respective languages. My job was to analyze

Translated by Ted R. Weeks.

the radio programs of the German armed forces and German press material, both of which were supposed to yield information on what was going on in Germany, particularly concerning morale. I worked with interesting people there. At the desk next to me sat Ruth Benedict, the famous anthropologist, who worked partly on Germany and partly on the Netherlands. I still remember our conversations comparing Westphalian and Dutch eating habits! Nonetheless, I must say I remember my time in Washington as a very frustrating experience. There were too many people, and there was a great muddle of bureaucracy, professorial vanity, and phony intellectuals—I didn't find it satisfying. So I wasn't too unhappy when my duties called me back to the Institute, to take an active part in a study on anti-Semitism among American workers. This study, financed by the American Jewish Labor Committee, was never published.

Dubiel: Marcuse told me that his job in the Office of Strategic Services consisted of identifying, along with other specialists, the groups in fascist Germany who contributed to its economic recovery. As you know, that happened as a preparatory stage of the later, poorly carried out denazification process. Did you also work in this context?

Lowenthal: Unfortunately, no. I would have much preferred to work in the Office of Strategic Services. But for personal reasons, that didn't work out. There were some really interesting people working there: H. Stuart Hughes, Carl Schorske, Felix Gilbert. They carried out interesting, historically oriented studies, whereas our work was then often very short-term and unmethodical. We neither did much good nor caused much harm, I believe.

Dubiel: I'm amazed that your work in the OWI was so disorganized. I've always thought that when governments hire intellectuals for such functions, they must have a clearly defined research plan with a clear organizational hierarchy and precisely defined questions and instructions.

Lowenthal: I don't mean that everything was totally chaotic. It

was, you know, wartime, and the American governmental apparatus was inflated with new agencies and personnel. And, to tell the
truth, it wasn't really prepared for such things as intelligence work.
In this respect, the United States had no real tradition in international politics, as existed in the European countries and especially in
the totalitarian systems. No, the work there was not especially
satisfying. That was not the case later with the Voice of America;
the work there was an intellectual and scientific challenge.

Dubiel: Could you explain that in a little more detail?

Lowenthal: My task consisted of setting up a research division
that was to evaluate the effects of the Voice of America radio programs. And I did just that, in fact, setting it up for a broad, international area. My immediate superiors in the State Department
helped me a great deal in this, and many American social scientists
assisted me to an extraordinary degree. We employed many experts
in the social sciences and maintained contracts with university institutes and commercial research firms. All of the plans for these
widespread activities were worked out in our office. Above all, we
approached the effects of mass media in a quite different manner
than was usual in American studies at that time. Unfortunately, this
new approach didn't last long; that was one of my biggest disappointments. American studies at that time were influenced essentially by the needs of the advertising industry. Our work had two
primary target areas. The first of these was the Soviet Union and its
satellites, and here our work was basically archeological. Naturally,
we couldn't examine the effects of the programming in the Eastern
Bloc directly, so we had to develop completely new methodologies.
One was the questioning of refugees. That was a very dubious
method because it involved such a selective sample. Other material
for our investigations came from the reactions of the Soviet Union
to our broadcasts, including its jamming of them.

The other important investigations involved communication
habits. One can't naïvely assume that all nations and cultures respond in the same manner, for example, that reactions in the Near

and Far East to printed or electronic media would be the same as in the United States. In this context we examined the formation of public opinion leadership: What sources supply public opinion with information, for example, in rural areas? How are opinions formed and disseminated? In the café, by the mule driver, or by the messenger who goes from the village to the big cities and brings back information? Our task consisted, as I already said, of evaluating the specific effects of the radio broadcasts, but we also studied other media. Of particular theoretical and methodological importance was the set of questions aimed at revealing the conceptions an average inhabitant of another country would have of America, of American culture and politics. How was one to know whether and to what extent a conception can be traced back to a certain source— a certain broadcast or a certain film? It was interesting to pursue in detail the question of how the image of America is influenced in different countries.

One other important aspect of our work involved our relationship with the producers of the radio broadcasts. Here our task was fundamentally to bicker, that is, to criticize what was being produced in the broadcasts. For that reason, we weren't exactly popular with the programming directors. After all, we were investigating the relationship of the radio producers to their public. We were, so to speak, their auditors.

Dubiel: I don't understand something here. Now, the Voice of America was an agency of the State Department. I thought that in the United States there were only private radio stations. Or is that a dumb question?

Lowenthal: The Voice of America was an arm of the State Department, later of the U.S. Information Agency. You're confusing that with the American radio industry, which covered the domestic market. We were forbidden by law to transmit any of the Voice's programs to America. The Voice's programs were—and still are today—broadcast by radio stations in Europe and Asia. Some were also broadcast from New York, for example, the German-language Stimme Amerikas—but you're much too young, you've certainly never listened to that. No, your question isn't dumb at all; there were and are private radio stations that had and have a commission similar to that of the Voice of America: Radio Liberation and Radio Free Europe. These are semiofficial government agencies whose credibility is, on the one hand, strengthened by the fact that they don't appear as direct agencies of American foreign policy. On the other hand, they are often rather excessive in their radicalness. You surely know that; sometimes the administration was caused a lot of embarrassment and effort because these semiofficial propaganda agencies went too far. For example, in 1956 during the Hungarian uprising, it was difficult to prevent Radio Free Europe from encouraging the Hungarian population to engage in further useless bloodshed.

Several things interested me as a sociologist in this work: the development of new methods in communication research; the relationship—of which I experienced a good deal myself—between the scholars engaged in evaluation and the producers of media programs; and finally, the contact with the hierarchical competitive struggles in the various sections in the State Department, especially in the Foreign Service. Diplomats and other high government officials who worked in Washington looked down on this enormous propaganda apparatus and the information service much more than the officials working out in the field did. To their way of thinking, this was no way to conduct foreign policy; they treated us with great condescension. Whenever they wanted to know something from us, they would always demand immediate answers. For example, I often gave lectures in the Foreign Service Institute, and I might suddenly be asked, "So what do we have to do to make the Russians like us or so that this or that happens, and how can you prove this or that assumption?" While they had disdain for our nondiplomatic activities, they nonetheless demanded quick answers to difficult, complex questions. I felt as if I were in an echo chamber, where from all sides I was pummeled with questions, none of which I quite understood. My biggest and most fundamental mistake at that time was to equate American with German government service. I was around fifty, and if German standards had applied, I probably would have stayed in the foreign service until retirement. Today I sometimes have to laugh at my naïveté then. I didn't realize the internal mobility and politicization of the governmental apparatus. I finally came into great difficulties when the Republicans took over the helm and, besides that, the entire agency was transferred to the organizational framework of the U.S. Information Agency. Then they made my life very tough, broke up my department, and reduced my research funding in order gradually to force me to quit. But I only resigned after I was offered a professorship at Berkeley.

Dubiel: How did that come about?

Lowenthal: Like a bolt from the blue I was offered a visiting professorship at Berkeley, for which I obtained—with some difficulty—a leave from the government. I was then invited to spend a year at Stanford's Center for Advanced Studies, where I did enough sociological research to be offered a professorship at Berkeley. In that connection a concrete example of the sociology of role change occurs to me. As director of research for the Voice of America I was often approached by the director of the Voice, who wanted to use our results, of course, only to the extent that they were advantageous for him, that is, in order to expand his staff or his budget. The senior officials in the State Department, however, wanted to know only the critical side. So I was tugged back and forth between the wishes of the director and those of his superiors: the one wanted only justification, the other only criticism. That was a precarious position. I have many more sociologically interesting stories from that job, but that would take up too much time here.

Dubiel: Leo, I have a burning question. At that time in the early fifties, with your political past and in that politically sensitive position, surely you would have been an ideal victim for McCarthy?

Lowenthal: Yes, in fact, one of the main targets of attack of McCarthy and his henchmen, those loathsome lawyers Roy Cohn and David Shine, was the information service of the American government. According to them, the Voice of America was controlled by Communists. They constantly harassed us in New York. They had set up their headquarters in the Waldorf Astoria in order to better interrogate us. (I believe I already told you that the main offices of the Voice of America were located in New York.) They continually summoned the political and technical directors and the various division chiefs of the separate departments, in both secret and public sessions. They never summoned me. That was astonishing, because I was, after all, the man from that odd institute in New York, I held a quite high position in the propaganda apparatus of the State Department, and I had a past they certainly knew about. I was convinced that they would interrogate me one day.

At that time I used to keep my writings stacked on the desk in my office. On top of the pile I had placed an offprint of an essay with the title "Portrait of the American Agitator." That was an advance copy of my later book *Prophets of Deceit*. If I had been summoned to testify in Washington, I would have taken that stack with me and placed it so that the committee and the television crew could have read the title. Then if some senator, outraged at the unambiguous allusion, had asked me to explain myself, I would have calmly said that I brought the books along for the sole purpose of demonstrating my scientific qualifications to the honorable senators. Unfortunately, I was never given that chance; I was never called to testify. I've often thought about it, but I've never quite been able to figure it out. Perhaps it had something to do with my institutional independence; after all, I could have just gone back to the Institute. I can only tell you the following story, which I learned from the executive director of the Voice of America. I simply said to him, "Ask around why I haven't been called to testify." So he asked one of those unpaid assistants of McCarthy's, the well-known William F. Buckley, a very rich, archreactionary journalist belonging to the farthest right wing of American journalism. And he said to the director, "Yeah, that Lowenthal. We had him at the top of our list, we looked into every corner of his past, but we couldn't find anything against him." I was aghast, of course, and said to my informant, "Do me a favor and go back and tell them that I'll help them find something!" But nothing happened.

In connection with the State Department's efforts to get rid of me, I had to go through another security investigation. That was a favorite way to humiliate the people they wanted to get rid of. As a rule, the investigators who carried out such supplemental security investigations held at least the same civil service rank as their "victim." At that time I was director of a department, so I should have been interrogated by the director of the security office of the foreign service or his representative. But in order to humiliate me even more, I was interrogated by a petty civil servant whose name I'll never forget: Mr. Spence. He was a kind of glorified nightwatchman at our New York office. It must have been a trauma for him, because from his perspective I was a bigwig.

On his desk were the questions—written by someone else—that he was to ask me. He sat at a little desk, in front of which were a few chairs and a comfortable armchair, in which I sat. Then came the stereotyped questions—I'll just mention a few of them. Among others: "Are you now or have you ever been a member of the Communist Party?" I could answer that with no. Then: "Do you now or have you ever had sympathies for the Communists?" There I said yes. He just about fell off his chair. He made sure that I had understood the question correctly. I said that I now no longer had sympathies for the Communists; my official position and area of activity spoke for this. But I was born in 1900. "In 1917, the revolution broke out. We were pupils in one of the most liberal high schools in liberal Frankfurt. We hated the Kaiser and the world war, and we saw the Bolshevik revolution as an act of liberation for humanity." And, I added, I would hope that the American government would never place anyone in a sensitive post who was of my generation and yet had never felt sympathies for international Communism. The man looked at me in astonishment and asked, "Should I write all that down?" I said, "You don't need to. I'll place a State Department memorandum in the files"—which I did, too, and nothing happened to me. And then the man, still following his instructions, accused me of having only investigated the material of right-wing agitators in my book *Prophets of Deceit*. I told him, "I'm sorry, but the American Jewish Committee paid me ten thousand dollars to write a book about anti-Semitic agitators." The Communists might well be very wicked, but in the United States they aren't anti-Semitic, at least not in terms of their ideology. The next question contained the accusation that in my lectures at Columbia University I had paid inordinate attention to the works of Karl Marx. To that I answered that when I accepted the job as lecturer at Columbia I had taken an oath to be scientifically objective, and consequently I would have been committing an act of considerable dishonesty if I had given a lecture on the history of social philosophy and simply ignored the most important social philosopher of the nineteenth century, Karl Marx, and his followers. And so the questions continued, each more stupid than the preceding one.

Dubiel: This interrogation, this security examination, then, was a degradation ritual to make you quit your job. But it surely had some connection with the McCarthy interrogations to which others were subjected? And didn't the fact that they suddenly no longer wanted you at this post have, possibly, something to do with your ideological and scientific background?

Lowenthal: I hardly think so. More likely it coincided with a new trend. First of all, they wanted a Republican to fill my post, and second, there was a strong bias against the scientific orientation of our methods. The Republicans were old-fashioned and set all their hopes on the intelligence apparatus. They were no longer willing to spend money on scientific research. It's also not true that so many people were fired because of the McCarthy trials. Very few who had secure positions were actually fired. This is all very interesting sociologically. If somebody were writing about the sociology of the state machinery, there would be a lot of material on that from the McCarthy years. There were many people who served as informers for McCarthy, among them officials from the Voice of America. But even more important than one's party affiliation, in an American-type government, is which governmental branch controls your office. Of course, Republicans and Democrats aren't friends, but Congress and the executive branch are even greater enemies. If—and this happened frequently during the McCarthy years—somebody from the executive branch would say something to the Congress people that could hurt the executive, that was the greatest crime. We had a man in our department, a unit supervisor—I don't want to mention his name—who was one of the head informers and was constantly going over to the Waldorf Astoria to relate his horror stories to Cohn and Shine, and probably to McCarthy as well. The man had a secure position; he couldn't be fired. I remember a meeting in which I took part. We realized that we couldn't fire him, but we had to "punish" him somehow. So he was transferred to Kabul, Afghanistan.

Dubiel: Can you talk some more about those events?

Lowenthal: The McCarthy committee wasn't at all liked by the members of the Senate Foreign Affairs Committee. When McCarthy began to interfere with the business of this important congressional committee, they formed their own subcommittee, the so-called Hickenlooper committee. This committee summoned me and asked me about the effects of the Voice of America in the Soviet Union. The next day the *New York Times* published my testimony on the front page. I thought I was going to be famous! But, as it turned out, it was a media flash-in-the-pan, even with my photo and testimony on the front page. The senior officials in the State Department were very annoyed at this sudden public visibility. I was severely reprimanded for my testimony. Well, all of that's probably not so interesting, but it is interesting that the two committees were at loggerheads: while the McCarthy committee had no use for me, the Foreign Affairs Committee treated me with a great deal of respect.

Dubiel: Could we speak now a little more generally about foreign policy in the United States?

Lowenthal: Well, I had my views on American foreign policy insofar as my work provided some insight into it. The interesting thing was how much the entire mode of thinking was influenced by domestic interests and conditions, by events in domestic politics and in business life. Let me give a few examples. I was always amazed at how little interest the Voice of America and other propaganda agencies had in South America. People would always say, "We've got them in our pocket." And I would respond in conversation, "Those are authoritarian feudal societies. There are surely groups other than these military *juntas* who in the distant future could determine the destinies of these countries." They ignored that. This attitude was manifested in the fact that only second-rate people were used for the programs destined for South America, and little attention was paid to them. Perhaps in this respect the behavior of my department was representative of the entire State Department. That's one good example. The other was Africa. For Africa there was simply nothing. I wrote memorandum after memorandum suggesting that we do some programming in Swahili, but nothing came of it (that changed later on). I must say that in my time, as I saw it, Africa scarcely appeared at all in the immediate realm of American foreign policy. What amazed me most was the undifferentiated thinking with regard to Stalin's anticipated death. This was in 1953; he was already very ill, and it was obvious that he would soon die. Endless position papers were written, full of speculations on what would happen after his death. Would civil war break out, would tensions between the military and the party become critical, would the political apparatus be able to take the strain, would unrest result, would it possibly even be a good opportunity for intervention? You can't even imagine all the nonsense written in those days. Of course, little Leo Lowenthal wasn't asked for advice, but if I had been given the opportunity, I would have predicted that nothing dramatic was going to happen. I would have said, "The whole governmental system has been in the saddle for almost forty years now, the majority of the people living there don't know any other system, the government and the military apparatus are dependent on each other; the country is in a stage of industrial reconstruction after a horrible war, nothing extraordinary will happen that could threaten the system." At that time, they took me for a fool, but I was right. It left a deep impression on me, this official wishful thinking and anticipation of the Soviet Union's collapse after the death of Stalin.

Dubiel: Leo, when you talk like this about American foreign policy from the perspective of your work, it occurs to me that though your description of foreign policy is critical, it is, so to speak, critical only of immediate circumstances. You mentioned that whole hemispheres, for example, Latin America and Africa, were ignored because the Americans supposedly "had them in their pocket anyway." You've also told me often enough about American blindness toward certain developments in Communist China and about the personalistic image many officials and politicians had of the development of the Soviet Union. You've mentioned to what extent American diplomats and other employees of the U.S. foreign service remained estranged from the country in which they were stationed, always assessing local conditions, so to speak, from the cultural-imperialist bias of the United States. They generally wouldn't learn the language well enough to communicate, had contact only with the country's upper classes, and consequently seldom gained a realistic picture of social conditions, even in the countries where they were considered friends and allies. None of this goes beyond the limits of immanent criticism. I could well imagine that you'd write memoranda about all of this, concluding with the recommendation that the foreign service be reformed. In short, what surprises me is that you didn't come up with a more radical critique of American foreign policy. Only once, when you were speaking about the disappointment of all of your political hopes—and you also brought postwar political development in the United States into this global disappointment—you came a little nearer to my expectations. My generation, that is, the social scientists who got their political education through the experience of the Vietnam War in the context of the student movement in the late sixties, had very specific and clear-cut criticisms of American foreign policy. So, the combination of this political socialization and a relatively good knowledge of Southeast Asia and Latin America has made me firmly convinced that the United States represents an imperialist power. For that reason, it's considered astonishing— and the target of these accusations has, of course, usually been Herbert Marcuse, but I've heard them made in reference to you, too— that people like all of you, with a clear-cut intellectual, socialist tradition, who are counted among the founders of Critical Theory, had no qualms about entering the service of a power that, just one generation later, was unequivocally seen as imperialistic. What do you say to the charge that the United States is an imperialist power?

Lowenthal: I'm not interested in posing as an ardent critic of American foreign policy. I looked at it from the vantage point of my specific function; after all, I was only the director of a certain department within the American propaganda apparatus that didn't make political decisions itself. I'm emphasizing this only in order to make clear that what I'm about to say is merely an aphoristic marginal note, not a conclusive assertion. The governmental activity didn't compromise either Marcuse or me. For practical reasons I was forced to find suitable employment. As you know, the Institute's funds had become diminished, and already beforehand I had actively tried to find an acceptable academic position, an endeavor in which I finally succeeded after this "detour" in government. The "cunning of reason" sometimes works for the individual, too. I've already told you the story about M. I. Finley, a respected professor of classics; when he was denounced by the Committee on Un-American Activities, he was fired from his crummy job at a tiny college and ended up being offered a great position in Cambridge. But, to get back to the subject, I'd have to say that neither during the war, when I worked for the Office of War Information, nor in the postwar period did I ever have the feeling that I was working for an imperialist power. At that time, American foreign policy was essentially reactive and in no respect active. I consider it false radicalism to say that the politics of the cold war were nothing but a manifestation of American imperialism. After all, there were two superpowers opposing each other, and it's difficult to make out just who—the United States or the Soviet Union—engaged in the more imperialistic politics right after the war.

Dubiel: Now you're starting to take the defensive, probably because the category of imperialism is so morally loaded. Because of that, your answer sounds a little like a justification. Let's take a sober look at the term. There are certain elements of definition on which we can quickly agree. And when these elements are applied to the process of foreign policy precisely in this period right after the Second World War, the term's meaning becomes clear. I am following the accepted formulas of established American political science. By imperialism, I mean the establishment of a permanent military establishment; the setting up of a defense industry that is independent of war cycles, that is, an industry specifically implemented for the production of military goods; the setting up of a permanent crisis staff that, in the American case, is ultimately more influential than the Secretary of State but is located not in the normal institutional apparatus of the government but rather, as it were, adjacent to it. (I refer here, of course, to the National Security

Council, which is basically a war agency—no Western European country has anything analogous.) I'm also thinking about simple historical facts that, as far as I know, became known only in retrospect—for example, that under Truman the military budget was suddenly doubled with the justification that the role of the United States as the guarantor of international stability or as the leader in world politics could not be made plausible except by a permanent war readiness. These are all things that became obvious only after a whole series of interventions. At least since Vietnam they have been unmistakably evident. My question is, was there at that time a consciousness, for you or among your colleagues, of imperialism as I've just defined it?

Lowenthal: I concur completely with your description. Nonetheless, in those days, as I was working for the government, I wasn't really conscious of it. What was always present, and still is today, although the Americans usually have to pay bitterly for it, is the belief that in order to carry out foreign policy effectively, it's necessary to form an alliance with whatever class happens to be on top at the moment, without an exact analysis of what sort of scoundrels those people may be and what sort of real support they enjoy in their society. I've often said to you that American foreign policy is essentially reactive. They let the world name the topics, as it were. It's a strange mixture of Calvinistic moralism and politics for capitalist interests, which are incorporated in an opaque and often very contradictory synthesis. Charlie Wilson's outrageous saying, "What's good for General Motors is good for the country," is a perfect expression of the American mentality. In this country, many people really do believe that what supports the economic system and its values is simultaneously compatible with a moralistic line on how to live one's life, equally in the private and in the public context. Consequently it happens that they have dealings with those scoundrels in Iran and those criminals in Vietnam and God knows where else. When they finally realize that it isn't working out, they

go off—in the exact same short-sighted and reactive manner—in
search of new allies, with whom the same process starts all over
again. The Americans are in this respect like a Hegelian thinker,
who always supports as "logical" whatever party happens to have
the power at that moment. This policy leads *nolens volens* to relativism and even amoralism. Most American politicians aren't even
conscious of this policy.

An undialectical concept of American imperialism is questionable. Essentially what that means is that American foreign policy is
on the one hand forever trying to counteract, by means of arma-
ments, alliances, and intervention, its constant fear of being out-
done militarily while on the other hand trying simultaneously to
forestall the ever-present threat of a global economic crisis, by gain-
ing new markets and protecting old ones. If you want to call that
imperialism, fine. I think it's nothing more than a clear-cut emana-
tion of the capitalist production system.

Dubiel: You're paraphrasing Lenin . . .

Lowenthal: Yes, and all this is by no means so different from
what is happening on the other side, in the Soviet Union and now
also gradually in China. Already in 1950 I said that the United States
and the Soviet Union are very similar systems, differing only in
details of institutional processes. I don't believe, for example, that
the National Security Council is so unique. I'm sure that similar
institutions exist in the Soviet Union and elsewhere.

Dubiel: That is to say, today you support—like many of your
former colleagues and allies—a sort of negative, critically interpreted convergence theory.

Lowenthal: You have to keep in mind that the United States's
role as a world power is very new. Just how long is this business
going to last? The Americans became an international power, involved in modern world history, only toward the end of and after
the First World War. That's just a bit over half a century ago. Many

peculiarities, particularly institutional ones, of American foreign policy are very simply explained by the fact that in this respect—unlike the Western European nations—the United States has no tradition reaching back into the nineteenth century or even earlier.

Dubiel: I'd like to offer one more observation I've made on the basis of a closer acquaintance with American postwar history. The ability to recognize precisely the imperialist character of American politics was, after all, very much hampered by the following circumstance: if you judge foreign policy strategies by the same right-left parameters that you can apply to domestic politics, then the pertinent contending factions of the postwar period present a very confusing picture. The people who already during the war and later in the postwar period were interested in a leading world role for the United States were, after all, the liberals with strongly moralistic—if not messianic—pretensions. In contrast, most of the conservatives at this time felt a strong interest in keeping America sheltered from world history. Today we tend to identify imperialist strategies with the right-wing, conservative, or even fascistic groups in the United States. And precisely this perception makes the assessment of American foreign policy so confusing for Europeans. But that also illustrates very nicely what you just said about U.S. foreign policy being a contradictory synthesis of Calvinist moralism and the politics of capitalist interests.

Lowenthal: Besides, Helmut, we don't want to forget that America's primary enemy in both world wars was Germany, first a Wilhelmine and then a fascist Germany. And if these enemies weren't a good moral justification for a policy of liberal intervention, then I don't know what would be. The anti-interventionists in the United States on the eve of the Second World War were practically fascists. This "America first" movement was a very precarious affair. The fascistic and anti-Semitic fringe groups I examined in my research were at that time, as you know, fanatically isolationist. Even within certain strata of the working class, insofar as these were anti-Semitic, there was the attitude: how does all of this concern us?

Dubiel: I'd really like to continue our discussion, but unfortunately our conversation has to fit into one book. So back to the biography. In the course of your work with the Voice of America you traveled more or less all around the world. What especially interests me now are the trips to Europe, your return to Germany in the early postwar years. Please continue.

Lowenthal: I first returned to Europe after the Hitler years, or as Germans usually say—regrettably—"after the war," in 1949 on business for the Voice of America. My first destination was England. At that time, of course, there were no jets that were able to make the whole journey nonstop. We had to land in Shannon, Ireland, and were forced, half-asleep, to disembark and wait in the airport café. As soon as I saw the waiter I was struck by an impression—of the servility and assiduity with which the dreadful coffee was served. As I contemplated this specific type of servility and assiduity, which I never experienced in quite the same way in America, I thought I noticed beneath the obsequious politeness something hidden, namely the resentment, the rage and envy, felt by the proletarian class toward the bourgeoisie that had just arrived in that expensive airplane. I hadn't seen that for fifteen years in America: Americans, after all, are fooled by a completely successful middle-class ideology—tomato juice unites us all beyond any class differences! Shannon was the return to an archetypical experience. My entire political memory was revived when I reexperienced this sharp class difference in a psychologically recognizable form. This was Europe.

Dubiel: Leo, a similar experience occurs to me, which complements yours in all aspects because it also took place in an airport, in Los Angeles. A black waitress in a cafeteria in the TWA building started up a conversation with two passengers, a well-off couple who had just returned from a vacation in Miami. The three of them exchanged remarks about their life stories, and the man, who clearly belonged to the upper middle class, told how he had acquired his business. At that point the black waitress responded, without a trace of reserve or distance, that she'd tried to make her fortune in business at one point, but "I didn't make it." In this small conversational scene, two classes were personally represented: upper middle and lower middle. They dealt with each other without a trace of psychological class barriers. Here in the United States there's an ideological egalitarianism that permeates every facet of social life. That really is different in Europe. Even in those societies where the integration of the proletariat into bourgeois society has taken place smoothly, as in the case of the Federal Republic, there are still remnants of a once-intact class consciousness. The status anxieties of the petit bourgeois, the helpless resentment against the upper class, which manifests itself in all that silly talk about "the little man"—it's all a perverted, lingering trace of this.

Lowenthal: That's just what I meant, you've formulated it perfectly. Suddenly, all of that was there once again: the class differences that express themselves in this reserve, in the distance, the gestures. These signs signaled to our group that we lived in another, socially different world.

Dubiel: Yes, Leo, in this we agree, but what can we do with it? It can be said that the American dream is the perverse apogee of a thoroughly ideological class harmony, which the ruling strata in the Federal Republic can only dream about. Their ideological motto of "social partnership" certainly hasn't taken root to the same extent; the residues of a once-intact class consciousness must still be too strong. But then again, I'm inclined to defend this psychological class harmony, without a theoretical backup for my position. The United States represents the most perfect bourgeois society the world has ever known, including its positive aspects. Everyday life here is so easy and pleasant, so free from the authoritarian-Wil-

helmine fuss that still characterizes much of political life in the
Federal Republic today. It's reminiscent of the concept of competition in the third volume of *Das Kapital:* bourgeois equality is such a
massive psychological reality in the United States that it really does
determine a good part of daily behavior. Here I'm ambivalent to the
point of helplessness. . . .

Lowenthal: Yes, when I first came to America, I said: this is
capitalism without a bad conscience. When someone in Germany
called someone a capitalist or spoke about capitalism, a friend-foe
relationship was immediately established. Here it's different. Nobody tries to deny that this is a capitalist society. This is probably
because America's emergence as a society occurred at the height of
the bourgeois age. America had no feudal mortgages on its future.
Here there are unfortunately no pretty ruins of castles or other
historical relics of earlier times, but similarly lacking is that feudal
ideal of obligations to those above and below, the ritual mainte-
nance of social boundaries. But I'd better get back, finally, to the
waiters in Shannon and to my first trip back to Europe. The airplane landed in London. There I saw for the first time the destruction caused by bombing. The city made a most depressing sight,
characterized by extreme lethargy: very little reconstruction work
was under way. One of my most embarrassing experiences—this
was once again at the airport, waiting for my flight to the Con-
tinent—was to see the stout, overly well fed, loud, and uninhib-
ited German-speaking businessmen. At that time I heard the absurd story that Germans were sending their English friends "Care"
packages—don't forget, this was 1949. There I thought to myself,
for once in my life I'm on the winning side, whereas otherwise I
generally feel more comfortable among the losers. And yet here it
was no use to me anyway, for the tables had already turned again.
From London I flew to Italy, and from there I traveled by train
through Austria to Germany. The next morning I woke up in my
sleeping car in Innsbruck and saw bombed-out Austrian buildings

for the first time. I admit quite freely today that at the moment I said to myself, "Not enough, not enough." Suddenly the whole rage, the fury, the grief at all the horror Hitler had brought about, exploded in me. An old acquaintance picked me up at the train station in Munich. He suggested that we go directly to the *Oktoberfest,* and I agreed, half out of politeness and half out of melancholy. On arriving there, I just about turned around and flew back to America. The whole crap had started up anew: there were those loud, fat, boozing oafs in the giant tents, making a ruckus drinking, eating sausages, and swinging their mugs, the oom-pah-pah bands were blaring. It was ghastly.

Another experience I remember was Dachau, where I went with a group of colleagues from my office. I was walking, in a kind of daze, in the little cemetery in front of the ovens, and I suddenly saw that one of my American colleagues was pulling out his camera to take a picture of me. I came at him like one possessed and shouted, "Jim, you can't take a picture of me here." He didn't understand that at all. The thought that I, a Jew who had survived through no merit of my own, would stand in front of the memorial at Dachau and have my picture taken for "fun," as it were, was more than I could stand. From Munich I traveled to Frankfurt, where I stayed awhile. Frankfurt was the headquarters of the High Command. Yes, Helmut, I had some experiences in Frankfurt, but should I tell about all that?

Dubiel: Yes, by all means.

Lowenthal: Well, then, I was quartered in a V.I.P. hotel, the Hotel Carlton by the train station. And there, after all those years, was the same manager who had been there in the early thirties, before Hitler. He recognized me right away; in earlier days I had frequently eaten there. He asked, "Herr Dr. Lowenthal, what brings you to Frankfurt again?" He was astonished when I told him that I was an official in the American foreign service. Then I asked him what I could do that evening—it was a Sunday. He suggested a cabaret, I think on Lindenstraße. When I checked my coat at the cloakroom, I heard from the stage of the cabaret a *soubrette* singing a melody from the *Threepenny Opera*. I must have muttered to myself out loud in English, "Well, that's how I went out and that's how I come back!" The cloakroom lady looked at me with astonishment. I had only wanted to say, half subconsciously, I left with Brecht, and here I was, returning with Brecht.

And another story occurs to me just now. The next morning I was picked up from the Hotel Carlton by an official American government car. The driver was a young German, about eighteen years old. When I walked out of the hotel, he diligently opened the rear door of the car, and I said to him in German, "No, that's not necessary; I'll sit up front with you." He was completely amazed. Then we began to talk. He was greatly impressed by the fact that I spoke German so well and especially by the fact that I could chat with him in the Frankfurt dialect. I told him that, as a German Jew, I had emigrated in time to avoid Hitler and that I had, so to speak, made my fortune in America. Then this boy said to me in Frankfurt dialect, "Ja, Herr Doktor, that was really dumb of Hitler to start in on the Jews. After all, everybody knows that Jews have money." That was one of the saddest experiences I had. This innocent boy, who must have been born around 1931, was chronically afflicted with this ideological poison that Nazism had spread and left behind. At that time I didn't feel capable of enlightening the boy. In any case, it was a depressing experience and colored my first impressions of post-Hitler Germany. Shall I go on?

Dubiel: Yes, yes.

Lowenthal: One of the few people in Germany who impressed me positively at that time was the then vice-chancellor of Frankfurt University, Franz Böhm. I can't remember when I had seen him last, but he knew who I was. Even before I got around to formulating my impressions, he said, "Isn't it depressing? Nobody ever knew about anything. Everywhere you find this feigned ignorance

about the goings-on in Germany during the Hitler years." Böhm
had great moral integrity. My meeting with him was actually my
only uplifting experience of that visit. During a business trip to
Heidelberg I also visited a prominent social scientist, who, as a
well-known Social Democrat, had immediately been fired from his
post by the National Socialists. So I went to see him, and, typical
for a German professor, he continually called me "Herr Doktor" to
establish the proper distance between himself, the "Herr Professor"
and a commonplace "Herr Doktor." When I asked him how he was
doing, he immediately began to complain about the American occupation authorities. He complained about the planned but long
since shelved school reform that would have done away with Latin
and the learning of other classical languages. I couldn't resist asking
him what he really had to complain about. After all, with the help of
the American victors he was back in his job, and he was doing well
materially. After this conversation about the school reform that
hadn't been carried out, he asked me what had impressed me most
in Germany, and I told him about my encounter with Franz Böhm.
I also repeated to him that again and again I had run into the phenomenon of Germans claiming not to have known anything about
the atrocities committed under Hitler. To this he responded with a
slightly smug smile, "Well, Herr Doktor, you in America carry
out so many empirical studies. Have you ever done a study on how
fast the living forget their dead?" After he used the almost incred-
ible pronoun "their" in connection with "dead" to refer to the Jews
and the other countless victims murdered by the Germans, I bowed
and took my leave. It was a shattering experience. But enough of
that now.

Dubiel: You wanted to tell about the behavior of certain American officials with whom you had dealings during your travels in
Germany.

Lowenthal: Yes, Helmut, I'll start off with an amusing story
that is very characteristic of the mentality of both the Germans and

the Americans. In my research department in New York we didn't
do any of our own research on the effectiveness of the Voice of
America programs because the American occupation authorities in
Germany maintained their own research department. It was precisely this agency that I was to visit. It had already struck me in
America that a surprisingly large number of listeners commented
unusually warmly and cordially on the Voice of America. I simply
couldn't believe that they had been listening so zealously or that
they had been thinking so benevolently about it. So I asked my
colleague—that was, so to speak, my official task—"What do you
do, exactly? What approach do you use? How do you find respon-
dents?" "Well," he said, "we send a postcard to the people whom we
want to interview stating that on a certain date an American official
of the High Commission will come to ask them a few questions."
My immediate response was, "Fine, I understand everything." The
Germans, the defeated, wanted to make a good impression when
they had dealings with Americans, and they could easily guess what
the Americans wanted to hear. This anecdote is equally characteristic for the authoritarian German character as for the indescribable
naïveté of the Americans, who, after all, must have known from
their methodological training what an interview prejudice is.

But there were also more serious stories. I flew with a military
airplane from Frankfurt to Berlin; that was the only way—it was the
time of the blockade. I flew together with a rather highly placed
State Department official who also worked for the U.S. Information Agency (USIA). The airplane had hardly taken off when he
turned to me and said, "Leo, since you're in Germany, why don't
you buy yourself some jewels?" I said to him that I had never bought
jewels in my life and that I didn't have the slightest intention to buy
any in Germany. At that time, despite the German currency reform—you're probably too young to remember that, Helmut—
the cigarette economy still prevailed in Germany, and it was easy for

the relatively well-off American occupiers to buy up jewels and other objects of value. In Berlin we were picked up by an official government car with a German driver, as usual. Even before we reached our office the car stopped in front of an apartment house in Charlottenburg. My colleague got out and said that it wouldn't take long and he would be right back. At this point the German driver, who had found out that I was of German origin, turned around and asked me, "Do you know what the gentleman is doing up there?" Without being asked he proceeded to inform me that my colleague's jewel dealer lived there. Helmut, this is by no means an isolated incident. Many of my colleagues urged me to buy jewels, furniture, and china at that time because everything was so cheap. I was appalled at this mentality, not because I had any great sympathy for the Germans but because the fact that government officials were so set on plundering the Germans for a few cents was really repugnant. Furthermore, these government employees, who often weren't career officials and who after the occupation years settled back into civilian life at home, had something in common with the senior diplomats and military men, namely, great ignorance about Germany. Hardly anyone made the effort to learn the German language or to establish contact with the German population. I remember how one high official of the USIA urged me to stay on in Germany because they could really use me there. I told him that I was in the process of setting up a large research agency in the United States, and that he wouldn't accept my conditions anyway. He asked, "What are your conditions?" I would have demanded a binding promise from all my employees that, first, they would not engage in black market activities; second, they would be able to converse in colloquial German within a year; and third, they would have to name me five German families with whom they interacted socially. This was, in my view, the only way to carry out the politics of information, or any politics whatsoever, in a democratic manner.

Well, I don't have to tell you that these conditions weren't accepted. Fine. A year later an equally high official in Austria made me the very same offer, and I smilingly named him the same conditions, and he naturally laughed, too. Those were sad experiences.

In 1951 I once again took an extensive trip to Europe, visiting, among other places, Scandinavia. I was in Sweden first, and I came away with a most uneasy feeling. I had always called this nation the land of "psychological isolationism." Modern world history had always bypassed the Swedes. They made a lot of money selling their ball bearings to both the Nazis and the Russians—to whomever was a good customer. They kept out of the war, the country blossomed, there were more Cadillacs to be seen on the streets of Stockholm than in New York. Already at that time Sweden was a consumer society, especially as seen by someone coming from England, as I did. By the way, I forgot to mention that on my first trip from England to Germany I could hardly sleep because of the constant noise of construction. The Germans were hauling rubble away until late at night, and early in the morning they would start up again. Not just I, but many people coming from England to Germany were struck by this. It was already possible to see how things would develop. Also, I often heard the Germans lament the magnificent buildings the Americans had bombed and destroyed. But on none of my trips, whether in 1949, 1951, or 1953, did I ever hear a German express regret at what the Germans had done during the war. And that was certainly not limited to the bombing of beautiful buildings.

From Sweden I continued on to Oslo. There I was picked up at the airport by an English-speaking driver. That was an amusing incident. I had never been to Oslo before, and yet when we drove into the city I knew the precise locations of the Grand Hotel, the Café Central, the theater, and so on. The driver asked me if I had been in Oslo often, and I had to tell him it was my first time. Then I explained to him that I had worked on Hamsun and Ibsen and was well acquainted with Norwegian literature. Seeing Oslo was something like déjà vu.

Dubiel: That's really a beautiful story.

Lowenthal: Another good story comes to mind, the one about the Edvard Munch collection. Have I already told it to you?

Dubiel: No.

Lowenthal: As you know, I'm a great admirer of Edvard Munch. In fact, I just made a special trip to Washington to see the Munch exhibition. At that time there was no Munch museum in Oslo, as there is today. The paintings were still in the National Gallery. Unfortunately, I was always busy during its opening hours. So I gathered up all my courage and called the director of the National Gallery and asked him if he could suggest a way for me to see the paintings in spite of my schedule. In response he asked me, "What are you doing right now?" I answered, "I'm on the phone with you." Thereupon he said, "Then hang up the receiver and come to the front door of the museum. I'll open up for you, and you can look at the Munch paintings to your heart's content." And that's how it happened. Sometimes I say jokingly that I hope that was the only time I consciously misused the "power" of my official position for private ends. But I'm not ashamed of it.

There's another interesting Norwegian story I'd like to tell. As you may know, Helmut, the Nazis wanted to make Oslo the center of their international radio communications, both military and civilian. At that time they forced the Norwegians to erect an enormous building full of state-of-the-art radio equipment. This monster was naturally much too big for Norwegian purposes, and when the director of the state radio agency showed me the many rooms and studios, they were mostly empty. I asked the director—it was an obvious enough request—to acquaint me with the department concerned with audience research. He replied emphatically: "We don't have one." I was astonished and said, "You, perhaps the most democratic nation of Europe, you don't have one?" "Yes, perhaps precisely for that reason we don't. Because we are such a democratic nation, we also have cultural-political and pedagogical intentions. If we were to test listeners' preferences to see what the people out there in the country, in the fjords, in the little towns, liked to listen to, they would surely ask for hillbilly music and the like. That's just what we don't want; we want to offer them a highly cultured program. So we don't ask them in the first place." I've often had to think back on this story; it's a wonderful example of the paradoxes of modern democracies.

Dubiel: Yes, when one takes a look at the programming of the mass media here in the United States, that sort of authoritarian nurturing of culture can appear thoroughly worth consideration.

Lowenthal: Perhaps I could tell one more story.

Dubiel: As long as I can light up another cigar.

Lowenthal: Go right ahead. For me as a sociologist, certain experiences in Spain and Greece, particularly in the countryside, were interesting. At that time it struck me—and this made an enduring impression—that the poorer people, especially the rural people, seemed considerably more satisfied with their lot than corresponding groups in Western Europe or, especially, in America. In these countries, which are still in the early stages of capitalist development, I always had the impression that where the entire hinterland wasn't yet completely in the clutches of capitalism, human beings lead a more relaxed and contented life. I can still see in my mind's eye—and this is the archetypical experience I wanted to tell about—a Greek peasant sitting at the side of a country road with a glass of wine, gazing into the distance. I saw that in Spain and Portugal, too. Agreed, the distance between what such people know and what would be available and possible for them at the height of capitalist development is so enormous that the "good life" doesn't even enter the picture, neither on the plane of their objective experiences nor on that of their psychological experience potential. For me, as I said, that was another of those archetypical experiences—in contrast to the waiters at Shannon airport. Greek or Portuguese peasants aren't Irish waiters.

Dubiel: Well, okay, Leo, but what of it? What can be done with this description of idyllic and bucolic ways of life? What does one do with this nostalgic romanticism, this romantic criticism of industrial society, which I'm also prone to express? I lived for a long time on a farm, but I'm always ashamed to articulate that kind of romantic critique of civilization out loud.

Lowenthal: Yes, Helmut, but one just can't help asking oneself—and here a conservative element comes into my perception—if the price one must pay for integration into modern society isn't too high. Perhaps in this idyllic, preindustrial way of life there lives on, in a murky form, a bit of that utopian dream about a human approach to nature.

Dubiel: I don't find that conservative at all. If one puts you in the theoretical context of your one-time colleagues at the Frankfurt Institute, then this memory of archaic forms of life and experience is something like a utopian *imago*. Utopian not in the sense of the labor movement as the designation for the anticipated highest level of social development, but rather in the sense of a comprehensive critical philosophy of history such as that offered by Horkheimer and Adorno in *Dialectic of Enlightenment*.

Lowenthal: After all, in a certain respect I've been a specialist for nature ideologies ever since my Hamsun essay. The conservative-reactionary content of Hamsun's glorification of nature really has nothing to do with what I've been saying.

Dubiel: This irritated antimodernism, which often occurs in the form of a critique of technology, was certainly more than just a conservative phenomenon, at least in German romanticism. That today, more than a hundred and fifty years later, this antimodernism has acquired a progressive function, that's the dialectic of history. This whole bundle of alternative movements, which you can see here in California more strongly than anywhere else—holistic medicine, macrobiotics, rural communes, baking one's own bread, natural childbirth—all those are, after all, just variations on that theme.

Lowenthal: But I reject all of those things: those are completely artificial things. You can't turn back history. It's not possible.

Dubiel: But just what do you mean, then?

Lowenthal: I don't want to say more than the following: this archetypical experience with the Greek farmer taught me—and this makes me simultaneously sad and happy—that human beings can also live that way, that their lives are in order without being driven by an unending restlessness, as ours are. Their way of life is a utopian spark that shows, I'll say it once again, what was once possible. Today on the spot where I saw the Greek peasant there probably stands one of those hideous hotels for mass tourism. I don't know whether this relationship to nature can ever be restored. I don't think so. But it really took hold of me, that scene then; I'll never forget that man on the bench in front of his house, there on the way from Athens to the foothills of Sunium.

4

Scholarly Biography

Dubiel: In the early twenties you wrote many articles—in part politically oriented, in part oriented toward the history of ideas— that could be summed up under the bibliographical rubric "Judaica." In Jewish newspapers and community bulletins you published articles on Lassalle and Marx, on Tolstoy and the German spirit, and on the Jewish philosophy of religion of Hermann Cohen. Some of these writings on the history of ideas were systematically collected in a long omnibus article, "Judaism and the German Spirit." All these articles, if taken together, recall a thematically similar short article by Walter Benjamin on the role of the Jews in the recent German history of ideas. Could you tell me what you consider to be the uniting link of these essays?

Lowenthal: My intellectual and political interest in Jewish affairs developed very strongly in my student days by contact with the philosophy of Hermann Cohen and under the influence of his student Walter Kinkel, by contact with the Zionist student movement in Heidelberg, and by the great influence of the charismatic Rabbi Nobel. I believed that Jewish philosophy of religion, especially that of Maimonides, contains a progressive rationalism with strong secular tendencies, which, though garbed in religious symbolism, also connote the idea of a paradise on earth. At the time I

Translated by David J. Parent.

was intent on capturing in this secularly oriented redemptive thinking the utopian element that Marx, Heine, and also Freud at least
inherently display. It is probably not by chance that I often gave
lectures in Jewish communities and synagogues, in part to earn
some money as a struggling young scholar, in part out of conviction
about the Jewish element in the utopian aspect in socialism. However much I once tried to convince Martin Jay that there were no
Jewish motifs among us at the Institute, now, years later and after
mature consideration, I must admit to a certain influence of Jewish
tradition, which was codeterminative.

Dubiel: I found among your papers the draft of a project with
the title "Judaism and Jewishness in Recent German Philosophy."
I read this short manuscript, as well as a few letters from Franz
Rosenzweig and Martin Buber, who reacted very positively to this
idea. Was it the intent of this project to gather together in one
volume your scattered works in this field as a sort of German-
Jewish intellectual history?

Lowenthal: Do you have a particular year in mind?

Dubiel: Yes, 1925.

Lowenthal: That was just one year before I became associated
with the Institute of Social Research. This project was an attempt to
find a basis for an intellectual, perhaps even an academic, existence.
At that time I was not thinking of a professorship; it had only been
two years since I had received my doctorate. With Buber's and
Rosenzweig's help I tried to obtain a grant for this project from the
Moses Mendelssohn Foundation, which was a kind of Jewish Ford
Foundation. I don't remember anymore why it failed. Maybe it
wasn't judged favorably; maybe Leo Strauss didn't like it—he was
very influential in the foundation at that time. In any case, my association with the Institute of Social Research began soon thereafter.
I would have liked to have worked on a philosophically and politically oriented study on the interrelations of Jewish and non-Jewish
philosophy and Jewish and non-Jewish intellectual life. That also

was connected with my earlier essay "The Demonic" and my dissertation on Franz von Baader. Even though nothing came of it, the moral impulses that motivated the project remained alive in me.

Dubiel: Leo, I would like a few more comments from you on those articles of yours that have a purely political orientation, especially those you wrote in the *Jüdisches Wochenblatt,* published by Ernst Simon. Judging by their titles, the articles are often primarily about current affairs—for example, "The Situation of the Jews in Poland" or "The Concession Law in Poland." But I'm especially interested in the essay "The Lessons of China," which contains a very sharp critique of the Jewish settlement policy in Palestine. As a reminder, I want to read you a few sentences from your article of June 25, 1925:

> China's revolution must be a lesson for Palestine. If, especially in earlier years, one looked at Zionism's ideological products, it would be easy to remark ironically on what bloody laughter it would cause in the world if, for instance, a remnant of Celts scattered on a remote island were to travel to France today and claim its territory as a national property belonging to them by historical right. Zionism's dangerous vice, its ethnocentric naïveté in historical matters, found in Jewish history a fertile field. . . . The Arab question was therefore approached in about the same way the Zentralverein Deutscher Staatsbürger Jüdischen Glaubens conceives of its relation to anti-Semites, i.e., how shall we deal with this unsavory, numerically overwhelming element? In other words, one could say that Zionism's borrowings from the arsenal of European diplomatic weapons were ill advised, that is to say, Zionism took out a larger loan than it had originally intended: for it engaged in European colonial policy against the Arabs. . . .

And on looking around with open eyes, one is keenly aware that Arab youths today are studying at European universities and working to prepare for the hour that has now struck in China. Here, too, a national majority is screaming for justice. Here, too, a tremendous "danger" is approaching. It will require the concerted moral energy of the entire Zionist generation living today, indeed the entire world Jewish community, to demonstrate a willingness to change not merely its tactics, but its mentality as well. I am not so politically naïve as to make a favorable prognosis without hesitation.

Lowenthal: You know that in my student years in Heidelberg I was a member of the Zionist student organization. But I had joined because I believed most strongly in Judaism's messianic mission, its utopian political task. I had hoped that Eretz Israel would be the model for a just society. However, my experience with Zionism followed a path very similar to my later experience with the Communist world movement and the Communist Party. I experienced great disappointment; I felt that the Zionist movement was suffering more and more from what my friend Ernst Simon at that time so convincingly called the "intoxication with normality." Ideologically, I was not so blinded as to refuse a critical analysis of the settlement policy of the Jewish organizations in Palestine. As I saw it, the Jewish land purchases were an alliance of big Arab landowners and Jewish money at the expense of the Arab peasants and farmworkers. I instinctively foresaw that this could lead to bad conflicts, if not catastrophes. My comparison related to the occupation of China by the European powers and the establishment of extraterritorial zones. I believed that a lesson should be learned from the Boxer uprising, that a population had to be listened to and could not simply be raped. This article, which I signed "Hereticus," resulted in my abandoning the Zionist movement and also, quite concretely, the newspaper. This does not mean, I would like to repeat, that I had given up my relation to Jewish motifs or my support of Israel.

Dubiel: As I was going through your papers from the 1920s I found, in addition to the manuscript of your dissertation, many other manuscripts testifying to your philosophical activity. One feels in all your writings not only that you studied philosophy but also that philosophical orientations are present in all your scientific works, even though you did not write a philosophical treatise in the strict sense, apart from your dissertation. In the 1920s you wrote about the political philosophy of the Enlightenment. I also found a manuscript on Thomas More and Campanella, and one entitled "Power and Law in Rousseau's Philosophy of State and in German Idealist Philosophy." Then I found a longer manuscript on Helvétius's philosophy, a manuscript that was projected to be your inaugural dissertation but could not be completed because of your emigration. First, comment a bit on the works just named.

Lowenthal: You have traced something decisive in my intellectual life. You know that here in the United States one often has to present one's professional calling card. Someone asks, "What do you do?" and then I say, "I'm really a philosopher." My relation to philosophy began very early through my father's influence, especially through his recommendation that I read Schopenhauer, and it continued throughout my intellectual youth. There is no semester in which I did not register for a few classes and seminars in philosophy. As a very young man I went to Giessen just to study neo-Kantian philosophy. Hermann Cohen was very reactionary and nationalistic, but it must not be forgotten that one of his greatest students was Paul Natorp, who at that time was a socialist. Walter Kinkel was himself a socialist. Natorp and Kinkel have shown that Kantian ethics and socialist consciousness are compatible. The interest in Enlightenment philosophy you were just speaking of came about mainly through my Marxist orientation. You know that Marx was indebted to the Enlightenment; he criticized the Enlightenment philosophers only because, although they postulated the right goals of society theoretically, they did not state practically how these goals can be translated into revolutionary praxis. This subject has always interested me; therefore, I studied the left wing of Enlightenment philosophy very intensively: Holbach, Helvétius, La Mettrie, Diderot. You see here in my library the first editions of Holbach, La Mettrie, and Helvétius, which were dearly paid for with my scanty savings. In the mid-1920s there were no good German books about the French Enlightenment in existence. There were hardly any modern translations—for example, no translation of the introduction to the *Encyclopédie,* no translation of Helvétius, hardly any of Diderot. If you look at my bibliography in the Helvétian manuscript, you'll see how scanty the secondary literature was. It was also politically interesting that in Germany the mostly trivial German Enlightenment philosophers, such as Wolff, were praised to the sky, but the French Enlightenment was almost totally ignored. After all, Helvétius was one of the sharpest critics of German class society.

Thus the philosophical motifs in me always remained alive. Look at my later literary studies. When I write about Corneille, I also write about Descartes. When I write about Molière, I also write about Gassendi, and when I write about popular culture, I also write about Pascal and Montaigne. For me, philosophy is still the queen of the sciences, and, like most who think as I do, I mourn the present situation in which philosophy is undergoing a decline. If metaphysics is still being taught in the universities here, then it is mostly by arrogant, old, boring "nuts," while fashionable interest is inclined toward linguistic analysis, which in most (although not all) cases is a technically oriented methodology of the sciences and shares with authentic philosophy only the name.

Dubiel: In the years 1928 and 1931 you wrote a few works that were not published, I believe, until 1971, under the title *Erzählkunst und Gesellschaft* [Narrative Art and Society]. These essays show Lowenthal as he would later be known. Indeed, these writings comprise a first and very self-confident realization of a program for a materialistically oriented study of literary history. The volume contains something like an ideologically critical reconstruction of bourgeois class consciousness in terms of its most prominent literary representatives.

Lowenthal: Yes, with the exception of the first essay in that volume, on the social situation of literature, which first appeared in 1932 in the *Zeitschrift für Sozialforschung,* the other essays originated from a compendious lecture series I had developed in the League for Popular Lectures. I lectured on all areas of European literature, although my main interest was German literature, because as a good Marxist I acted according to the principle of beginning with criticism at home, and at that time Germany was causing me to lose a lot of sleep. In its methodology this work is characterized by an as yet—how should I put it?—unmediated Marxism. Maybe I am doing myself an injustice by this judgment, for in these works I also apply the psychological mechanism of mediation, particularly by taking into account the socially codetermined private reactions of the literary personae. Most of what I wrote or began writing in Germany before my emigration expresses the attempt to track down the decline and disintegration of bourgeois consciousness and to delineate it in a critique of ideology. My special interest concerned the documents of literature and the documentations of literary influence. And if you take a look at the subtitles added fifty years later to these sections, they express this theoretical intention: for example, for the chapter on Goethe I choose the title "Bourgeois Resignation"; for Gottfried Keller, "Bourgeois Regression"; and so forth. These studies are part of a larger project to describe and analyze the specific course of German bourgeois consciousness and why there was no bourgeois revolution in Germany. As I said, these essays were motivated by political critique. As far as I can remember I stopped working on this material in 1930, because I was then too burdened with Institute business, especially with the founding of the *Zeitschrift für Sozialforschung.*

Dubiel: On reading these old works I had the impression of a specific continuity and discontinuity, similarity and dissimilarity, with the essays that appeared a few years later in the *Zeitschrift*. As regards your early work, I would speak of a methodological indifference. But the studies that appeared in the *Zeitschrift* can be summed up under the intention of a study of literary history based on the materialistic and social-psychological study of the history of literature. I like the freshness of those early works and the unself-consciousness with which cultural processes were related to the substructure. I always asked myself, how does he do that, what methodological authorities does he refer to? Do these works comprise a sort of *Nullpunkt* [moment of absolute beginning], or in what theoretical, or more precisely, literary-critical, tradition does he really stand? You yourself name Georg Brandes in connection with these questions, and of course Franz Mehring; you also name contemporary Russian literary studies—very heterogeneous points of reference in time and content. So, in brief, I had the impression that you were just rolling up your sleeves and beginning to write.

Lowenthal: Precisely, Helmut, a fresh dilettantism, if you wish, though originating in a political attitude and on the basis of a more or less solid knowledge of literature, but still in the sense of a fresh impressionistic discourse—I let myself be carried by my own enthusiasm. That was the case to some extent with the work on Baader and the works on Enlightenment philosophy. Although at that time I did not yet know Walter Benjamin's wonderful statement that history is always written by the victors, I was always interested in writing the history of the losers. Baader was such a loser—a lone figure of German Restoration philosophy.

In this book we have been talking about, *Erzählkunst und Gesellschaft,* I speak of the literature of the Young Germany [Junges Deutschland] movement in light of the history of the revolution that didn't take place. The essay on Mörike traces the state of melancholy of the great German poets, who did not get from their public anything near the resonance that would have been matter-of-course in France or England. There was no public in Germany such as Victor Hugo had in France or Shelley and Byron had in England. And last but not least, I wrote on Friedrich Spielhagen, who, though he was no great artist, was a very conscious, independent, and radical analyst of bourgeois society. I was intrigued with dealing a blow to the widespread reception of Gottfried Keller's and C. F. Meyer's so-called greatness and with honoring the lost and neglected streams of German literature.

Dubiel: Thus documenting again and again the thesis that there was no genuine bourgeois consciousness in Germany, or in sociological terms, that there was no significant and influential carrier group of a liberal worldview.

Lowenthal: And consequently no carrier group of a political liberalism, either, or any historical chance of an alliance between socialists and enlightened liberals, who could have prevented the disaster in Germany. That is again the theme of my works on fashions in biographical subjects.

Dubiel: Leo, I'd like to come now to the essays you wrote in the *Zeitschrift:* first the essay "On the Social Situation of Literature," which appeared in 1932, then the 1933 essay on Conrad Ferdinand Meyer, then the 1934 study on Dostoevsky, the 1936 essay on Ibsen entitled "The Individual in Individualistic Society," and the famous 1938 essay on Knut Hamsun. The 1932 essay does, to a considerable extent, contain a methodological program in which literary history is conceived as the critique of ideology. Compared to those earlier works in *Erzählkunst und Gesellschaft,* one might say that the articles in the *Zeitschrift,* under the influence of Max Horkheimer's ideas on the critique of ideology, have a sharpened methodological consciousness. Would you agree with that?

Lowenthal: Yes, one can certainly say that. You know how these things originated historically. The first volume, no, the very first number of the *Zeitschrift,* was supposed to contain a sort of program, a position adopted by all the major collaborators of the

Zeitschrift concerning what united them—namely, the materialistic conception of history—focused on and applied to the fields they understood best. Horkheimer wrote about philosophy, Adorno about music, Pollock about the economy, Fromm about psychology, and I about literature. I challenged established literary scholarship, its idealistic arrogance, its distinctively political reactionary function. At the same time I tried to develop a kind of program for a set of studies I considered important. When the next essays appeared—you have just named them, the one on Conrad Ferdinand Meyer and the other on the Dostoevsky reception (this was, so to speak, a pioneer work)—they also fit into the analysis of the decline of the bourgeoisie: C. F. Meyer's heroes and their exemplary attempts to magnify themselves as symbols of the superior, sovereign, and leading class; and the enthusiastic reception of Dostoevsky, who was the most widely read author after Goethe, or at least the most published novelist in Germany, as a reflection of what Fromm called the anal and sadomasochistic character of the petit bourgeoisie, if not of the broad strata of the middle classes in general.

Dubiel: Does your work on Ibsen also fit into the framework of the critique of the disintegrating bourgeois consciousness?

Lowenthal: Yes! I was not naïve about Ibsen's patriarchal character. The essence of Ibsen's drama, his method, as it were, consists of taking bourgeois consciousness completely seriously on the level at which it articulates itself and then showing how hollow, fallacious, and in every sense untenable it is. Death, deception, bankruptcy, and the smashing of all interhuman relations among friends, between husband and wife, between parents and children, are the price that must be paid for the bourgeois system of competition. His decisive statement is that the bourgeois principle of competition penetrates into the intimacy of human relations and destroys them and—very important in Ibsen—that those who are furthest removed from the competitive struggle and at the same time most deprived of rights in a society based on the principle of competition, namely women, are the bearers and heralds of a better system. This then belongs to the context of my theory of marginality, which we should speak about when we come to *Literature and the Image of Man*.

Dubiel: Yes, let us now speak about your Hamsun study. This study to some extent goes beyond the methodological program of a critique of ideology. I have frequently found it listed under the rubric "Theory of Fascism" and not as an inherently literary-sociological work, which it claims to be. To my disgrace I must admit that in my late puberty I was a great, almost rapturous admirer of Hamsun. . . .

Lowenthal: A pardonable offense! You weren't the only one!

Dubiel: Your essay had an enormous prognostic quality. For Hamsun's sympathy with the Nazis became manifest—as far as I remember—only in 1940, when the German troops invaded Norway.

Lowenthal: Yes, precisely. This prognosis of mine did not go uncontested in our circle. Marcuse and Walter Benjamin both defended Knut Hamsun. But I insisted that the subtitle of this essay, "On the Prehistory of Authoritarian Ideology," was not accidental. I tried to document my thesis not only with what Hamsun had produced in manifest political statements, but also by an immanent analysis of his characters and his principles of literary construction. It was an immanent critique, an experiment carried out in the spirit of Adorno's beautiful statement: "Art does not come to society, but society comes to art: society should originate in the work of art and not the other way around." In the Hamsun essay, and even in the Ibsen essay, one of my methodological convictions is developed—namely, that the private is unmasked as the socially mediated. Works of art can give us information about the social dimension in the private sphere of men, how society is present in the love relationship of two people, in friendship, and in an individual's return to nature. Hence, literature is treated as the documentation of social representation in the psyche of the individual. In later works I once formulated this to the effect that literature provides the best source of data for information on a society's pattern of socialization.

Dubiel: May I rephrase this in order to appropriate it? So literary sociology is meant not in the sense of a sociology of literature, its production and circulation; rather, it means understanding literature as the material, along with other cultural documentation, in which social and cultural structures can be identified. Such a kind of literary study uses literature as the medium and material for an analysis of society.

It was also then, the second half of the 1930s, that those discussions about the relation between aesthetics and politics appeared in the *Zeitschrift.* I am referring to Benjamin's essay "On Art in the Era of Its Technical Reproducibility" and Adorno's essay criticizing it, "The Fetish-Character in Music and the Regression of Hearing." Also, if I'm not mistaken, Herbert Marcuse's essay on "Affirmative Culture" appeared in the same volume as your Hamsun essay. All these essays, even if they are not as explicitly interrelated as is often underscored in contemporary literature, really constitute the three sides of a problem triangle. This could be designated as, first, the relation of art and science; second, the relation of art and mass culture; and third, the relation of art and politics. I want to describe quickly, in very crude simplification, three possible approaches to this problem and then hear from you how you classify yourself in this scheme.

Marcuse defended the thesis, and actually maintained it until his death, that art has a dual function in bourgeois society, an ideological one and a utopian one. Art is ideologically functional in the sense that it constitutes the realm of all collective imaginations and desires, whose political realization is denied in society. All unrealized possibilities of action in bourgeois society are repressed in their political-practical frame of action and banished to the realm of art.

The great classical bourgeois works of art represent at the same time the bourgeoisie's utopian consciousness. Marcuse, at least in his writings of the 1930s—and this distinguished him then from Benjamin and especially from Adorno—was not interested in the way the aesthetic consciousness of bourgeois society could be transposed into politics directly and without consideration of the evolutionary difference between culture and politics. I am alluding to the fascist propagation of mass art, indeed to the aesthetization of political life and war that Benjamin noted about fascism in general. Thus, fascism represents the false abolition of the relation between art and politics. Benjamin—this is his most famous thesis—ultimately interpreted the development of the relation of esoteric art to a mass culture made technically possible with political optimism. In crude terms, by smashing the uniqueness and almost cultic aura of works of art through new techniques of reproduction, new historical chances for the politicization of art are released. All the same, no one saw more clearly than Benjamin himself the danger posed by the political instrumentalization of mass art in fascism. Adorno, who formulated exactly the opposite thesis, thinks of mass art as the degeneration of art only in the framework of a repressive ideological exercise of domination, and consequently he attaches political intentions only to that art and those forms of art that refuse to serve mass culture. The utopian functions of art noted by Marcuse in the late-bourgeois epoch, that is, under the conditions of a mass culture, can be realized only through extremely esoteric art.

I came across this problem in an unexpected way when I read your book *Literature, Popular Culture, and Society*. I hadn't known that the phenomenon of mass culture is not at all a phenomenon that first emerged in late-bourgeois society. In fact, you show that mass culture, and also the political problem of the relation of the esoteric and exoteric, goes back far into the eighteenth century. The whole problem we are speaking of is not necessarily typical only of mass societies. The three authors I was speaking of apparently assume that the whole problem first arose when the means of reproduction were technically revolutionized. Now, Leo, can a point be given in the history of bourgeois society, and particularly in aesthetics, when autonomous art was forced to define its relation to mass culture? Or is it just a matter of the gradual evolution of an intrinsic, ever-present tension?

Lowenthal: I would say this is another leap from quantity to quality. But I first want to respond to what you said before. I naturally find it very hard to take as clear a stand as you demand. Of course I agree with much of what Adorno, Benjamin, and Marcuse said, although I never wrote about it systematically except in the foreword to the book you just mentioned. So first of all on the Benjamin thesis, to the extent that we perceive his position accurately: he really seems to say that the dissemination of works of art made possible by mechanical and electronic means of reproduction can also have a positive political effect. I consider this wrong. It runs counter to all our political experiences. But it is possible that we have misunderstood him. If you read this Benjamin essay closely, he himself moves very quickly away from the positive aspects of the technical revolution and describes the aesthetization of politics as it had become manifest in fascism. He definitely saw this more clearly than others. But he also said that in Communism art is equally politicized.

Art is really the message of resistance, of the socially unredeemed. Art is in fact the great reservoir of creative protest against social misery; it allows the prospect of social happiness to shine dimly through. I myself indeed tried to show that even in works of art that in their ideological coloring, with regard to author and target group, are very conformist and conservative—such as Lope de Vega in Spain, Corneille and Racine in France, also Goethe in many respects—the protest shines through in many a passage. The most important thing about bourgeois art is that it depicts the individual as threatened by bourgeois society. The best works of art are, in my opinion, those that do not stand in a conformist framework: Cervantes, most of Shakespeare, Racine, and later Ibsen, not to mention Romanticism. It is precisely the marginal minor characters in such great works that often become decisive bearers of utopian protest. I therefore have essentially tried, as Adorno says, to proceed "micrologically" and to analyze intimate, private, personal situations and modes of behavior in order to uncover in them just those unredeemed utopian elements that await social happiness. For I really believe that Walter Benjamin's thesis that history is always written by the victors is refuted in works of art. The work of art gives voice to the losers in history, who, it is hoped, will someday be the victors. A secular philosophy of redemption is visible in this theoretical nexus of aesthetics and politics. In mass culture, on the contrary, nothing is ever redeemed, everything always stays the same because it ought to remain the way it is. In Hamsun, for example, even the minor characters are scoundrels; there is absolutely no redemptive phenomenon, no assertion anywhere that things could and should be different. And that was a touchstone for me to use in distinguishing between what is and what is not genuine art.

But now to the other part of your question, the relation of art and mass culture. As long as art has existed as an institution, there has also been its opposite, in Greek antiquity as well as the Middle Ages—for example, the entertainments in the church square after the religious service presented by jugglers and performers to entertain the masses. But the essential thing is the development of this relation of high and low art, which can be observed in the sixteenth and seventeenth centuries, when in many countries of Europe the predominantly agricultural mode of production was complemented by the urban forms of production of manufacturing and industry. In short, with the beginning of bourgeois forms of life and thought, an ambiguous philosophy about the role of art also begins to develop—or perhaps one should say the role of leisure, of which art seemed to be an essential part. In my book I expressed this symbolically through the counterposition of the philosophies of Pascal and Montaigne. Montaigne suggests that man needs relaxation and distraction under the pressure of modern life, whereas Pascal says that if you seek distraction you lose your life's meaning. This motif of Montaigne's, that the greater burden of life in the bourgeois age is eased through distraction, namely, distraction through art, occurs again and again in literature—for example, in Schiller in the speech of the "weary citizen"; and Goethe, too, in his "Prologue at the Theater," speaks of how "the men arrive bored, the women to show their beautiful fashions."

Dubiel: But the joke in this linkage of art and leisure against mass culture is probably that this function of distraction must not be detached from the ethical function of art, isn't it?

Lowenthal: Quite right, exactly. Art is here a kind of mental hygiene, an ethically important leisure occupation. In the eighteenth century in England, where bourgeois forms of life and ideology developed the fastest and strongest, there was clearly a great movement among the intellectuals to elevate the citizens' taste. Many of these authors, like Richardson and Oliver Goldsmith, are quite schizophrenic on this point; they are uncertain whether what they produce as literature is art or not, written for the market or for art's sake. Goldsmith says that the time of literary patrons is over and that the market is now the patron. Marjorie Fiske and I studied the literary scene in eighteenth-century England. There already existed literary genres that have become quite popular today, such as, for example, books on love, on how to win friends, on how to obtain a big dowry, popular and popularized versions of Homer and other items of classical literature, a whole world of journals and libraries with literature for entertainment. In short, all these phenomena of an ultimately market-oriented mass culture were already taking shape at that time.

Dubiel: Can you give a reasonably accurate dating of the origin of this contrast between art and mass culture?

Lowenthal: Certainly! That begins with the *Spectator* and the *Tatler,* Addison and Steele's journals, and it reaches its peak in Romanticism and also in German classicism. Wordsworth and Coleridge then first declared war on melodrama and shallow entertainment-literature. They decried the fact that now everything is written from the standpoint of quick comprehension and enjoyment so that one wouldn't have to exert oneself.

Dubiel: But the development of this relation of high and low art, of esoteric art and mass culture, can be derived not only from the perspective of the development of mass art itself, but especially also from just the opposite perspective. For the phenomenon of an autonomous art following only its own laws is a relatively late product of bourgeois consciousness. So, if it is true that an esoteric art conscious of its own laws arose only relatively late, then that must affect their relation to so-called low art. I mean that in the period we were talking about, the seventeenth and eighteenth centuries, the difference between high and low art must have been much more indefinite than in the late nineteenth century.

Lowenthal: Yes, much more gradual, of course. In any case, the concept of mass art is rather complex. When we speak of masses we mean of course only certain bourgeois strata in a few urban cultural centers, although Ian Watt maintains the interesting thesis that the reading strata in eighteenth-century England included not only the well-to-do housewives but also their personal maids. But aside from that, of course, there can be absolutely no question of reading in petit-bourgeois circles and the proletarian masses, for they were completely overworked and did not even have the money to buy themselves candles for reading. There is a marked change, however, in the course of the nineteenth century as literary and reading material rapidly increased. We enter the era of a big culture industry that is made possible because printing techniques become cheaper. More and more books, booklets, magazines, and newspapers became available in large quantities before radio and cinema were introduced.

On art and culture industry all of us generally held the same position, although there once was a period in the development of Marcuse's thinking in which he put greater value on partisan literature and spontaneous political art. He later abandoned this view and came around again to a firm belief in the utopian character and independence of the great work of art. Adorno's position that art has been pressed more and more into defensive positions is in my view perfectly justified. The greater the dangers and seductions become for an artist, who after all is also a member of the bourgeois-capitalist world, to earn money through circulation figures, film rights, and so on, the more difficult it becomes to preserve the integrity of artistic consciousness. The artists and writers of the nineteenth century worried about this constantly. I mean, it is trivial, but in such a situation the technique of esoteric communication becomes the weapon for the integrity of the artist; I am thinking of Kafka, Joyce, and Proust, who are "inaccessible" in a certain respect, but precisely this "inaccessibility" is their goal. The same thing applies to abstract painting. But bourgeois society has a big stomach; we have always underestimated how much it can assimilate and digest.

Dubiel: If we examine the objects of your literary analysis, it is always a matter of paradigms of the bourgeois consciousness that didn't come about in Germany. That is really relevant only in the framework of the critique of ideology. In positive paradigms, for example in Ibsen, it is only the depiction of immanent bourgeois self-critique. What we have just formulated in positive terms about the political purpose of esoteric art is, in your case—in contrast, for example, to Adorno—not positively stated in individual studies. You have never written about avant-garde literature. Sometimes I wonder, when you make such an emphatic distinction between the cognitive and the symptomatic significance of art, whether that can still be maintained for avant-garde literature.

Lowenthal: Yes, I plead guilty. Adorno urged me repeatedly to write about contemporary literature. I didn't do it. Perhaps I am more a literary historian in the conventional sense. At any rate, to this day I refuse to make binding "sociological" statements about modern literature. I have two reasons for that. The first is that modern literature has not yet passed through the sieve of history and it is more difficult to distinguish what, in the Lukácsian sense, will one day be typologically significant for a knowledge of social contexts. The other reason is that, for me, sociology of literature is supplementary to a purely aesthetic contemplation. If, for example, I want to examine changes in the relationship of genders or of generations, I do not need literature, which, after all, provides only indirect access. I can study these phenomena empirically. They are accessible, whereas the human phenomena I have analyzed in my writings have become inaccessible; my studies are, if you wish, great obituaries on the patterns of socialization and acculturation of former centuries. I can only repeat: other sources are available to analyze our modern situation.

Dubiel: I just want to make sure I've understood you correctly. The specific nature of your social-scientific study of literature consisted of using literary historical documents as material for your sociological interpretations. To judge the representativeness and validity of this material, the sieve of history—as you so beautifully put it—is indeed indispensable. Now this type of study of contemporary and avant-garde art is impossible, not because it would be impossible to distinguish whether we are dealing with real art or not, but because it cannot be determined to what extent these documents of modern art really stand in a reciprocal connection to significant social tendencies. I have sometimes been bothered by the self-assuredness with which Adorno identified, for example in Stravinsky, certain decoded sound patterns with political options. Adorno did not seem to have the same scruples you have just formulated. The combination of immanent analysis of avant-garde art and political attribution he practiced sometimes seems questionable to me.

Lowenthal: Well, I don't know. Of course I was very happy when he was so friendly as to add a footnote on Sibelius to my essay on Hamsun, showing that the same symptoms I discovered in Hamsun's work could also be seen in Sibelius's. I wanted to point out one other aspect, since we happen to be engaged in assigning grades. I always asked myself whether I'm not smart enough to apply my analysis to modern materials. Let's take Kafka. People say that this or that in his work reflects the alienation of the modern world, the entanglement in the bureaucratic maze of highly industrialized civilizations, the administrated world. They say that absurd theater critically reflects the impossibility of real communication in the modern world. And that Thomas Mann reflects the disintegration of the bourgeoisie. So what? What has been said? Certainly nothing about the artistic value of these products, and from an advanced vantage point of social philosophy you're still in the realm of banalities.

Dubiel: I'm glad that our prejudices on this point coincide.

Lowenthal: I would only apply to this literature something I have already experienced elsewhere. It is quite different when I write about Shakespeare. I know what happens to Romeo and Juliet only from this source itself.

Dubiel: Leo, I would like to talk with you about your two biographical studies. By that I mean first the essay on the "Biographical Fashion," which appeared in 1955 in the first volume of *Sociologica,* the festschrift for Horkheimer, although it was written much earlier. The English version of this essay appeared in a festschrift for Marcuse. The other essay I am alluding to is one with which you made a name for yourself here in the United States, "Biographies in Popular Magazines." How did you come to write these?

Lowenthal: Well, the essay that appeared under the title "Biographical Fashion" deals with popular biographies of German writers, such as Emil Ludwig and Stefan Zweig. I would like to mention here two motives for writing it. The first is interest in the genre; I wondered what kind of literary form popular literature uses. One of the least understood problems of the sociology of literature is precisely genre. This was first developed magnificently in Lukács's *Theory of the Novel*. Generally in the sociological analysis of literature it is a matter of content aesthetics. My biographical works are thus a parallel case to my Dostoevsky study. Dostoevsky was the most widely received novelist in Germany, at least shortly before the end of World War I. And biography was the most widespread form of nonfiction writing. And so I asked myself why, which leads to my second motive for writing about this. If you ask what really was the common denominator of the people at the Institute, the answer would probably be the shared concern for the fate of the individual. Horkheimer's "Egoism and the Freedom Movement" or Marcuse's "Affirmative Culture," some works by Fromm, and my own literary studies are variations on the theme of the increasing fragility of the bourgeois individual. And here, biographies seem to me to be an especially characteristic genre, in which individuality makes an appearance and is at the same time destroyed. The German popular biographies combine two extremes: while describing the heroes with tremendous superlatives as creators of something unique, they at the same time bring those same heroes down to the level of ordinary people. This *coincidentia oppositorum,* that they are on the one hand unique and on the other hand like everyone else, deadens our consciousness of history and politics. The repetitiveness of this literature has a lulling effect. Just as, for example, entire passages in various novels of Hamsun could be interchanged, so could various biographies. The representation of Hindenburg at that time was barely different from that of Jesus. With great glee, I compiled entire lists of superlatives and other stereotypes that were repeated over and over again. Historical data was debased to the level of commodities for mass consumption. I finished writing the essay in the 1930s. We did not publish it then out of courtesy, for a good many of the authors I analyzed were German-Jewish emigrants who were having great difficulties at the time. Some even committed suicide. I first published it only after the direct references to contemporary authors had lost their sting.

Dubiel: Let us now get to the second work on biography, "Biographies in Popular Magazines." The extraordinarily positive reception of this essay by American social scientists somehow illustrates its genesis. Wasn't this essay the result of a suggestion by Paul Lazarsfeld?

Lowenthal: Lazarsfeld knew of the unpublished essay on biographies we were just talking about. He asked me whether I would be interested in doing that sort of thing in the framework of American literature. This coincided with my experience at the time, that every single issue of the *Saturday Evening Post* and *Collier's,* extraordinarily popular consumer magazines then, always contained biographies. I looked at all the issues from 1901 to 1940 from the methodological viewpoint of their "symptomatic" significance and reflected on the extent to which these market products might be indicators of social processes. I found that in the first twenty years of this century the heroes of these biographies were taken from the field of production: successful merchants, professionals, inventors, and entrepreneurs. In brief, it soon became clear to me that these biographies served as political-educational stimuli. Their motto was "It can be done"—in short, the unbroken Horatio Alger myth. These heroes were models, and to follow them meant to join the competition of the free enterprise system. Not everyone could be a general, but every dishwasher had a chance to amass the bank account of a millionaire.

That situation changed radically at the end of the thirties. The so-called heroes were suddenly people from show business: movie actors, radio stars, famous impresarios, singers, in other words, people from the entertainment field. A good number of sports heroes were also featured, as well as a whole group of freaks, meaning people who were carrying on some kind of business or had invented something odd or comical. In short, the heroes were no longer the heroes of production. The theme was no longer the industry of individual enterprise but a matter of characters who were supposed to entertain us. But that was only one side of it; the other side was the change in categories through which people were portrayed biographically. Their consumer habits, their hobbies, were particularly stressed. Whereas in the first phase you had producers, about whose productive qualities statements—however banal— were made, in the later period the consumer hero, with consumer needs and preferences, became the theme. This corresponded exactly to two modern tendencies: first, that in the society of corporate capitalism the rise of the entrepreneur increasingly becomes a pure fiction; and second, that bourgeois society turns into a consumer society. People are interested essentially only in consumption. This theory of consumption-heroes can be harmonized with David Riesman's typology, and also with Fromm's "market-oriented personality." Anyway, Robert Merton, one of the most cultured and progressive American sociologists of the late forties, praised this essay as one of the few successful examples of a synthesis of the European theoretical stance and American empirical research. I was very proud of this. My friend Paul Lazarsfeld, who unfortunately died a few years ago, then said to me, in his typically empiricist-positivist way: "So far you have shown what a bad biography is; now you ought to demonstrate what a good biography is." Thus he failed to see the political and analytical meaning of my study.

Dubiel: I would now like to discuss the *Prophets of Deceit*. This study appeared here in America in the year 1949, as a single volume in the series *Studies in Prejudice*. In 1970 *Prophets of Deceit* was reissued in the United States with a very now-oriented introduction by Herbert Marcuse. I will first try to characterize this book, and if this description stimulates or annoys you, feel free to react to it. It is a reconstruction of the typology of fascist agitators, collated from speeches and articles by American agitators of the interwar period. Do you agree with my characterizations that in this book you essentially limited yourself to grasping typologically and collecting the usual topoi, figures of argumentation, and rhetorical figures of agitators?

Lowenthal: Yes, we tried to collect the rhetorical stimuli on the basis of speeches, pamphlets, journals, and similar materials. I would characterize the technique of agitation basically as turning psychoanalysis on its head. Moreover, I would say this of mass culture in general. It makes people neurotic and psychotic and finally completely dependent on so-called leaders. I tried to translate the manifest stimuli of these agitators into what they actually mean. My purpose was to unmask the aggressive and destructive impulses hidden behind that rhetoric. The American edition has as an introduction a kind of ideal-typical montage of an agitator's speech. This montage, incidentally, was constructed by Irving Howe, one of the best-known intellectuals of this country, following our detailed instructions. At the end of the book we added a speech that decodes the introductory one, to show what the agitator really means: kill the Jews, destroy the democratic institutions, follow me and no one else, and so forth.

Dubiel: An essay from this time that impressed me very much, despite its small size, appeared—as far as I remember—in January 1947 in *Commentary*. Its title was "Terror's Atomization of Man." In it you write about the disintegrative tendencies of man under the terroristic conditions of concentration camp internment. As far as I know, this essay goes back to a lecture you gave at Columbia University during the war.

Lowenthal: Yes, that was in 1944 as part of a whole series of lectures at Columbia University on National Socialism by Pollock, Marcuse, Otto Kirchheimer, and myself. This essay, which stemmed from that lecture—I don't find it easy to talk about—is an analysis of the first terrible reports about what was going on in the concentration camps. I got hold of this material even before the end of the war. I then tried to describe how, under the conditions of totalitarian terror, the victimized individual completely disintegrates, how he almost takes on the features of the murderer, how under such conditions any sense of solidarity with other people ceases to exist so that humans seem to regress to an animal phase. I was much inspired by Bruno Bettelheim's important article on behavior under extreme conditions. Apparently my lecture was very effective. The audience consisted mainly of Columbia University students and professors, that is, people of good will who were very shaken by what they heard. One of the best-known professors, Robert Lynd, author of the famous study *Middletown,* told me that I absolutely had to publish my lecture manuscript. At his suggestion it was then sent to the *American Journal of Sociology* in Chicago for publication. The editor at that time was a teacher of a whole generation of sociologists in America. He sent the manuscript back to me with the statement that unfortunately it could not be published because the empirical data base was too slight. I then wrote back to him and sarcastically excused myself that I was not in the concentration camp myself and so could not have gathered my data right on the spot. I often since had to shake my head at this political and historical naïveté not untypical of American social scientists. I then sent the piece to Elliot Cohen, the editor and founder of *Commentary,* and that is where it was published.

Dubiel: Leo, can you again give us some information on the *Studies in Prejudice* series in general? The institutional framework in which these studies were made was the research department of the American Jewish Committee. Did this integration of many members of your former group with another research team really mean a substantive break with your theoretical past?

Lowenthal: No, the task of this research department consisted basically in applying to the area of anti-Semitism all the decisive theoretical and empirical insights we had developed in the Institute over the decades. It was also similar to the format at the Institute and on the journal in that essentially the work was done by members of the group, but other intellectually friendly scholars could be called upon to collaborate. We had already worked with Marie Jahoda before; then Bruno Bettelheim, with whom we had also had contact, joined, and Morris Janowitz in Chicago, and the psychoanalyst Nathan Ackermann. We wanted—quite in line with Critical Theory—to accomplish scientifically meaningful work in a manner that would allow its application to political praxis. Horkheimer's dream, which was never fulfilled, was that each of these books in the series *Studies in Prejudice* should be rewritten in the form of small booklets in popular format for distribution in a given situation of anti-Semitic political outbreaks or the like here in America—namely, to teachers, students, politicians, that is, to so-called multiplicators. That was sort of the idea of a political-educational mass inoculation program, a "fire brigade," as the Americans say. Unfortunately, it never materialized.

Dubiel: That's interesting, I didn't know that. I do remember the introduction to *The Authoritarian Personality,* in which the idea of a preventive democratic mass-education is formulated, but I considered that to be just a rhetorical ornament.

Lowenthal: No, that was meant quite seriously. You're talking about a foreword by Max Horkheimer not only to *The Authoritarian Personality* but to all the volumes of *Studies in Prejudice*. We meant that quite seriously.

Dubiel: Were these various volumes of *Studies in Prejudice* conceived in relation to each other only in their original conception, or also in the actual execution of the research—be it methodologically, or by the exchange of materials, or in drawing up the analytical framework? Did you, for example, try to coordinate your work with that for *The Authoritarian Personality*?

Lowenthal: Now, these are all very different questions. On the whole it was a research strategy about which Horkheimer consulted a few leading people in the American Jewish Committee and us. *The Authoritarian Personality* is really a direct continuation of our interests, which started with the *Studies on Authority and the Family*. In California Horkheimer met Nevitt Sanford, the founder and first president of the Wright Institute and a good friend of mine. Sanford took a great interest in our problems and subsequently brought us together with two of his colleagues, Else Frenkel-Brunswick and Daniel Levinson. I participated in the preliminary discussions for *The Authoritarian Personality*, and at Horkheimer's request came to California to discuss with Sanford the general organization of the entire research project.

Dubiel: *Prophets of Deceit* became quite well known in its time. You once showed me the folder with the reviews of this book. It got a lot of attention, not only in scientific circles but also among the nonscientific general public. Might one say that *Prophets of Deceit* is better known in the United States than *The Authoritarian Personality,* or is that a false compliment?

Lowenthal: I must reject that compliment in all modesty and with indignation. The most important book was *The Authoritarian Personality,* which still has strong influence today. Compared with that, *Prophets of Deceit* had a relatively modest influence; one might even say that it stood in the shadow of *The Authoritarian Personality*. But I don't want to understate my book's influence. It did have an influence, especially among students and instructors in the field of mass communications research.

Dubiel: Now we come to the 1950s. The appearance of *Studies in Prejudice* coincides with the beginning of your work with the Voice of America; we spoke about your various activities there on another occasion. I suppose it would be accurate to describe the nature of your work basically as research organization, as a result of which you produced only a few scholarly products during that period. Do you agree that we now skip that time?

Lowenthal: Yes, let's speak of the time after that, when I have a much better conscience about my output. That was 1955–1956, when I was working in Stanford at the Center for Advanced Studies. My ever-faithful friend Paul Lazarsfeld, who had been instrumental in getting me invited to the Center, said to me then: "In this research year you have the alternative of either embarking on what the Americans call 'having a good time,' and at the end of the year you can become a dog-catcher in Palo Alto; or you can write a few books and subsequently become a professor." Lazarsfeld's advice really proved to be sound. Since I was not very interested in catching dogs, I sat down to write. In that year I wrote the book *Literature and the Image of Man.* The German title, *Das Menschenbild in der Literatur,* originated in part from the revision and systematization of older essays that had already appeared in the *Zeitschrift.* The Shakespeare chapter in the book was completely new, as was the one on the French drama. The chapter on Goethe already existed in a rough version but had not yet been published. In addition I wrote the longer study with Marjorie Fiske on the relation of art and mass culture in England during the eighteenth century. Immediately afterward, in the fall of 1956, I was appointed professor at the University of California in Berkeley.

5

Berkeley

Dubiel: I think it's safe to say that you're the only member of the Frankfurt circle who became a typical American professor, with all the connotations of that title. To be sure, cognoscenti also know Horkheimer's name, since he taught for a time in Chicago; Adorno's name is also quite familiar here in the United States. After all, his name appears first among the authors of *The Authoritarian Personality*.

Lowenthal: You shouldn't forget that Herbert Marcuse was a professor at Brandeis and after his retirement continued as a professor at the University of California in San Diego.

Dubiel: I was just getting to Marcuse. Marcuse, I'd say, is more of a cosmopolitan phenomenon that can hardly be ascribed to American social science. After all, he's really a partisan in this entire "scene"; he can scarcely be considered part of American social philosophy.

Lowenthal: I disagree with you there; as professor of philosophy at Brandeis he was for many years a regular member of the teaching faculty. I occasionally heard his lectures when I visited him at Brandeis. I think you're exaggerating somewhat.

Dubiel: Okay, I'm speaking comparatively. He's much less integrated into the social science community of the United States

Translated by Ted R. Weeks.

than you are. Your integration into this community—here I'm recalling our earlier conversations—can be traced all the way back to the Institute's years in New York. For example, you found it much easier to work with Lazarsfeld than Adorno did. That was most likely no coincidence. Lazarsfeld, even though he was of Austrian-German origin, and Adorno represent, to a degree of almost ideal purity, the incompatibility of American and German scholarly culture. In your case, from the very beginning that was different.

Lowenthal: Well, I come from the same scholarly tradition as Adorno. I think it was just easier for me to combine the theoretical and historical outlook with the empirical requisites of sociological research. Robert Merton put it this way: the German style of social-philosophical thinking is not incompatible with the American methodology. He referred to my study on popular biographies as a paradigmatic example of such a successful synthesis. It may also have something to do with the fact that in my own career I've been forced to deal with concrete things. I was a teacher and a social worker, and I was strongly involved in the practical affairs of the Institute, both financial and administrative; I was simply more concerned with social reality than Adorno was. And this was most likely also reflected in our academic behavior. Besides all this, there's the fact that one of the key areas of my work, both theoretical and applied, lay in the field of mass communications, which for a long time was one of the most important themes of American social science. The war provided a great impetus for differentiated studies, stimulated especially by the demand for effective propaganda techniques for both domestic and international use. And the applications were not limited to politics and the advertisement industry; pedagogical innovations, too, came to be regarded more and more as problems of the electronic media and thus played an increasing role in the theoretical and empirical fields of interest to American social science. Through happenstance and interest I became closely linked with these areas of research. Finally I also learned—it wasn't particularly difficult—to assert my own individuality as a sociologist, while at the same time familiarizing myself with what seemed to be significant and important in American social research. Later I attempted to convey this synthesis to my students. When in 1955 I became a visiting professor and then, the following year, a regular faculty member at Berkeley, circumstances forced me—more than my colleagues at the Institute—to come to terms with the methods of American social science, which I had already been familiar with from my work for the government.

Dubiel: That's just what I wanted to ask about. I'll start off with a general question. In Germany you're perceived as a German professor who lives and works abroad. That was also my perception; I was actually quite astonished when I came here and discovered how matter-of-factly you are perceived here, both in the literature and in the conversational remarks of your colleagues, as an American intellectual. So, in this vein, first of all a superficial question: with whom and with which theoretical-political factions among American social scientists do you have particularly good contacts? According to theoretical-political interpretations of American sociology, such as those of Alvin Gouldner, structural functionalism, which prevailed here in the fifties, is always contrasted with symbolic interactionism, which followed later. You're in the no-man's-land between these two camps. Do you sympathize more with one of them, or do you reject this entire interpretation?

Lowenthal: How should I put it? Both approaches are equally close and both are far from my own. In a certain way, after all, functionalism is related to Marxist methodology, only with the difference that the development of functionalist theory essentially serves the purpose—and this, of course, gives it an ideological tinge—of constructing a balance of the various functions of a society in order to produce an almost conflict-free societal system.

Everything always fits together, doesn't it? But functionalist theory also contradicts the rather hollow metaphysical perceptions of society, and in this respect it definitely has a sort of materialistic character.

Symbolic interactionism isn't completely alien to me, because I'd say that it's concerned essentially with problems of mediation. What we so sorely missed in Marxist theory, namely the mediation between the fundamental economic and social forces and actual human deeds, is, after all, a theme that is developed in interactional theory. The part of interactionism I can't accept, however, is the dissolution of social reality into symbolic forms of interaction. That leads to a trivialization of the problems—for this very reason I am most critical of the currently fashionable ethnomethodology, which sometimes, strangely enough, refers to itself as "phenomenology." In the work of Goffman and his students, interactionism has led to a sort of neo-idealism. The only reality that still exists for them is formed by human self-perception. One may well ask at this point, where does reality then remain? When you read, for example, Goffman's book *Asylums,* the very institutions that the book purports to treat end up disappearing. They're merely a welcome empirical occasion for making unempirical observations. For that reason I call this a type of neo-idealism.

I'm quite familiar with these new currents, but I'm often polemically disposed toward them. This is certainly related to the fact that these aren't the intellectual traditions I grew up with. Those, for me, were Marx, Dilthey, Simmel, and Hegel, neo-Kantian philosophy, Rickert, and Max Weber. Half-unconsciously, I probably still defer to my ancestral fathers, whether they were friendly fathers to me or not. Thus I occasionally pass rather condescending judgments on the Americans, for which you've sometimes reproached me, Helmut. However, I must immediately add—and in this respect I'm different from my former colleagues at the Frankfurt Institute—that through my more prolonged exposure to American intellectual life, I've learned to understand that the way in which we criticized pragmatism, for example, or George Herbert Mead's theory, was simply superficial. I've come to recognize that these are, after all, completely respectable theoretical approaches and methods of research, even if my background doesn't allow me to adopt them. I mean, what disturbed me most of all about American social science was the so-called empirical research enterprise, where one had the feeling that the research was actually being done only for the sake of the method and not for the sake of the objects of research. Almost always, the historical context of the phenomena under study seemed to me to be totally lacking. Empiricists always acted as if the phenomena popped into reality at the precise moment when the researchers focused on them with their methodological instruments. Every new research project defined new realities. But that's all changed now. In general, much in American social science is changing. You yourself have been here a while, and you can see how great the interest and commitment are among our younger colleagues and students for theory, history, and philosophy.

Dubiel: I'd like to pursue this question. This was one of my first enduring impressions when I came here as a German social scientist, an intellectual tourist, so to speak: that the European, particularly the German, prejudices and categories I brought along—such as "excess of empirical research," "opposition of structural functionalism and interactionism," and so on, are hardly relevant. Thus I'm interested in hearing your advice on this aspect. From your perspective as an outsider, can you recognize a new typical structure? Do you see any emerging new theoretical-political obstacles? Or is American sociology now in a phase—as I think is true at present for sociology in the Federal Republic—where "anything goes," that is, a phase of very strong dissolution of the structures and boundaries that had prevailed in the fifties, sixties, and early seventies?

Lowenthal: I think that all these categories of different

"schools" are just as outmoded as the categories of intellectual disciplines. But this is similar to the Marxist scheme of superstructure and base; it just proceeds very slowly. You know my cynical remark that the division of the social sciences into different academic departments is just a means of limiting structural unemployment among intellectuals. Today, for example, it really makes no sense to say, this is a political scientist, this is a sociologist, this is an anthropologist, this is a social psychologist. Those are all outmoded terms.

Dubiel: Does what you say have descriptive character, or are you speaking normatively?

Lowenthal: It's not just normative, it's simply the way it is. Just take a look. I mean, it's already obvious in personnel matters: a few years ago Reinhard Bendix, who used to be a sociologist, decided to switch over to the political science department, and Martin Trow, who also used to be a professor of sociology, is now a professor of public policy. As for me, I could just as well be in comparative literature. . . .

Dubiel: So you mean to say that this interdisciplinary intertwining of the different social science disciplines is more strongly developed here than in Europe, even the Federal Republic?

Lowenthal: Just take a look at such institutions as schools of business administration, law schools, and medical schools—you can see how many sociologists are wanting to get in there. You know how closely associated I am with legal-sociological studies here. It's a novelty that sociology is being taught at the law school now and that sociologists are becoming professors there.

Dubiel: Has there been a negative reaction on the part of the medical or law faculties?

Lowenthal: Of course, some resist it; to be sure, not always the best!

Dubiel: Can this be attributed to a certain ideology on the part of these disciplines? I'm only asking because in our small social science province of the Federal Republic—and specifically as a consequence of the student movement—a situation arose wherein, often under pressure from students of various disciplines, sociological approaches were established, sometimes even in the form of new professorships. This was particularly strong in the humanistic disciplines, but also in medicine, and somewhat less in jurisprudence. For quite some time now, however, a very strong affective reaction against sociology has been apparent in broader scientific circles.

Lowenthal: No, that doesn't exist here. Nor was it the case, according to my observations, that the process I described was instigated solely by student pressure, although that may have had something to do with it. I believe that what resistance there is, especially in the juridical institutes, represents rearguard battles. The need for more psychological and sociological orientation is growing. Maybe you're right, after all, that student interests are behind it. Many medical students want to study more social medicine and public health policy, law students want to learn more about community law in order to better represent the legal interests of the poor. Many business students here want to contribute to the building of more social involvement within large conglomerates. I think this sort of development will continue and expand. The danger at the beginning of this development lay in the old, petrified tradition that a good sociologist *must* work in a department of sociology, and it was often difficult to attract the best people to these other areas. The old traditionalists tended to look down on these "interdisciplinary sociologists." That's changing in places like Chicago, Harvard, Stanford, and here.

Dubiel: In the Federal Republic there are, or at least there were a little while ago, certain people who perceived this trend as a danger. Under the motto "sociology without sociologists," they saw this migration into other fields or into "hyphenated sociologies" as a manifestation of the dissolution of general sociology. In my view, this is based on the need, particularly in sociology, for a paradigmatic, disciplinary unity that unquestionably doesn't exist, at least not yet.

Lowenthal: That doesn't exist here, that fear that sociology will dissolve. I've always said that these disciplines such as sociology or political science are conglomerates, organizational units of very heterogeneous elements. No, that need to hold the ranks together in order to survive as a profession, that doesn't exist here.

Dubiel: I didn't mean that so much in the professional sense, but more in terms of the interest to have clearly defined disciplinary identity. This interest probably originates in the analogy, most likely false, to the development of the natural sciences. Sociology is, to paraphrase Thomas Kuhn, an immature science. If we go on working for, say, a hundred years on the fundamental concepts of general sociology, then . . .

Lowenthal: Now this is really the dialectic of world history. When I came here in the thirties, that was still the prevailing model: sociology was supposed to be a natural science. That's changed completely here. Today people would laugh in your face if you even expressed such ideas at all. What you really can observe here in America today is an increasing penetration of sociology by philosophical and psychological concerns. At the good universities and in good departments, the leading sociologists intellectually are no longer purely research technicians. Rather, they're also always interested in the interdisciplinary, theoretical, political, and sociopolitical contexts.

Dubiel: Well, that's certainly not the rule in the Federal Republic. There are many sociologists whom I wouldn't count among the intellectually leading figures but who tend to determine the image of sociology because of their advisory role in politics, their professional politicking, and their role in the major foundations; and the orientation of these people bears a striking resemblance to American sociology of the thirties. Their scholarly approach is very pragmatic, to the point of limiting themselves to technical issues; they mostly have very specialized areas of interest and are more like administratively oriented research technicians than theory-oriented intellectuals. This development, however, is determined in a very dialectical manner by the classically bad reputation sociology has in Germany, which in some respects is still a belated effect of fascism.

Lowenthal: I can certainly believe that. We really experienced a culture shock when we came to America. You know, in our time, sociology, like psychoanalysis, was generally considered esoteric. Thus it can't have been a coincidence that both of them came together at our Institute. Sociology and psychoanalysis were avant-garde pursuits. They smelled of leftist politics, of Jewish intellectualism.

Dubiel: Well, that really hasn't changed fundamentally in the Federal Republic. The prejudice against sociology was simply reinforced by the postwar development of Critical Theory and then especially by the student movement in the 1960s. Perhaps this fascistic image of sociology would have changed gradually over the course of the decades, but the student movement then, in reaction, so to speak, reactivated it once again. Even the established and politically flexible sociologists have to fight this prejudice in politicians, and so they are constantly obliged to present a low profile. That is, we're just "methodological technicians"; we're just supposed to furnish data; the information we provide is only to assist decision-making processes; and so on. And good old Max Weber is splendidly suited to give theoretical blessing to this self-castration.

Lowenthal: That's interesting. Is that really the case? Well, I can't see it that way in the people I know there. I don't see that in Jürgen Habermas or Ralf Dahrendorf or Ludwig von Friedeburg, or even in René König, who, after all, is more American than many an American. But perhaps these people aren't representative. Even though I've traveled several times to the Federal Republic, and various German colleagues have been here in Berkeley, I don't know enough people there to be able to form a definitive judgment. But it's interesting to see how you portray it.

Dubiel: Leo, now I'd like to address another matter. It's somehow delicate. . . .

Lowenthal: Women, money, wine?

Dubiel: No, no, not that. You know, Adorno once coined the beautiful formulation that he could imagine the political message of Critical Theory only in the form of a message in a bottle. He was probably amazed at how quickly and with what a bang that bottle was uncorked by the German student movement. My question is this: are there intellectual currents here in America that uncorked that bottle, and how do you assess them? I'm referring now to the editorial groups of the journals *Telos* and *New German Critique*. The NAM (New American Movement) group, which is influential in certain circles in the United States, also involves the tradition of Critical Theory in its theoretical positions. Of course, these are very small groups, but the public response to them and their influence on publishers are extraordinarily great. It simply astonishes me as a German to see what recondite and difficult writings are being published here now. Yesterday Benjamin's book on Baroque tragedy came into my hands—you should give yourself the pleasure of reading its English introduction. In short, Leo, how do you evaluate this whole neocriticism, as I shall call it, here in the United States?

Lowenthal: I'll answer very impudently. In America, the intellectual currents come and go just like the political ones. At the end of the First World War, America got involved in a big way in the business of imperialistic and economic international politics for the first time. What I experienced as a negative shock in the thirties was in response to an intellectual and cultural provincialism, relative to the technological and political development here. Intellectually, America was then practically a province. Just in our own field, think how late the works of Max Weber and Durkheim were translated. If Parsons hadn't come along, perhaps they still wouldn't be translated. Think of Dilthey, who to this day isn't properly translated. Not much of modern German literature has been translated, and the great documents of the French counterrevolution are still, with few exceptions, mostly unknown.

So, the key word was provinciality. Today, one can't speak of that any more. A sense of disappointment, disillusion, and outrage over what had happened in America after the Second World War slowly spread among the more enlightened young people. The broader public was not convinced that the Americans had defeated Hitler and Mussolini; fundamentally, it appeared to have been merely a matter of destroying armies, not a political system. Leftist intellectual circles reacted to this disappointment with a strong interest in political philosophy. And in this context the Frankfurt School was discovered. Most likely the new interest derived largely from the great popularity Herbert Marcuse enjoys in this country; at least, that's what I suspect. Then, of course, there's the factor of the ideological disputes on the left, which, to be sure, never had a mass political basis. There were, for instance, the many Trotskyist-oriented discussions at the end of the thirties. Today it's like that again, except that now it's much more cosmopolitan. This is the context in which we find a fairly broad reception for many of the ideas of the Frankfurt School, as well as for those of a good number of French thinkers. Intellectual curiosity is great and nearly unquenchable. But all this excited curiosity and intellectual activity can't replace real, politically oriented activism. Ultimately, none of this has any real political meaning.

Dubiel: All of what you say could be perfectly well applied to German circumstances. These extremely heated discussions of sectarian circles are only possible in the hothouse of complete political isolation.

Lowenthal: But I always have the feeling that that could quickly change in Germany. A great economic crisis or who knows what could change that.

Dubiel: In reading *Telos* I'm amazed to find a lot of paradigms that were in vogue in Germany over a decade ago. For example, the endless discussion about whether your circle was the representative of authentic Marxism or whether it consisted of infamous Marxist dissidents; you know, that overheated atmosphere in which the Benjamin legend arose, I find it here once again. It's really astonishing. In Germany, it was at least related to the rising student movement and the problems involved in orienting a social movement. Here it really isn't anything more than an excited academic affair.

Lowenthal: I have nothing to add to that; you're quite right. They really are small groups, but in America even small groups count simply because the country is so large and it all eventually adds up. In some sense all of this is a "catching up" phenomenon. European intellectual circles used to be strongly characterized by intellectual partisanship. As a philosopher in Germany, for instance, one belonged either to the Marburg School or to the Southwest School, and one engaged in disputes and polemics; one was either a Kantian, a liberal, or a Marxist. And this current endorsement of Critical Theory—which, as a concept, has become so diffuse that I myself don't know anymore what its constituent elements are—is probably an attempt to found a philosophical-ideological party, a search for a unified scientific-political perspective. It's a protest against every form of scientistic positivism, and here Critical Theory functions as a guideline.

Dubiel: That is to say, a stimulus to different scientific-political and ideological orientations.

Lowenthal: Yes, but a stimulus that is attractive precisely to many extraordinarily bright people. In my experience, it's always the best students who become partisans of Critical Theory. That's my impression. I don't think that happens just by chance.

Dubiel: Leo, let's talk about the student movement. We're in Berkeley, you've taught here since the fifties, one could say that things began here when you were at the high point of your university teaching career. It can also be said that Berkeley, at least chronologically, was the leader of the worldwide student movement.

Dr. Victor Lowenthal,
Leo Lowenthal's father, c. 1934

Rosy Bing Lowenthal,
Leo Lowenthal's mother,
c. 1940

Leo Lowenthal in the Goethe Gymnasium, Frankfurt am Main, 1912
(third row, third from left)

Leo Lowenthal in the Kaiser's army, 1918 (top row, center)

Lowenthal as a young schoolteacher, Liebig-Oberrealschule,
Frankfurt am Main, c. 1928

Theodor W. Adorno, c. 1921,
age 18

Lowenthal as a schoolteacher, Liebig-Oberrealschule, Frankfurt am
Main, 1930

The young Siegfried Kracauer,
Frankfurt am Main, c. 1925, age 36

Max Horkheimer, New York (?),
c. 1940

Right, Lowenthal's mentor, Luise Habricht, Giessen, c. 1919, age 40

Below, Lowenthal's mentor, Walter Kinkel, Professor of Philosophy, University of Giessen, 1919, at about age 45

Lowenthal and son Daniel on the roof of the
Institute building, 1927

Lowenthal's first wife, Golde, and son Daniel, c. 1936

Leo and Golde Lowenthal, 1936

Lowenthal at the Voice of America, c. 1950

Marjorie Fiske, Lowenthal's second wife, c. 1955

Lowenthal at the Center for Advanced
Study, Palo Alto, 1955

Lowenthal and Herbert Marcuse at Lowenthal's wedding to
Susanne Hoppmann, 1977

Lowenthal and Jürgen Habermas in Crete, 1980

Leo and Susanne Lowenthal, Laguna Beach, California, 1979

Lowenthal and Martin Jay, Berkeley, 1984

Susanne and Leo Lowenthal and Helmut Dubiel, Munich, 1980

Lowenthal receiving the Federal Republic's Distinguished Service Cross from President Richard von Weizsäcker, Berlin, 1985 (Photo courtesy of Elke Petra Thonke, Hölderlinstr. 11, Berlin)

Lowenthal: Yes, that started, I believe, around 1960. The first student demonstrations then must have been on the steps of City Hall or the courthouse in San Francisco, protests against the Committee on Un-American Activities, a kind of successor to the McCarthy committee. I congratulated the students in my classes. I said, "I'm glad that you've finally awakened from the great hibernation of the fifties." And then when the Free Speech Movement started in 1964, drawing its support mainly from the civil rights activists from the South, I was really enthusiastic. As acting chairman of the Sociology Department, I endorsed the faculty protest against the university administration. I then joined a faculty committee that worked very closely with the student organizations, and we, together with the students, assumed an adversary position toward the chancellor, the president of the university, and the governor. And, in the end, we won, too. But about that later. First I became a member of the so-called Muscatine committee [Select Committee on Education, chaired by Charles Muscatine], belonging, so to speak, to its left wing. This committee had the task of working out suggestions for educational reform, which were later published in the book *Education at Berkeley* in 1968. I can only speak for myself, but for a time I had the feeling that this movement would really gain political momentum and that perhaps a third party would develop in America. Whether one could have called it "socialist" I'll leave aside. At least, that was my hope then. But it didn't happen.

Dubiel: When did the first signs appear? Are there any key events?

Lowenthal: In 1966, that is, two years later. I realize this now in light of experiences I had in 1966 during an extended trip through the Federal Republic, when I often had contacts with West German students. But especially here in Berkeley, I soon gained the impression that it was essentially more a matter of satisfying certain psychological needs than of realizing realistic political goals. There are enough examples of how, as time passed, these private psychological projections often translated themselves into frustrations and tragedies in student circles. At first I thought that this would be different in Germany, that the student movement would be much more strongly linked with other political movements. Isn't that a fair assessment of what happened?

Dubiel: No. Various disoriented parts of the student movement joined various other feuding groups. But one can't say that the student movement as a whole placed itself in the service of another political force. I don't quite understand your criticism, though, Leo. Just what sort of an argument is this about psychological satisfaction?

Lowenthal: Perhaps I put it badly. I noticed that it never really came to a consolidated, politically oriented movement. I saw that many of these young people enjoyed the state of upheaval they had caused on campus with their activities, that they experienced this as an atmosphere that mitigated certain psychological frustrations in the academic as well as the personal sphere and allowed them to retreat into the background. But this hardly translated into a viable political movement. At first I thought that this conflict between protesting students, who were supported in part by openly protesting employees, and the police, with their constant hail of tear gas grenades and so on, could develop into a real movement. But that didn't happen. You see it yourself every day: Telegraph Avenue is now a bazaar; People's Park is a collection of little vegetable gardens. But at that time I was happy about it, and I was a part of it, too. Then in 1970, the invasion of Cambodia took place, and those were the days when the students wanted to "reconstruct" the university. Well, I have to admit that I wasn't completely sold on the idea of an intra-university democracy. The students at that time had a kind of vague notion of a Soviet council–type community of professors, staff, and students. When my students refused to meet on campus for our seminar because it was impossible to do any work there what with all the police and tear gas, we met privately. Out of this grew my private seminar, which today, nine years later, still exists. Another example of the cunning of reason!

Dubiel: Today, in retrospect after ten years, one really has to say that it was an extremely dramatic and critical political situation. I think it's pretty much agreed that the antiwar movement reached its high point with the protest against the invasion of Cambodia. Ronald Reagan was governor at that time, and the unrest on the Berkeley campus was his most important and most attractive campaign issue. Even though the student movement in the Federal Republic lasted longer and possibly also reached somewhat deeper, it never reached such a dramatic critical point in its development as here. In the entire area around Berkeley and San Francisco the antiwar movement was very strong; on campus, it was a situation more or less of civil war.

Lowenthal: You're right there. What I described previously was, so to speak, the one side. The other side was, of course—and this mustn't be underestimated—that it had led to a great protest movement throughout the country, which was joined by other important groups of the population. I think that one can really say that the Vietnam War was brought to an end by the pressure of student and nonstudent movements, that the ending of the Vietnam War was, to a great extent, a victory of the American student movement. But out of the actual Free Speech Movement, nothing developed. After the awful war came to an end, everything else also came to an end; the movement practically disappeared overnight. The campus became quiet, and although people say that there are a number of underground activities, one doesn't see much of them. Since then there have been recurrent efforts, especially centered around the problems of minorities and women, to repeat the victory that the struggle against the Vietnam War ultimately gained, but so far they have failed.

Dubiel: Yes, I've also observed that here. I always explain this phenomenon to myself in simple theoretical terms: one can't determine the cycle of social movements independently from world history. For that reason, such immanent appraisals of political movements that don't take into account the opportunities offered by historical events are always somehow inadequate. So, with the end of the Vietnam War, it all fell apart. But at the same time—and this is the tragedy of the American student movement—this tremendous political success formed expectations among the American left by which the success of other activities is measured even today. It's no wonder, then, that here apathy goes deeper, that the nostalgic mystification of the sixties is much more intense than in Germany. I've attended several conferences of the American left here—they were nostalgia festivals! You might recall that last September here in Berkeley there was a big festival at which the sixties were to be officially buried. Now the motto is: the sixties are now!

Lowenthal: All that confirms precisely what I've been saying: these are just psychological calisthenics, nothing more.

Dubiel: No, it's not that simple. You can't just ascribe everything to the psychological mechanisms of these people. It certainly has more to do with the fact that the cause they're representing does not at this moment inspire general social sentiments sufficient to rally the masses behind it—it simply lacks political explosive force. These are obviously highly respectable needs, which, however, don't seem to be symptomatic of a general social conflict structure.

Lowenthal: And you want to accuse me of having become a pessimist! Is that the behavior of a youth who claims to be politically motivated, that you have to search around to see whether there are any political situations with which you can identify? What happened to spontaneity? After all, world history continually confronts us with new tasks and challenges.

Dubiel: Leo, I don't think it's that simple. In history there just doesn't arise that often a constellation of situations, a series of events that come together in such a way as to make it possible for a large political movement to react to it with closed ranks, or even to forfeit the opportunity to react. In that respect—this would make a nice afterword—your own life was full of such mostly negative situations, which we often, in retrospect, recognize as dramatic historical crises: the October Revolution, the German revolution of 1918, fascism, the end of the war. This kind of historical explosion isn't experienced every day. But that leads me to something else. As you know, in my book I took great care to examine the formation of political consciousness in your circle in the thirties and forties. There I found an increasing development away from a skeptically distanced support of the "progressive forces of humanity," which was a sort of embarrassed rhetorical flourish showing that you could not fully identify with either the Social Democrats or the Communists, all the way to an apocalyptic skepticism toward world developments as a whole. Even today I often find traces of that skepticism, that world-historical pessimism, the most concrete examples of which I found in the early forties. You probably remember the evening we spoke about Iran with Herbert Marcuse. There I noticed that attitude, which doesn't lead merely to skeptical comments on all specific political events; more than that, it provides a pitch-black background against which everything appears totally gloomy and hopeless. This view of world developments as an inescapable continuity of doom—which is documented in numerous places in the writings and letters of the members of your circle—apparently stayed with you all, including you, Leo. In many conversations, when we've touched on essential matters, I've often perceived you as someone who sits, so to speak, in the foxhole of a world-historical pessimism and describes everything from this perspective. Would you say that this is a fairly accurate description?

Lowenthal: Yes, maybe.

Dubiel: Well, as a younger man I can, for simple psychological reasons alone, scarcely adopt that view. At the same time, however, I see—and here I may sound a bit nasty—that you've set yourself up rather comfortably in this world. Lukács once characterized this life-style with the malicious *mot* "Grand Hotel Abyss"—you know, that formulation was coined referring to Horkheimer and Adorno. You appreciate your comfortable life-style, you like to eat well, you enjoy good wine. In short, you live in very pleasant circumstances in a very pretty house in one of the most attractive areas of the United States. What I'm driving at is this: in contrast to former times, the experiences on which you base that pessimism are no longer connected with the immediate sufferings of today's generations. Then, in a very dramatic and brutal way, the opposite was the case. To be a socialist and a Jew in fascist Germany, to have to emigrate because of that—just yesterday I was reading your letters from the late thirties when you were trying to get your parents out of Germany via Lisbon—your individual fate was inextricably linked with world history: you had just escaped Hitler. Others in your circle, Benjamin, for example, weren't so lucky. The most dreadful repercussions of world history affected your intimate circle; the anguish of the world of that time was existentially tangible for you. Now for my question: is your present pessimism or profound skepticism just a deeply rooted aftereffect of the shock of those days that you have never completely overcome, or are there also present-day political developments that provide a possible source of your pessimism? Forgive me, Leo, that I've talked for so long, but this is an important question for me.

Lowenthal: First of all, Helmut, I'd like to state one thing very energetically. I'm sorry to see you in the company of those who take us to task for the alleged contradiction between radicalism and the enjoyment of the good life. We were always of a different opinion: luxury is not an evil. The proletarian resentment of the upper strata is not productive for theory. Enjoyment leads to a higher sense of differentiation, unless one becomes the victim of unbridled hedonism. So, Helmut, I think that the environment in which one lives should be as beautiful as possible, and traveling well and comfortably, enjoying a good meal and good wine, socializing with friends—all these things are surely positive experiences. This is how human beings should live. Whom would it help if I were to voluntarily lower my standard of living—as if only the very rich were entitled to the so-called good life!

Dubiel: I'm a little intimidated to say anything more. Perhaps here I'm also a victim of that fundamentally Protestant sympathy with the proletariat. . . .

Lowenthal: I don't sympathize with the proletariat. Marx didn't sympathize with the proletariat either: the proletariat was to be abolished! Proletarian life-styles are hardly a model worth imitating, nor are petit-bourgeois life-styles that attempt to emulate the life-styles of the upper classes. Today, however, many members of these upper classes engage in the glorification of a rural communal life in primitive circumstances. I reject that as well. I would say quite directly that luxury is the anticipation of utopia. Perhaps Marx might have found more sophisticated formulations and made more subtle distinctions had he lived in better circumstances. But back to your question. So then, pessimism is a term I would rather not use. I'd prefer to just say, sadness. Pessimism presupposes an anthropology I don't share. I still have not completely shed the utopian ideas that motivated me as a young man of seventeen or eighteen. Fundamentally, if I may put it arrogantly, I never abandoned politics and the revolution; rather, the revolution abandoned me. I'm not against progress, and certainly I'm glad to see the "good guy" and the "good cause" win a victory in the political arena, but this only amounts to avoidance of a greater evil. I think that the shock to which you referred was caused not only by the disappointment over a failed universal revolution after World War I but also by the disappointment resulting from the developments after World War II.

Dubiel: Do you mean the lack of ideological consequences of the battle against fascism?

Lowenthal: It's rarely been much fun to find oneself on the side of the winners. Usually one feels better in the company of the losers. The end of the war was experienced as the defeat of the German, Japanese, and Italian armies because of their inferiority to the military power of the allies. The military inferiority was there, of course, but the demonstration of that was hardly the purpose of that war. We had hoped for a real change in the world, not only in the countries formerly ruled by fascists, but also in the United States, which, after all, is hardly in a state of moral and political innocence. It was a great disappointment for us to realize that the war was waged practically without ideology. "Getting it over with" seemed to have been the principal goal.

Dubiel: If you, Marcuse, Pollock, and Neumann had no scruples as intellectuals to work for the American government during the war, you were probably also motivated by the belief that this was also a war of ideologies.

Lowenthal: Certainly. As for me, that was still the case when I was working for Voice of America.

Dubiel: Was this, then, the second shock, after the traumatic experience of emigration and the eventual failure of the Weimar Republic—I mean, the shock that America, although it entered the war, did so with cool rationality and not in the name of the unequivocally superior cause?

Lowenthal: I don't want to exaggerate. You overinterpret me a bit. First of all, it is a positive fact in world history that Hitler's Third Reich lasted not a thousand but only twelve years and that Mussolini and other political criminals have disappeared. Of course, new ones emerge all the time, but those were the worst so far. No, Helmut, what makes me so sad is that there aren't any real political movements with which I can identify, at whose disposal I could place my meager resources. I feel very isolated. For a time I tried to identify with the organization Americans for Democratic Action, the left wing of the Democratic Party. But that turned into an exercise in futility, a pastime for left liberals devoid of theoretical basis. I can't do that, I simply can't do that.

Dubiel: This reminds me of a passage in a letter by Horkheimer that I just came across. In the postscript to a letter dated September 1, 1939, he writes—I'm paraphrasing—the most dreadful thing about the present historical situation is that one cannot have even the slightest sympathy with any of the fighting powers. He wrote this on the eve of World War II. Could you today subscribe to this position?

Lowenthal: Helmut, I can only restate my position of political nonidentification. If you wish, you might interpret this as a weakness. This attitude probably goes back to what I have just described to you, namely that in my memory I'm still so strongly rooted in my political youth, that is, the period from age seventeen to twenty-two when I really believed in utopia. I believed in the possibility of a successful revolution and the realization of its goals. I really believed that we could change the world. Already then such deep-seated utopian expectations served as a rationalization for disengaging myself from the tedium of concrete political activity. Perhaps my youthful hopes have been so profoundly disappointed that I can no longer muster the patience to identify with movements that are dedicated to mere improvements. Of course, my heart beats faster when the utopian seems to throw off sparks, if only for a moment; but disappointment follows all too quickly. Just take a look at the world today. Tell me, just where should one plant one's political sympathies and hopes?

Part II

Memories and Memorials

6

Sociology of
Literature in Retrospect

BY LEO LOWENTHAL

For more than a half century I have primarily concerned myself
with the sociology of literature and the problem of mass culture.
With financial support from the Institute of Social Research at the
University of Frankfurt, I began in 1926 with studies on German
writers in the nineteenth century.[1] Discernible in these studies is
the socially critical spirit that motivated this group of then still
young scholars to reject conventional research methods and to seek
a new and bolder mode of analyzing material in the social and
human sciences—in short, to dare to break through the walls of the
academic ivory tower, where specialists pursued their professional
interests without any social or moral consciousness. I had the
privilege of being one of the first members of this group, which I

Originally published as "Literatursoziologie im Rückblick," in Heine
von Alemann and Hans Peter Thurn, eds., *Soziologie in weltbürgerlichen
Absicht: Festschrift für René König zum 75. Geburtstag* (Opladen, 1981),
pp. 101–13. Translated by Ted R. Weeks.
1. Cf. Leo Lowenthal, "Studies on the German Novel in the Nineteenth Century," in *Literature and the Image of Man*, vol. 2 of *Communication
in Society* (New Brunswick, N.J., 1986), pp. 221ff.

joined in 1926 at the invitation of Max Horkheimer and Friedrich Pollock.

The years of my academic training were devoted to the study of sociology and literature. Later, in my first independent work, I attempted to apply what I had learned from Marx, Freud, and the great philosophical tradition of Europe to a new appraisal of European literature since the Renaissance. Like many other intellectuals in my circles of that time, I was convinced of the decadence of Western society. All of us felt Hitler's threatening advance, and the rest of the so-called civilized world we considered to be impaired. We strove, each according to his own knowledge and inclination, to interpret historical and contemporary problems in such a way as to reveal their socially regressive or progressive character. We rejected the concept of a "value-free science" as an unpardonable renunciation of the moral responsibility of those who, amid the general misery of average people, had the good fortune to lead the life of an intellectual. If some of the formulations in what follows appear partisan or even angry, I offer no apologies. On the contrary, I would be pleased by such accusations. There was reason enough for anger—in the scientific enterprise as well as in public life.

Since my school days I have been attracted to literature, and it is certainly no coincidence that I spent several years as a German teacher at a *Gymnasium* in Frankfurt before joining the Institute. I suspect that from the outset I tended toward literary criticism, for as a high school student and young teacher I had experienced the utterly banal approach to the teaching of literature practiced by most instructors and supported by the officially approved textbooks. More than anything, however, I was irritated by the utterly conventional choice of literary texts. Because I lived through the years after World War I as a politically rebellious, if not out-and-out revolutionary, young man, it seemed to me quite natural to apply the practical experience gained in school and in politics to my theoretical endeavors within the academy.

I soon discovered that I was quite isolated in my attempts to pursue the sociology of literature. In any case, it was almost impossible to find allies in approaching this task from the perspective of a critical theory of society. To be sure, there were Franz Mehring's articles, which I read with interest and profit; but despite the admirable decency and the uncompromising political radicalism of the author, his writings hardly went beyond the limits of a socialist journalist writing in essentially the same style about literature as about politics and the economy. Georg Lukács hadn't yet published his impressive series of essays on Marxist aesthetics and literary interpretation. Of course, I was deeply touched and influenced by his fine little book *The Theory of the Novel* (1920), which I learned practically by heart. Besides Levin Schücking's small volume on the sociology of literary taste, the only other major influence I can recall was Georg Brandes's monumental work on the literary currents of the nineteenth century.

Nonetheless, I had the courage, or even the hubris, to plan an ambitious, socially critical series on French, English, Spanish, and German literature, the beginning of which was to consist of the above-mentioned studies. My attention was especially focused on the writers and literary schools that the German literary establishment either punished by total silence ("Young Germany" and Friedrich Spielhagen, for example), raised up into the clouds of idealistic babble (Goethe and the Romantics), or relegated to quasi-folkloric anthropology (C. F. Meyer and Gottfried Keller).

In these studies, I limited myself to the narrative forms of literature; for reasons I hold to be sociologically and artistically valid, I believe that novels and stories represent the most significant aspect of German literature in the nineteenth century. While I am in no way ashamed of these documents of my youth, I am conscious of their weaknesses. If I were to write them over again, I would certainly be less sure of some of the direct connections I drew between literature and writers on the one hand, and between literature and the social infrastructure on the other. In later publications I attempted to analyze with greater circumspection the mediation between substructure and superstructure, between social currents and ideologies; but my views on the social world and the necessity to combine social theory and literary analysis have not changed in any essential way. In the last decades the sociology of literature has become progressively more fashionable. The writings of my contemporaries have often amazed me because some—frequently in unnecessarily complicated and esoteric language—are so concerned with "mediation" that the connections between social being and social consciousness become almost obscured.

I

The first issue of the *Zeitschrift für Sozialforschung*—the only one we managed to publish in Germany before the Hitler-night descended—gives an indication of what Critical Theory means: namely, a perspective, based on a shared critical fundamental attitude, that applies to all cultural phenomena without ever claiming to be a system. It includes critical analysis of philosophy, economics, psychology, music, and literature.

Critical Theory—a term, by the way, that we began to use only in the late thirties—should not, then, be understood as anything more than this collective "common denominator." As the only survivor of the founding years in the twenties, I feel almost ill at ease. . . . Why should I survive and not the others, who in 1926 invited me to join an intellectual alliance they had created in an institutionalized form two years earlier? We did not speak of "Critical Theory" at that time, and the thought of a "school" was certainly far from us. We were and remained "Nay-sayers," in the tradition of Hegel's particular form of negation; each one of us tried to express what was wrong in his particular field and, therefore, in our society. We were consciously on the periphery of established power. Even now, as you will see, this position on the periphery, this marginality, remains for me in my work, and perhaps even in my own perception of life, the most important category. What I have tried to do in the last fifty years is guided by my unbroken commitment to the European literary heritage and simultaneously to the critique of the production of commodities and words for a manipulated and manipulable mass market. I shall now try to sketch my critical approach.

II

First, the most important thing to stress is that art and consumer goods must be held strictly apart. I cannot accept any of the current radical attempts, either in Germany or in the United States, to do away with this distinction. To be sure, the consumption of high art can also turn into mass culture and play its part in manipulating society. I need only remind you of Wagner's role during the Hitler years, about which Adorno has written extensively. More peculiar examples are found in the history of theater direction, for example, when bourgeois common sense trivializes the socially inherent tragedy of marriage and love. Here I am thinking of an eighteenth-century English production of *Othello* in which the Moor does not kill Desdemona in the final scene but rather realizes his own mistake and asks her forgiveness so that they can be eternally happy on earth; or, for another example, when in a turn-of-the-century staging of Ibsen's *Doll's House* in Munich, Nora, at the end of the play, closes the door not from the outside but from within and returns to her boring husband—for, after all, a woman's place is in the home. These are certainly examples that reflect the social climate. In contrast, certain materials, originally produced as articles of consumption, can sometimes—if seldom—pass into the realm of folk art, or rather of folkloric mythology. But those are borderline cases. And I must not neglect to point out certain differences between the American and the European scene. In the United States the sociology of literature is more or less limited to content analysis and the study of the effects of mass culture, with particular emphasis on commercial and political propaganda. The model used in these studies is behavioristic, that is, unhistorical; sociology of literature in the sense of an analysis of art remains suspect. I sense today in Europe an inclination to perceive a work of art merely as a manifestation of ideology, which strips it of its specific integrity, that is, its historically conditioned, but also rationally creative and cognitive, role. To put it in a more provocative form: Marxist literary criticism is not merely totally adequate, it is indispensable in the analysis of mass culture. It must, however, be applied with utter caution to art itself and must, as a critique of social illusions, limit itself to the residues that are unequivocally ideological in nature.

To put it in even stronger terms: art teaches, and mass culture is learned; therefore, a sociological analysis of art must be cautious, supplementary, and selective, whereas a sociological analysis of mass culture must be all-inclusive, for its products are nothing more than the phenomena and symptoms of the process of the individual's self-resignation in a wholly administered society.

III

I would like to speak first of the sociology of literature as art. Adorno once said, "Works of art . . . have their greatness only insofar as they let speak what ideology conceals. They transcend, whether they want to or not, false consciousness." Literature is not ideology. We are not engaged in research on ideology; rather, we have to focus our attention on the special truth, the specifically cognitive aspect, that the literary work imparts. This does not mean "new criticism"; on the contrary, it implies studying the social history of art and its reception, as suggested in Marx's comments on Greek tragedy and the novels of Balzac. At this point I would like to identify the great themes of literature as I perceive them from a sociologically critical perspective. To begin with the most general: literature is the only dependable source for human consciousness and self-consciousness, for the individual's relationship to the world as experience. The process of socialization—that is, the social ambience of the private, the intimate, and the individual—is raised to consciousness by the artist, not only for his time but also for our time, and thereby functions as a constant corrective to our false consciousness. Awareness of this aspect of art has come to be an important issue on the intellectual agenda only in the past fifty years, when the Western world entered into a severe crisis with the rise of totalitarianism. The sociology of art is indeed one of Minerva's owls. The sociology of literature, rightly understood, should interpret what seems furthest removed from society as the most valid key to understanding society, especially its defects. Psychoanalysis, by the way, in revealing the social dimension of the most intimate aspects of body and psyche, is a good model for what I am attempting to express. Of particular importance to me is the role of a critical sociology of literature in the analysis of the social ambience of the intimate and the private, the revealing of the sociological determination of such phenomena as love, friendship, the human being's relationship to nature, self-image, and the like. This approach does not mean reductionism, however. Literature is no mere site to be plundered. I reject all attempts to regard literature as a tool for learning facts about such institutions as the economy, the state, and the legal system. Social scientists and social historians should be forbidden from regarding literature as a source for raw materials. Literature teaches us to understand the success or failure of the socialization of individuals in concrete historical moments and situations. The novels of Stendhal, for instance—in particular, *Lucien Leuwen*—would be a perfect source for studying the transitions of forms of experience from a feudal to an aristocratic to a bourgeois type of individual.

If what I have said thus far seems too formalistic, let me assure you that a critical perspective is absolutely necessary. When I speak of the history of the individual's socialization, I also speak of the history of his sufferings, and of his passions. The literature I am familiar with, that of Western Europe since 1600, is the history of human passion in our everpresent crisis, the long-endured story of tension, promises, betrayal, and death. The literature of bourgeois society makes the permanent crisis of the individual apparent. A criterion of literature as art demands assessing whether and to what extent the crisis is manifested as being permanent. And thus we enter the precarious realm of the fringe, or marginality.

The most extreme form of the marginal existence, that is, the conscious or unconscious critique of society, is expressed in the emphatic utterances of those characters who know humanity's death sentence to be already sealed before we enter the so-called fullness of social life. Stendhal has one figure, with whom he identifies, say somewhere in *The Charterhouse of Parma*: "I can see nothing other than a death sentence which characterizes a real human being. . . . Everything else can be bought." And a half century later, Walter Pater assures us in his *The Renaissance: Studies in Art and Poetry*:

> Well, we are all *condamnés,* as Victor Hugo says: we are all under a sentence of death but with a sort of indefinite reprieve—*les hommes sont tous condamnés à mort avec des sursis indéfinis:* we have an interval, and then our place knows us no more. Some spend this interval in listlessness, some in high passions, the wisest, at least among "the children of this world," in art and song.[2]

This means, in the language of a neo-Romantic, that art alone communicates what is truly good in human life and experience; it is a promise of happiness that remains unfulfilled.

Here I come to the most significant aspect of marginality, namely, the sociology of the artist himself. He has a skewed view of

2. Walter Pater, *The Renaissance: Studies in Art and Poetry* (London, 1912), p. 238.

the world. By looking at the world obliquely, he sees it correctly, for it is indeed distorted. The artist is no Cartesian but rather a dialectician focusing on the idiosyncratic, on that which does not fit into the system. In short, he is concerned with human costs and thus becomes an ally of Critical Theory, of the critical perspective that is itself a part of critical praxis.

The marginal in the work of art is represented by groups, situations, and protagonists.

First, from the perspective of Critical Theory, the literary artist becomes our ally as the spokesman for the *collective of outcasts,* of the poor, the beggars, the criminals, the insane, in short, of all those who bear the burden of society. Here, however, the true dialectic of art is immediately apparent, making it meaningless to interpret it, in the sense of Adorno's remark cited above, as mere ideology. In the writer's representation—which comes nearer to reality than unmediated reality itself—the collectivity of those excluded from profits and privileges is shown to be the true first nature of humankind. In the collectivity of misery, the possibility of true humanity is revealed not as distortion, but as an immanent indictment. It is a dialectical irony that those who least correspond to a trivial bourgeois-ideological concept of the individual bear the mark of liberated, autonomous humaneness.

Here I may perhaps refer to my analysis of the works of Cervantes as an example of social groups on the periphery:

> There are two, not mutually exclusive, ways of looking at the marginal figures of Cervantes; they are the refuse of a society that has cast them aside, and they are, by virtue of their own right, moralists. . . .
>
> All these marginal creatures, the beggars, the crooks, the gypsies, the insane, constitute "overheads" of society, to which they are either unwilling to belong or from which they are forcibly excluded. But while they are accused, indicted, and confined, they themselves in turn are accusers. Their very existence denounces a world they never made and

which wants no part of them. The artist, in giving these people a voice, may seek to inspire uneasiness on the part of those who have profited by the prevailing order. The author's voice is the voice of the losers. The other aspect in which the marginal figures may be viewed leads us back to the concept of the utopian. The marginal figures not only serve the negative function of indicting the social order; they also positively demonstrate the true idea of man. They all serve to show the possibilities of Utopia, where everyone has the freedom to be his own deviant case—with the result that the very phenomenon of deviation disappears. The outcast society of robbers and thieves who are plying their trade on the fringes of Seville, and the society of gypsies encamped on the outskirts of Madrid, are grotesque utopian prototypes: everybody works according to his own talents, and everything is shared by everybody. . . .

The meaning of Cervantes' critical idealism is even clearer in *The Little Gypsy.* . . . The tribal chief says: "We observe inviolably the law of friendship; no one solicits the object of another man's affection; we live free from the bitter curse of jealousy. . . ." Thus at the threshold of the new society Cervantes describes the law by which it operates and confronts it with its professed measure: the autonomous and morally responsible individual. And this responsible and independent man is to be found only at the margin of society, which at once produces and expels him.[3]

The most extreme case in which a critical perspective attempts to highlight the cognitive character of peripheral groups portrayed by literature is that of woman. Ever since the Renaissance, the literary artist has made female protagonists the true revolutionary critics of a defective society. Ibsen once said, "Modern society is not

---

3. Leo Lowenthal, *Literature and the Image of Man,* pp. 43–46. (Translation emended.)

a human society; it is merely a society of males." However, this disenfranchisement of woman has not only negative but also positive consequences.

Ibsen's men never practice what they preach, and the only principle by which they live—the materialism of personal gain—they never admit. The women, too, are materialistic, but their materialism is clearly of a different nature, and it is, above all, openly articulated. It is a conscious dramatic irony that morality is preached by the egotists, whereas egotism is preached by the moralists.

Second, *situation-marginality* and group-marginality are very closely related. Significant examples are found in Shakespeare's plays, especially in *The Tempest, King Lear,* and *Timon of Athens,* where the characters are driven out into the wilderness of unsocialized nature. Here nature is not perceived as raw material to be abused and exploited by a class society's lust for power—an exploitation that parallels that of the marginal groups of society of which I just spoke. When in these plays nature emphatically appears in the form of the untamed elements, it heralds at the same time a reconciliation of nature and man. Outraged nature forms an alliance with outraged man in order to indict an evil society. In *The Tempest* this is made very clear, as unmastered nature leads the human being's second nature, his reified and socialized mask, back to his true nature. The marginal situation of absolute poverty (not to be confused with Robinson Crusoe's situation), which initially besets Prospero, Lear, and Timon, eventually turns into a blessing and thus represents the anticipation of utopia. Implicitly or explicitly (and this I can only boldly assert without proof), utopia—the reconciliation of human nature and nature—remains the fundamental theme of authentic literature.

Third, where the *protagonist* himself appears as a peripheral figure, the synthesis between marginal groups and marginal situations has been reached, or at least anticipated, all the way from Rabelais's *Pantagruel* to, if you will, Günter Grass's *The Tin Drum,* and into the present—here, the identity of the average person in class society and that of the protagonist are totally incompatible. Don Quixote is symbolic of a critique of bourgeois society, of its manipulated conformism from its late feudal forms around 1600 up to the present day. He is the ahistorical symbol of a genuine historical materialism. In every situation he is insane—that is, he is sane; in every encounter he is irrational—that is, he is rational. He is the only one who is really happy, nearly fulfilled—precisely because he sees society from an oblique critical perspective and "straightens it out" by his fantastic deeds. By converting his critical idealism into practice, he represents the fulfillment of the potential of every individual. Although he is destroyed and finally dies, he still stands for the premonition of what life could be. His fantasies anticipate what remains invisible in this damaged world. To quote Hegel:

> We find in Don Quixote a noble nature in whose adventure chivalry goes mad, the substance of such adventures being placed at the center of a stable and well-defined state of things whose external character is copied with exactness from nature. . . . In all the madness of his mind and his enterprise he is a completely consistent soul, or rather his madness lies in this, that he is and remains securely rooted in himself and his enterprise.[4]

In short, in him, through him, the identity of theory and practice is realized.

Before I turn briefly to the topic of mass culture, I would like, as a transition, to refer once more to Stendhal, who to my mind is the master analyst of the experience of socialization, and who, if in a now dated way, anticipates a social climate in which genuine experience becomes completely overpowered by conformism. And this is indeed the essential characteristic of mass culture. When, in *Lu-*

---

4. G. W. F. Hegel, *The Philosophy of Fine Art,* trans. F. P. B. Osmaston (London, 1920), vol. 2, pp. 374–75.

cien Leuwen, Lucien can endure the decadent restoration society as little as the *juste-milieu* of the new bourgeois world, he toys—as does the hero of *Wilhelm Meister's Travels*—with the idea of emigrating to America. This quotation speaks for itself:

> All Lucien's sensations had been so dreary since he came to Nancy that for want of anything better to do, he let this republican epistle absorb his attention. "The best thing to do would be for them all to sail to America. . . . And would I sail with them? I am not quite such an imbecile! . . . I should be bored in America among men who are, it is true, perfectly just and reasonable, but coarse, and who think of nothing but dollars."[5]

Bordeom is indeed the key word; it is the form of experience in which nineteenth-century artists express the perspective of Critical Theory in relation to the emerging manifestations of modern life.

IV

When I think about my own works on the analysis of mass culture, it is easy for me to appreciate the term "boredom," because this term offers access to the most significant factor: the crippling of imagination that obstructs artistic experience and gives free rein to the forces of manipulation. The extent to which the "administration," or suppression, of the imagination is part of the business of mass culture can be made clear in a few examples. In the United States, as well as in Germany, book clubs are a big business. One enterprise, called "Time Books," offers a "Time Reading Program." For a modest sum, three or four books are delivered each month and, with them, participation in a "planned approach" to

5. Stendhal, *Lucien Leuwen,* trans. Louis Varèse (New York, 1950), vol. 1, p. 35.

reading, which guarantees that "though your time may be limited, you will be reading widely and profitably . . . many books that are truly timeless in style and significance." The reliability of selection is beyond doubt: "This plan draws its strength from the fact that the editors spent thousands of hours finding the answers to questions that you, too, must have asked yourself many times. . . . It is part of their job to single out the few books that tower over all others." Significance, quality, and relevance of the publications are assured: "In each case, the editors will write special introductions to underline what is unique in the book, what impact it has had or will have, what place it has earned in literature and contemporary thought." In addition, a kind of religious sanction is bestowed upon the wrappings: "The books will be bound in durable, flexible covers similar to those used for binding fine Bibles and Missals."

Another example: the Literary Guild, one of the most successful American book clubs, recently offered inexpensive special editions of *Anna Karenina, Madame Bovary,* and Dumas's *Camille.* The advertisement reads about as follows: "These three classical novels, which are now published together in an attractively bound set, tell the story of a trio of tragic and unforgettable ladies who risked their lives for love and thereby lost everything. Tolstoy's Anna Karenina, a woman who gives up her aristocratic society for the cause of an insuperable passion; Dumas's Camille, a lady who makes the highest sacrifice for the man she loves; and Flaubert's Madame Bovary, a tender dreamer whose romantic longing leads to an act of violence." These descriptions illustrate how art is degraded into commodities of mass culture. After all, the triumphs and tragedies in love experienced by Faust's Gretchen or Anna Karenina are not eternally valid statements about the nature of woman; they are, rather, to be seen as specific perceptions about women in certain circumstances. It would not be such an outrageous act of manipulated mass culture if, instead of tossing such books cheaply onto the mass market, the experts were to proclaim that these ladies are all neurotics and would certainly be better off today after psychoanalytic treatment! In short, the organization and "administration" of the imagination is taken over by agencies of social control, and here reductionism, including that of the behavioral sciences, is a justifiable method, indeed the only appropriate method.

Mass culture reinforces and signals the instructions in the late-capitalist world that promote a false collective. In this sense, I have always regarded my studies as political. Two examples in particular come to mind, which appear to me symptomatic of the shattered bourgeois self-consciousness and the insurmountable impotence that characterized the mood of wide strata of the middle classes. One of the examples is related to literary reception, the other to genre, both of which are closely related.

One of my studies had as its subject the reception of Dostoevsky in Germany at the turn of the century, as documented in a volu-minous corpus of books, as well as in articles, journals, and news-papers. It soon became clear to me that the massive reception of Dostoevsky's works was not necessarily a function of their aesthetic quality but rather of deeper social-psychological needs. With the probable exception of Goethe, Dostoevsky was the most written-about literary figure at that time. The analysis of the material re-vealed that the reception of Dostoevsky's works illuminated sig-nificant idiosyncrasies of German society in a time of total crisis: infatuation with the so-called irrationalism of the artist; the alleged mystery in the life of the individual; the wallowing in the "dark regions of the soul," the glorification of criminal behavior—in short, indispensable elements that were later incorporated in the psychological transfiguration of violence by National Socialism.

That studies on reception can have social-political significance was confirmed years later when I took a closer look at the reviews of the writer I had predicted—years before the event—would be a Nazi-sympathizer: Knut Hamsun. A history of the reception of Hamsun's works can reflect the development of political consciousness all the way from liberalism to the slogans of the authoritarian state. Indeed, bourgeois literary criticism was not nearly as surprising as the Social Democratic responses. The observations on Hamsun that appeared in *Neue Zeit,* the leading theoretical journal of German Social Democracy, reveal as early as the nineties a clear political stance: Hamsun's novels are to be rejected; they do not portray living human beings but rather vague attitudes that have nothing to do with tendencies directed toward positive change.

The volumes of *Neue Zeit* from the early years of World War I and the immediate postwar years, however, contain glowing descriptions of the same writer who twenty years before had been so unambiguously rejected. What was previously judged as "empty atmosphere" and "mere nervous stimulus" was now perceived as "gripping depictions of life and soul in which the most vivid reality with all its lights and shadows is transposed into the allegory of innermost life." The author who impressed the earlier critics as an "amorous exclamation point in a melancholy easy chair" had now grown to such "solitary greatness" that one might not compare him with others without doing him an injustice; what had in his novels previously been seen as "ephemeral as the atmosphere" suddenly became "a parable of the eternal." After World War I, this hymn of praise was joined by the liberal spokesmen of the bourgeoisie, as well as those of the proletariat that Hamsun so despised. Conventional bourgeois criticism and *Neue Zeit* criticism both belong to the same constellation: that of political resignation and a susceptibility to ideological seduction within broad social strata in Central Europe.

My studies on genre examined the biographical fashion. I attempted to analyze, in two different societies, popular biographies as an illuminating criterion for significant transformations in political and social structure. The first study was carried out in Germany before 1933. It is difficult today to imagine the flood of popular biographies that inundated Europe and Germany at that time. Already by 1918, the popular biography was the classic example of

German bourgeois escapist literature. Biography is both the continuation and the inversion of the novel. In the bourgeois novel, documentation functions as raw material. In the popular biography, on the contrary, the various kinds of documentation—that huge pageant of fixed data, events, names, letters, and so on—come to take the place of social relationships, which have become the individual's fetters; the individual is, so to speak, nothing more than a typographic element, a column heading that winds its way through the book's plot, a mere excuse to attractively arrange a certain body of material. The heroes of the popular biography have no individual destinies; they are nothing but functions of the historic. Latent relativism, although rarely the manifest credo of this literature, is always present. Conscious cynicism of the masters is completely absent, but what remains is the need to cloak the helplessness of the losers. The aestheticism of the nineties, the *fin de siècle,* could be called the very epitome of activity when compared to the fatigue and weakness emanating from the writers of popular biographies. In these testimonies to the immortality of mortality, in this maze of superlatives and uniquenesses through which reason can never hope to guide us, the writers are every bit as lost as their readers.

Popular biographies in the United States operated in a different social context. I attempted to show in my work on the triumph of mass idols in several American high-circulation magazines the structural change in the treatment of popular biographies in the period of transition from liberal capitalism to manipulated collectivism. I called it the transition from the idols of production to the idols of consumption. Whereas around the turn of the century the so-called heroes were the representatives of production, at the end of the thirties and the beginning of the forties these "heroes" were increasingly replaced by athletes and entertainers, especially those of the cinema, who appeared to be "newsworthy" because of their private affairs rather than their productive functions. The identification offered to the reader was no longer with entrepreneurial success but rather with the imitation of consumption. Ultimately, the German and the American phenomena share certain identical characteristics, although in different political contexts. As I put it then:

> The distance between what an average individual may do and the forces and powers that determine his/her life and death has become so unbridgeable that identification with normalcy, even with philistine boredom, becomes a readily grasped empire of refuge and escape. It is some comfort for the average person who has been robbed of the Horatio Alger–dream and who despairs of penetrating the thicket of grand strategy in politics and business, to see his heroes as a bunch of guys who like or dislike highballs, cigarets, tomato juice, golf and social gatherings . . . just like he himself. He knows how to converse in this sphere of consumption and here he can make no mistakes. By narrowing his focus of attention he can experience the gratification of being confirmed in his own pleasures and discomforts by participating in the pleasure and discomforts of the great. The large confusing issues in the political and the economic realm and the antagonisms and controversies in the social sphere are all submerged in the experience of being at one with the lofty and powerful in the sphere of consumption.[6]

V

With the power of a seemingly prophetic insight, Shakespeare, in act 3, scene 2, of *Hamlet*, suggests the threat to the autonomy of the individual through social manipulation, although he certainly

6. Leo Lowenthal, "The Triumph of Mass Idols"; first published as "Biographies in Popular Magazines," in *Radio Research, 1942–1943,* ed. Paul F. Lazarsfeld and Frank N. Stanton (New York, 1944); later published in *Literature and Mass Communication,* vol. 1 of *Communication in Society* (New Brunswick, N.J., 1985), pp. 203–35.

could not have guessed that finally, nearly four hundred years later, the Guildensterns would defeat the Hamlets.

Hamlet:	Will you play upon this pipe?
Guildenstern:	My lord, I cannot.
Hamlet:	I pray you.
Guildenstern:	Believe me, I cannot.
Hamlet:	I do beseech you.
Guildenstern:	I know no touch of it, my lord.
Hamlet:	'Tis as easy as lying; govern these ventages with your finger and thumb, give it breath with your mouth, and it will discourse most eloquent music. Look you, these are the stops.
Guildenstern:	But these cannot I command to any utterance of harmony; I have not the skill.
Hamlet:	Why, look you now, how unworthy a thing you make of me. You would play upon me; you would seem to know my stops; you would pluck out the heart of my mystery; you would sound me from my lowest note to the top of my compass; and there is much music, excellent voice, in this little organ, yet cannot you make it speak. 'Sblood! do you think I am easier to be played on than a pipe? Call me what instrument you will, though you can fret me, you cannot play upon me.

Guildenstern represents, if you will, mass culture, which mediates social domination, which tries to force the individual to obedience and plays with him as on a passive, but well-prepared, instrument.

What finally happened is clearly expressed in the words of the American poet, Randall Jarrell, who has the following to say in his book *Poetry and the Age*:

The poet lives in a world whose newspapers and magazines and books and motion pictures and radio stations and television stations have destroyed, in a great many people, even

the capacity for understanding real poetry, real art of any
kind. . . . the average article in our magazines gives any subject whatsoever the same coat of easy, automatic, "human"
interest.[7]

Jarrell contrasts Goethe, who stated, "The author whom a lexicon
can keep up with is worth nothing," with Somerset Maugham,
who once said, "The finest compliment he ever received was a letter
in which one of his readers said: 'I read your novel without having
to look up a single word in the dictionary.'" And Jarrell closes with
the observation that "popular writing has left nothing to the imagination for so long now that imagination too has begun to atrophy."
In short, the wasting away, the end of imagination, is the end of
freedom.

I cannot say anything definitive about the possibility of genuine
artistic experience in the present day. Although the acquaintance
with great art is certainly growing, an acquaintance without genuine experience, rooted in critical openness, only serves to support
the system. Acquaintance and experience are mutually exclusive. I
am very concerned about the dwindling possibility of the aesthetic
experience as experience of freedom in today's world. I can say no
more. What I have tried to convey here was perhaps not so much a
summary of my work in the sociology of literature as a chapter of
a perhaps too presumptuous intellectual autobiography, an autobiography, however, that—and I will not be falsely modest—does
not lose sight of the marginality of the field. As an intellectual,
one certainly can, and possibly ought to, live on the margins. And
for me, sociology of literature has served me in that respect quite
adroitly.

7. Randall Jarrell, *Poetry and the Age* (New York, 1953), p. 18.

7

Theodor W. Adorno:
An Intellectual Memoir

BY LEO LOWENTHAL

Adorno was a genius, and his work, which is now published in more than twenty volumes, encompasses the intellectual universe of Western civilization, concentrating on but not limited to philosophy, the social sciences, musicology, and significant events of public life. It would be absurd for me to try to convey a systematic summary of Adorno's unique enterprise. Rather, I shall discuss it in a fragmentary style. In doing so, I find myself in tune with Adorno's own approach: to disavow consistently any legitimacy for a system. The famous *Dialectic of Enlightenment,* written with his friend Max Horkheimer, has the German subtitle *Philosophische Fragmente* [Philosophical Fragments], which was unfortunately omitted in the English version. His first writings on Richard Wagner were entitled "Fragments on Richard Wagner," and many of his books were called "notes" or "essays" or something similar. Adorno looked to Nietzsche, Karl Kraus, and Walter Benjamin as models of

Originally published in *Humanities in Society* 2, no. 4 (Fall 1979): 387–99; from a paper presented at the Adorno Symposium, May 18, 1979, at the University of Southern California.

this literary form. The style has a characteristic open-ended, prob-
ing quality, and its format is essayistic, aphoristic, or fragmentary.
In Adorno's case it was justified by his famous philosophical *bon mot*
on Hegel's system: "The whole is the false."

We met in late 1922, brought together by the eminent writer,
philosopher, and sociologist Siegfried Kracauer. Ten years later
we found ourselves working together in the Institute of Social Research in Frankfurt, and we continued a close association for about
twenty years. Our relationship was stormy at times, as is almost
unavoidable in a community of high-strung intellectuals. It fills
me with emotion to find, for instance, that Martin Jay, who is by
now the preeminent historian of our Institute, in an article called
"Adorno and Kracauer: Notes on a Troubled Friendship" (a subtitle
that ironically might serve as a proper characterization for the mutual relationships of all of us) noted that in 1927 Adorno "brooded
over his chances for successful habilitation and complained about
his rivalry with a mutual friend, Leo Lowenthal, in the ranks of the
Frankfurt Institute"; or that four years later, in 1931, "possibilities of
Kracauer contributing to the new Institute journal were discussed,
with Adorno lamenting that his hands were tied by Leo Lowenthal,
whom he described as 'king of the desert' [*Wüstenkönig*] at the Institute."[1] Well, I never had a crown, and Adorno gained his professorial appointment.

Maintaining a fragmentary format, I would first like to discuss
the areas and problems on which Adorno and I either engaged in
brotherly collaboration or shared scholarly interests, and then I
would like to make some observations on the frequently rebellious
criticism raised by some of his students and disciples.

1. Martin Jay, "Adorno and Kracauer: Notes on a Troubled Friendship,"
in Jay, *Permanent Exiles: Essays on the Intellectual Migration from Germany to
America* (New York, 1985), p. 222.

As some of you know, the Institute continued the publication of its journal—which originated in 1932 in Germany, where it lasted only one year—first in Geneva and then in New York as an essentially German-language outlet for our work. It was, in the true sense of the word, a joint enterprise, because all the major articles were subject to critical scrutiny by the entire group. To give a personal example, in 1937 I published an essay on Knut Hamsun with the subtitle "A Prehistory of the Authoritarian Ideology," at a time when Hamsun's membership in the Norwegian Nazi-Quisling Party was still unknown. Adorno wrote a lengthy footnote for my essay, in which he drew close parallels between Hamsun and Sibelius, whose music expressed similar elements of contempt for men oppressed in the glorification of a rigid, pantheistically colored concept of nature. Collaborative closeness is also documented by the first three theses on anti-Semitism that are incorporated in the *Dialectic of Enlightenment* and, above all, by our studies in the seductive and potentially dangerous devices of the American fascist agitator. This work culminated in my book *Prophets of Deceit,* to which Adorno anonymously contributed a draft of an introduction in addition to copious substantive comments and suggestions. Conversely, I had the privilege of participating in the original draft of the research plan for the famous *Authoritarian Personality,* on which Adorno was a senior author, and of contributing my own comments and suggestions on his chapters of this monumental work. In a similar spirit of collegial and intellectual solidarity, Adorno wrote the major text of a section in an essay of mine on popular culture, which we properly called "Some Theses on Critical Theory and Empirical Research."

It is indeed in this area of popular or mass culture—or, as Adorno called it, "the culture industry"—that our interests frequently converged. It is, by the way, not without irony that many topics for this symposium mention Adorno's work on mass culture, a term that he, with his discriminatory perception for linguistic nuances, intensely disliked. In 1967 he expressly stated this in a postscript to the essay published in the *Dialectic of Enlightenment* twenty years earlier:

> The term "culture industry" was perhaps used for the first time in the book *Dialectic of Enlightenment,* which Horkheimer and I published in Amsterdam in 1947. In our drafts we spoke of "mass culture." We replaced that expression with "culture industry" in order to exclude from the outset the interpretation agreeable to its advocates: that it is a matter of something like a culture that arises spontaneously from the masses themselves, the contemporary form of popular art. From the latter the culture industry must be distinguished in the extreme.[2]

I am proud that Adorno approved and used my shorthand definition of fascist agitation as well as culture industry as "psychoanalysis in reverse," that is, as more or less constantly manipulated devices to keep people in permanent psychic bondage, to increase and reinforce neurotic and even psychotic behavior culminating in perpetual dependency on a "leader" or on institutions or products. We both saw modern anti-Semitism and culture industry as ultimately belonging in the same social context even though at times they go different political ways. What is at stake here, as Adorno never grew tired of repeating, is the ever-increasing difficulty of genuine experience mediated primarily through art, whose independence and integrity has been increasingly sabotaged by the sophisticated apparatus of social manipulation and domination. Significant is the inexorable paralysis of productive imagination and artistic experience leading to a conversion of cognitive effects into sales psychology. Culture industry provides the inescapable commodity charac-

---

2. Theodor W. Adorno, "Culture Industry Reconsidered," *New German Critique* 6 (Fall 1975): 12.

ter of all its products and imperceptibly extinguishes the differences among these products themselves and the general or specific advertising purposes for which they are created. We agreed that the culture establishment refused to take any responsibility by ignoring completely the meaning of mass culture and conveniently indicting its technology alone for its miserable productions; we agreed that the dividing line between art and commodity culture must not be obfuscated and that the unholy alliance of social domination with the naked profit motive hardly promotes a state of consciousness in which, in Adorno's words, *Freizeit* would turn into *Freiheit*—leisure into freedom.

I would like to let Adorno speak with his own words, first in regard to the dividing line between art and culture industry: "The entire practice of the culture industry transfers the profit motive naked onto cultural forms. .... . The autonomy of works of art, which of course rarely ever predominated in an entirely pure form, and was always permeated by a constellation of effects, is tendentially eliminated by the culture industry, with or without the conscious will of those in control."[3] I might add as a melancholic personal comment that I find it ever more difficult to persuade my students, despite their predominantly radical persuasion, to accept these irreconcilable differences—another illustration of how the infamous positivist value-neutrality is affecting and infecting the best of us.

Adorno stressed the inescapable fate of people to succumb to the culture industry whether they want it or not:

> The phrase "the world wants to be deceived" has become truer than had ever been intended. People are not merely, as the saying goes, falling for the swindle—if it guarantees them even the most fleeting gratification, they desire a deception

3. Ibid., p. 13.

which is nonetheless transparent to them. . . . Without ad-
mitting it, they sense that their lives would be completely
intolerable as soon as they no longer clung to satisfactions
which are none at all.[4]

It was once a theoretical dream of our inner circle that, in addition to the social theme of authority, we would engage in a joint
study of all aspects of the decay of the essence and concept of the
individual in bourgeois society and its conversion to mere illusion
and ideology. However, whereas the theme of authority received
profuse elaboration in what are now almost classic books, that of
the individual remained merely a guiding perspective. Adorno, for
instance, continually emphasized the hollow cult of the so-called
personality and the exultation of the allegedly autonomous individual in the era of monopoly capitalism. I pursued the same theme in
my own studies on the literary genre of biography—in this country
as well as in Europe—and its role as a sham device that pretended
human specificity when in fact the true meaning of the particular
has been perverted. When I wrote on the cultural changes in the
selection and treatment of biographies in popular magazines, from
what I called "heroes of production" to "heroes of consumption,"
Adorno admonished me in a letter of November 1942 to emphasize
the theoretical function of biographies in present society and particularly within the context of mass culture. He said, and I could not
agree more, that "ultimately, the very concept of life as a self-devel-
oping and meaningful unity has as little reality today as the concept
of the individual, and it is the ideological function of the biographies to conjure up the fiction on arbitrarily selected models that
there is still such a thing as life. . . . Life itself in its completely
abstract appearance has become mere ideology."

While my own emphasis in the analysis of this trivial genre was
on the shallow solace it offered the politically impotent and histor-

4. Ibid., p. 16. (Translation emended.)

ically disoriented middle classes in Europe before the advent of
fascism, Adorno's profound reflections stressed the awesome para-
dox that the same apparatus of culture industry that extinguishes
private idiosyncratic consciousness falls all over itself in an endless
praise of personality and individuality. In his words, culture industry's "ideology above all makes use of the star system, borrowed
from individualistic art and its commercial exploitation. The more
dehumanized its methods of operation . . . the more diligently
and successfully the culture industry propagates supposedly great
personalities and operates with heartthrobs."[5] Narcissistic as it may
sound to some of you, this report of brotherly collaboration and
intellectual exchanges should be understood solely as a foil: I wish
to bring into relief Adorno's great contribution to a critical understanding of modern society's inescapable network of domination
and of its seemingly inescapable reinforcement of the psyche of
man, without which this very mechanism of domination would
cease to be effective. This theme inspired his continual admoni-
tion: "Don't participate"—arguably the leitmotif of his life's work,
against which all the weakness of personality or idiosyncrasies of
life-style weigh very little.

Thinking about Adorno's merciless, but always theoretically
founded, indictment of the social phenomena themselves, as well as
their faulty, distorted, and manipulated pseudo-interpretations in
bourgeois philosophy, social research, and literary criticism—just
to name a few of the dubious intellectual enterprises—I cannot help
but be reminded of the original theological meaning of the Greek
term *skandalon*. Every thought he ever had and every word he ever
said created a new *Ärgernis* [irritant] for his foes and friends alike.

At this point I would like to break off my brotherly tribute to this
genius, whose much too early demise might not be unconnected to
the *skandalon* he adhered to without compromise until the end at his
post as Germany's most prominent academic teacher and outstand-

5. Ibid., p. 14.

ing citizen of the Western European avant-garde. He would have
been the first to understand that the implacability implied in each of
the intellectual positions he held needed constant refinement and
defense against facile acceptance by followers and angry misin-
terpretations by adversaries. Nothing is more ironic than the term
"Frankfurt School," which presupposes a body of learnable statements and doctrines that one could live with, comfortably or un-
easily—whatever the case might be—henceforth. I truly believe
that no one who, either directly or indirectly, belonged to our circle
at its beginnings over a half century ago would ever have felt comfortable with this term. As a matter of fact, the by now indeter-
minably large corpus of books, articles, doctoral theses, symposia,
and seminars has almost "industrialized" the Frankfurt School;
many of these works seem to be little short of talmudic disputations
about the meaning of this or that theorem at different periods or
about the relation of this or that writer or scholar in this or another
phase. When Adorno chose as the subtitle of his first major collection of fragments and aphorisms the words "Reflections from
Damaged Life," he did not offer to repair such damage. But many, if
not most, of his disciples—indeed, students of all shades of the
school—could not and cannot accept the absence of political and
cultural remedies. I cannot help but think that their call for action is
not so far removed from the all-pervasive advocacy of fashionable
pseudo-psychological cures that are about to poison many of our
contemporaries. If I appear irate, you are not misreading me, but it
is an ire grounded in compassion for the restless youth and the now
equally restless middle-aged who have looked in vain to Adorno for
salvation; he was not, and did not want to be, a messiah.

In stressing some of their collective misreadings, I may perhaps
be able to add to an understanding of Adorno's intellectual heritage.
I start with the *ad hominem* argument: Adorno as a human being.
One of the most popular objections to radical thinkers has been
the vulgar argument that they should practice what they preach—
although they are not really preaching anything—by staying away

from all the amenities of the good life. Brecht's comments on the financial resources of the Institute and the upper-class backgrounds of some of its principal members (which I believe to be in poor taste) are well known. I take more seriously the elegant observation of Lukács, who, in the preface to a new edition of his *Theory of the Novel* in 1962, commented as follows:

> A considerable part of the leading German intelligentsia, including Adorno, have taken up residence in the "Grand Hotel Abyss," which I described in connection with my critique of Schopenhauer as "a beautiful hotel, equipped with every comfort, on the edge of an abyss, of nothingness, of absurdity. And the daily contemplation of the abyss, between excellent meals or artistic entertainments, can only heighten the enjoyment of the subtle comforts offered."[6]

I have never heard that miserable living conditions and substandard nutrition are necessary prerequisites for innovative thought. If Marx and Nietzsche at times suffered insults of material deprivation, their theoretical creativity survived, not because of but despite such painful conditions. I might also add that Georg Lukács found his own ways of comfortable survival in a political environment where many other heretic Marxists, who were not privy to Lukács's strategy of adaptive behavior, had their heads chopped off. This is an example of an older contemporary, though, not of a "rebellious son." The sons' favorite outcry, to which all of us have been exposed at times, is against the cardinal sin of what they call "elitism." In a lengthy essay by W. V. Blomster entitled "Sociology of Music: Adorno and Beyond" there is a section called "Adorno: ad personam":

> In an age when psychological interpretations of almost all phenomena are irresistible, it is astonishing that so few ques-

6. Georg Lukács, *The Theory of the Novel,* trans. Anna Bostock (Cambridge, Mass., 1971), p. 22.

tions have been asked about the man Adorno and the degree
to which his own psychological constitution might have conditioned—indeed, limited—his work in music. Although
this may seem at best a peripheral concern within this study,
several observations demand inclusion here. . . . There are
moments of uneasiness in working with Adorno when one
finds in his position the imprint of that "authoritarian personality" which he himself fought so vehemently. . . . Little remains to be said upon Adorno's elitism and snobbishness;
precisely in his work in music, however, it is felt that a greater
humility might have vastly increased his effectiveness.[7]

Blomster is in error. The litany about elitism has been sung for a
long time in many quarters, young and old, particularly when it
comes to the considerable demands made upon the reader to engage
in great efforts to follow the thought but not the thinker. I will
return to this issue toward the end of this essay. May it suffice for the
moment that it is exactly this kind of biographical and psychological reductionism that Adorno always opposed in his extensive studies of the literary arts (I might say, I learned a good deal from him
whenever I succumbed to an *ad hominem* shortcut in my own critical
work in literature).

I take more seriously a second paradigm, according to which
Adorno cut the connection between theory and practice so sacred
to Marxist doctrine. Hans-Jürgen Krahl, for a short while a prominent spokesman of the German New Left before he died in a tragic
accident, took Adorno to task for allegedly cutting this umbilical
cord. Although, according to Krahl, Adorno understood the ideological contradictions of bourgeois individualism and his "intellectual biography is marked by the experience of fascism," he nevertheless remained entrapped in the very contradictions he overtly
diagnosed.

7. W. V. Blomster, "Sociology of Music: Adorno and Beyond," *Telos*,
no. 28 (Summer 1976): 109.

Adorno's cutting critique on the ideological existence of the bourgeois individual irresistibly trapped him in its ruin. But this would mean that Adorno had never really left the isolation that emigration imposed on him. . . . Production of abstract labor is mirrored in his intellectual subjectivism. This is why Adorno was not able to translate his private compassion for the wretched of the earth into an integral partisanship of his theory toward the liberation of the oppressed.[8]

It seems to me that Adorno gave the correct answer with his often-quoted sarcastic observation that he did not know that Critical Theory had given license to throwing Molotov cocktails. True, had Adorno and his friends manned the barricades, they might very well have been immortalized in a revolutionary song by Hanns Eisler. But imagine for a moment Marx dying on the barricades in 1849 or 1871: there would be no Marxism, no advanced psychological models, and certainly no Critical Theory. The call to arms the ultraradical disciples directed at their teachers—legitimate as their intentions may have been—has merely produced excesses, the consequences of which have become only too obvious in the troubled state the New Left finds itself in today.

This leads to another, more serious, aspect of this perverted rebellion. In an introduction to a short piece by Adorno called "Culture Industry Reconsidered," Andreas Huyssen, an editor of *New German Critique,* in fall 1975 endorsed Hans Mayer's misguided formulation about Adorno's "secret hostility toward history."[9] I do not want to be disrespectful of Huyssen, whose good intentions are shown in his praise of Adorno as "one of the first to use critical Marxist thought to illuminate Western mass culture,

8. Hans-Jürgen Krahl, "The Political Contradictions in Adorno's Critical Theory," *Telos,* no. 21 (Fall 1974): 164.

9. Andreas Huyssen, "Introduction to Adorno," *New German Critique* 6 (Fall 1975): 3; Mayer's charge is made in *Der Repräsentant une die Märtyrer* (Frankfurt am Main, 1971), p. 165.

which for years had been dismissed by conservative culture critics
with elitist moralizing"; however, his reproach of Adorno, that he
"consistently avoided historic specificity in his work," is plainly
absurd. There seems to be an attempt on the part of these youthful
followers (or nonfollowers) to demand an activist pseudo-historic
participation, almost on a day-to-day basis and in a spirit of team-
dictated partisanship. At least, that is how I interpret Huyssen's
condescending remark that, although Adorno's "thought unmistakably developed in reaction to critical events," his hostility to
history was nonetheless severe: "This hostility in turn reflects his
rejection of the determinate negation as a key concept of the philosophy of history and indicates his insistence on negativity and
refusal as crucial elements of a modern aesthetic."[10] This perplexes
me! Every member of the Institute's inner circle not only was im-
mersed in Hegelian philosophy and the classical aspects of Marxian
dialectics but also continuously emphasized "determinate negation" as the key concept of any critical theory. Huyssen himself, a
few pages later, after the first outburst seemed forgotten, correctly
quoted the following words from Adorno's essay "Culture and Administration":

> The authentic cultural object must retain and preserve what-
> ever goes by the wayside in that process of increasing domi-
> nation over nature which is reflected in expanding rationality
> and ever more rational forms of domination. Culture is the
> perennial protestation of the particular against the general, as
> long as the latter remains irreconcilable with the particular.[11]

I do not really know how to explain this vogue of vague accusations except as what I suspect to be an understandable "morn-
ing-after" malaise in the wake, and at the wake, of the student

10. Huyssen, "Introduction to Adorno," pp. 4–5.
11. Theodor W. Adorno, "Culture and Administration," *Telos,* no. 37
(Fall 1978): 97. (Translation emended.)

movement. When hope for radical political change in our day or tomorrow collapsed, Critical Theory offered itself to many of the young as a convenient scapegoat. To the great pain and sorrow of its creators and practitioners, above all Adorno, it was forgotten that critical thought itself is adequate practice. It clashes with and is resisted by the cultural and, in part, political establishment, which always wants to convert the *skandalon* of nonconformist theory into a mere scandalous aberration and to recommend—and, if possible, contribute to—the liquidation of leaders and followers of Critical Theory. In that respect, Adorno's work and life in post-Hitler Germany serve as eloquent testimony to his historical sensitivity and his knowledge that only by a determined no, which he so admirably practiced, could historical progress and regression be kept alive in critical consciousness.

The attempts to catch Adorno in his alleged contradictions caused by lapses in historical consciousness are a continuation of my theme of filial rebellion. The same Mr. Huyssen perceived an irreconcilable contradiction between an Adorno who spoke, in the *Dialectic of Enlightenment,* of the autonomous individual as "a phenomenon of the bourgeois past" and one who, in his later essay "Culture Industry Reconsidered," allegedly revived this "autonomous individual" as a "precondition for democratic society." But if one reads the text carefully, it becomes apparent that, first of all, Adorno never intended to "reconsider" his theory of cultural industry but rather, as the German text clearly states, to write a "résumé," that is, a summing up of what he explicated, with Horkheimer, in the original essay. Furthermore, Adorno expressly says at the end of the new essay that culture industry's anti-enlightenment and mass deception has "turned into a means for fettering consciousness." He then dialectically states that autonomous individuals would only develop if there were no culture industry "obstructing the emancipation for which human beings *could be*"— not, as a translator incorrectly renders it, *are*—"as ripe as the productive forces of the epoch permit." The point here is unmistakable:

capitalism will not provide the emancipation that, according to every good Marxist, including Adorno, would technically be possible every day, since "the productive forces" would allow the termination of misery and domination. In contrast to his critic, Adorno remained rather melancholic, if not desperate, about the seemingly unresolvable—for the time being at least—intertwining of the establishment and its nonautonomous subjects (in the true sense of the term *subjection*). This is the opposite of a "retraction" of the original thesis of "enlightenment as an instrument of rationalized domination and oppression."

More painful even than the eagerness to trip Adorno in contradictions is the eagerness to take him to task for overlooking some very obvious historical phenomena. In a recent book by Otto Karl Werckmeister, *Ende der Ästhetik,* which, to my knowledge, has not been translated, we read:

> When Adorno until the very end defended modern art [meaning avant-garde art] against an imagined front of cultural conservatism, as if modern art still needed social certification, he missed the consequences of its complete assimilation in the late-capitalist culture. Culture and police both watch over the borderline of reality and art. On this side of the border, Adorno's negative-utopian glorification of art and the affirmative ideological function of art in bourgeois culture are much closer to each other than Adorno's concept of their absolute contradiction.[12]

To this schoolmasterly reprimand for having failed to do his homework, I can only say that the whole theory of avant-garde modern art, in which Adorno was really the leader of our group, consists precisely in defending the thesis that avant-garde art is the only reservoir of genuine human experience, and therefore of opposi-

12. Otto Karl Werckmeister, *Ende der Ästhetik* (Frankfurt am Main, 1971), p. 31.

tional consciousness, which itself is in constant danger of being suffocated through the loving profit-tentacles of the culture industry. Indeed, nobody was more aware than Adorno of the enormous dangers to the survival of "auratic" art (to use Benjamin's term).

Let me give you one last example of this chorus of critics (some of whom, I am sorry to say, I cannot differentiate from Beckmesser in the *Meistersinger*). It is fairly well known that Adorno's work in musicology and the philosophy and sociology of music developed the theory of the indispensable unity of performance and the intent of the composition. In particular, he spent a good deal of his efforts demonstrating the distortion of serious music by the technology of electronic reproduction, including, but not limited to, broadcasting and recording. I am not a musicologist, but I know something about the necessary relationship of a work of art and the social frame within which it is presented or performed, and I must assume by analogy that the horrors of televised Shakespeare are comparable to the distortion of musical listening of which Adorno speaks. (It is, by the way, at this juncture that I would like to say that I believe in the superiority of Adorno's aesthetic theories over those of Walter Benjamin. But this is a topic for others to ponder.) In a slick German literary journal I found a review of volume fourteen of Adorno's writings in German—which, incidentally, came out not too long ago in English under the title *Introduction to the Sociology of Music*. The reviewer, Helmut Heissenbüttel, did not like Adorno's typology of the music listener, and he quickly expressed regret that poor Adorno did not live to the day when the recording industry permitted variations of musical interpretation through the plethora of available records. This, he believed, is now possible thanks to the enormous accessibility to recorded performances composers have provided of their works, which are codified in record catalogs. Heissenbüttel cited with approval the so-called Bielefelder Catalog, "which appears every year with semi-annual supplements," and he reminded readers that in America the Schwann Record and Tape Guide appears every month. Missing heretofore, then, were reliable

guides that listed not only what was available but also what to select
and why to select it. This gap has now been filled. I quote from
Ulrich Schreiber's *Schallplatten Jahrbuch I* [Record Yearbook I]:

> What is decisive for the listing of a record in this guide is not
> its market value but the contribution it makes to the forma-
> tion of knowledge about the composer, about an epoch in the
> history of music, about musical interpreters and strategies of
> interpretation. Thus a record [*Schallplatte*] is here being taken
> seriously as an aesthetic, not an economic, phenomenon. For
> the first time, a comprehensive attempt is being made in Ger-
> man to assign to the record its significance in musical life and
> to use the medium "record" for a demonstration of changes in
> the history of musical tasks and consciousness. The records
> that we recommend for the reader of this guide do not add up
> to an eternal inventory of classical music, nor are they merely
> commodities for consumption. It is the essential task of this
> book to mediate meaningfully between false extremes.

I can only marvel at Heissenbüttel and his uncritical endorsement
of Schreiber's thinly veiled industrial enterprise, this epitome of
what Adorno called manipulated listening, *gegängelte Musik*. This
naïveté is topped by an insult: Heissenbüttel spoke of Adorno as
a caricature of the expert who has now been replaced by a true
"leader," the *Schallplattenführer*—in short, Leader Schreiber. Some
of us have always been critical of guidelines as predigested experience of works of art, enterprises that, of course, only serve the
purpose of rendering the oppositional character of the artwork into
a harmless, so-called aesthetic experience.

Let me juxtapose Schreiber's words on the merits of a *Schallplattenführer* with a Time-Life Corporation advertisement, which
guarantees that

> though your time may be limited, you will be reading widely
> and profitably . . . books that are truly timeless in style

and significance. This plan draws its strength from the fact that the editors spent thousands of hours finding the answers to questions that you, too, must have asked yourself many times. . . . It is part of their job to single out the few books that tower over all others. In each case, the editors will write special introductions to underline what is unique in the book, what impact it has had or will have, what place it has earned in literature and contemporary thought. . . . The books will be bound in durable, flexible covers similar to those used for binding fine Bibles and Missals.

I invite the audience to make a comparative content analysis between the shrewd public relations agents of the Time-Life Corporation and the Heissenbüttel-Schreiber alliance.

On this note I shall terminate my sampling of manifestations of oedipal rebellion against Adorno. I would like to say one final word about comments that persist from all quarters about the difficulty of reading Adorno.[13] It is true, Adorno's texts are very difficult. He never intended to make it easy for his professional and intellectual colleagues or for all his readers and listeners. He would not tolerate—another variation of the Adorno *skandalon*—that what he had to say should ever fit into a mode of easy consumption. On the contrary, the demands he made of himself and his audience are only another variation of his theme of striving for genuine experience in production as well as in received productive imagination. His sense of responsibility for language, his hostility to the all-embracing emergence of a one-dimensional, nonconnotative, unambiguous language of efficiency and predigested derivative thought that leaves no room for the unique and idiosyncratic, for productive imagination and the dissenting voice, reminds me of a letter Coleridge wrote to his friend Southey almost a hundred and seventy

13. I am well aware that this criticism is often raised against Western Marxism as a whole.

years ago, defending his style of "obscurity" and contrasting it "with the cementless periods of the modern Anglo-Gallican style, which not only are understood *beforehand,* but, being free from . . . all the books and eyes of intellectual memory, never oppress the mind by any after recollections, but, like civil visitors, stay a few moments, and leave the room quite free and open for the next comers."[14] I do not know whether Adorno knew of this letter, but I am sure he would have smiled with approval if I had told him about Coleridge's praise of "obscurity" as a witty rejection of linguistic consumerism. And so we come to another thinker who was, like Adorno, the embodiment of the *skandalon,* Friedrich Nietzsche. In his preface to *The Dawn,* he wrote:

> I have not been a philologist in vain; perhaps I am one yet: a teacher of slow reading. I have even come to write slowly. At present it is not only my habit, but even my taste, a perverted taste maybe, to write nothing but what will drive to despair everyone who is in a hurry. . . . Philology is now more desirable than ever before . . . it is the highest attraction and incitement in an age of "work," that is to say, of haste, of unseemly and immoderate hurry-scurry, which is intent upon "getting things done" at once, even every book, whether old or new. Philology itself, perhaps, will not "get things done" so hurriedly; it teaches how to read well, that is, slowly, profoundly, attentively, prudently, with inner thoughts, with the mental doors ajar, with delicate fingers and eyes.[15]

Those of us who knew Adorno will always carry this image of him with us: his "mental doors ajar," and touching everything he did "with delicate fingers and eyes."

14. Coleridge to Southey, October 20, 1809; in *Collected Letters of Samuel Taylor Coleridge,* ed. Earl Leslie Griggs (Oxford, 1959), vol. 3, p. 790.
15. Friedrich Nietzsche, *The Dawn of Day,* trans. Johanna Volz (London, 1910), pp. xxviii–xxix. (Translation emended.)

8

Recollections of
Theodor W. Adorno

BY LEO LOWENTHAL

What I have to say will come as a relief for those of you who have been participating in this conference for the last couple of days, for I will engage you less intellectually—tragedy is followed by comedy, and you will probably want to laugh about some of my remarks. But classical comedy always has a serious personal perspective, too. I am in a difficult situation, being asked as a survivor to talk about people who are no longer with us, because survival always poses the problem of distinguishing between an event of a purely biological nature and one that, considered from an intellectual standpoint, is not strictly arbitrary. My countryman Goethe frequently grappled with exactly this problem—if I may, for a moment, appeal to such a great standard.

A second personal remark: when one has lived as long as I have and belonged to a group that has gained such historical significance,

Originally published as "Erinnerungen an Theodor W. Adorno," in *Adorno-Konferenz 1983,* ed. Ludwig von Friedeburg and Jürgen Habermas (Frankfurt am Main, 1983), pp. 388–401. Translated by Sabine Wilke. Lowenthal's talk was given at the Suhrkamp Verlag reception following the Adorno Conference in Frankfurt on September 11, 1983.

one is constantly considered a kind of fragment of history. And indeed, in recent years I have experienced firsthand how history is actually written. Without wanting to cast aspersions on the integrity of friends in the audience who are historians, I must say that I am filled with increasing skepticism. Just recently a portrait of Adorno and myself was created on the basis of passages from letters;[1] that portrait, however, is less true to the relationship as a whole than the one I am going to sketch tonight—also on the basis of letters. This experience has led me to reflect on the question of documentation. One may reconstruct history from documents, or one may rely on memory; I, however, have the great fortune to possess both documents *and* a memory, and these serve mutually to correct each other. But this leads to a third personal problem: I am supposed to say something about my recollections of Teddie (it will be difficult to speak of "Adorno" the entire evening, since he is someone I knew since he graduated from high school), and when I speak of my recollections of Adorno, I certainly want to avoid the intrusion of a narcissistic tone. Yet, it is unfortunately impossible for Leo Lowenthal to remember Adorno without here and there mentioning a word (or two) about himself and his work. I would like therefore to ask at the outset for your understanding of such a contradiction.

I would like to present, essentially through letters, several aspects of the life we shared, especially in the twenties, thirties, forties, and fifties. Obviously, this selection has a fragmentary character for the simple reason that we lived together so many years: in Frankfurt, in New York, now and then in California. The accidental, however, is not merely accidental.

I was introduced to Adorno when he was eighteen years old by

---

1. See Martin Jay, "Adorno and Kracauer: Notes on a Troubled Friendship," in Jay, *Permanent Exiles: Essays on the Intellectual Migration from Germany to America* (New York, 1985), p. 219.

Siegfried Kracauer, who played a major role in our friendship—a friendship with all the positive and ambivalent traits such relationships have. I start with a letter from December 4, 1921, which I have already published, in which Kracauer conveys the following impression of Teddie: "Something incomparable puts him in a position over both of us [Kracauer and myself], an admirable material existence [note a slight ambivalence: Adorno was a very spoiled young gentleman from a well-to-do family] and a wonderfully self-confident character [here now the positive]. He truly is a beautiful specimen of a human being; even if I am not without some skepticism concerning his future, I am surely delighted by him in the present."

Anyway, the Adorno of these years—I don't know whether there is anybody here who knew him back then, I certainly doubt it—was a delicate, slender young man. Indeed, he was the classical image of a poet, with a delicate way of moving and talking that one scarcely finds nowadays. We would meet either at a coffee house—mostly at the famous Café Westend at the opera, where intellectual *enfants terribles* met—or at one or the other of our parents' places. Naturally, I knew Adorno's parents well, also his aunt Agathe. It was an existence you just had to love—if you were not dying of jealousy of this protected beautiful life—and in it Adorno had gained the confidence that never left him his entire life. For a short period of time, however, my relation to his parents was disturbed by a dissonance perhaps not uncharacteristic for the history of assimilated German Jews. When I accepted my first paying job in 1923—I had just received my Ph.D., a year before Teddie—bearing the overrated title of "Syndic of the Advisory Board for Jewish Refugees from Eastern Europe," Oskar Wiesengrund told his son that Leo Lowenthal was not welcome in his house as long as he had something to do with Eastern European Jews.

There is a remarkable irony in the fact that Adorno asked me many years later, he himself being ill in Los Angeles, to give the eulogy at his father's funeral. A certain knowledge of the mentality of the German-Jewish middle class, and particularly upper middle class, is required to entirely understand the atmosphere at the time. This might also account for why—this is how I explain it to myself—Adorno had such an incredibly hard time finally leaving Germany (we had to drag him almost physically); he just couldn't believe that to him, son of Oskar Wiesengrund, nephew of aunt Agathe, and son of Maria, anything might ever happen, for it was absolutely clear that the bourgeoisie would soon become fed up with Hitler. This kind of naïve unfamiliarity with the real world—particularly that of Germany and the at first complicated and then not-so-complicated relations of Christians and Jews—must be borne in mind if one is to fully understand Adorno's personal history.

For the moment, I would like to return to several experiences from an early period, when Teddie was about nineteen or twenty, making use of some passages from letters, to which recollections can so superbly be related. I have many recollections. For example, Adorno and Kracauer tell me about their reading of Ernst Bloch and Helmut Plessner; about Bloch they have as yet very little negative to say; Plessner, however, is said to write in an awful jargon, but nevertheless views many problems correctly. Soon they drag Benjamin over the coals in a way that will surprise you (more on that in a minute); I, too, am chided, because at that time I identified strongly with apocalyptic and messianic motifs. I had just finished writing an almost unreadable "master work," "The Demonic: Project of a Negative Philosophy of Religion"—I barely understand a word of it now—and, shortly thereafter, a dissertation on Franz von Baader, both composed in an expressionist style, which caused my friends to constantly poke fun at me. For example, on April 14, 1922, from Amorbach during a hot summer: "It would be a pleasure to take a bath [*Bad*], which doesn't mean that you have to plunge right into Baaderlake." And they also wrote to me that I was a professional apocalyptist, and for professional apocalyptists there was unfortunately no vacancy in Amorbach; but for the sake of a meeting they would be willing to try and find a room in the next town. That was about the tone in which we talked to each other. Yet openly friendly sentences, like this one, for example, from a letter from August 11, 1923, were heard as well: "Although you are constantly with us in our thoughts, it would naturally be nice to have your empirical person around also."

The year 1923 was when Adorno and Kracauer undertook a common reading of Goethe's *Elective Affinities* and subsequently the first draft of Benjamin's essay on the same work—to which I will return in a minute. On August 22, 1923, Adorno wrote that he was "so pleasantly tired that I don't even want to get down to *Elective Affinities.*" But they were still reading Franz Rosenzweig's *Star of Redemption,* about which Teddie had made this comment when Kracauer told him about it: "These are linguistic philosophemes I would not understand even if I understood them"; and in that letter of August 1923 he added: "We would certainly have the real chance to recover if we did not have to fear the mighty dollar's putting a premature ending to our idyll." That was about six weeks before the upward evaluation of the dollar, so I understood his comment only too well. The day before the dollar was revalued I was, for the first time in my life, in Brenner's Park Hotel in Baden-Baden— back then it was still called Hotel Stephanie (we were always bon vivants) or, as Lukács says, the Hotel Abyss; but only for a day, for when the dollar was stabilized, I had to clear out of the hotel and take the train back to Frankfurt—third class. Kracauer and Teddie had similar experiences at the time.

Back to more serious talk, though: Kracauer wrote again about Rosenzweig on August 31, 1923: "As a thinker [he] is and remains an idealist . . . and even his star won't redeem him from that—just as I don't believe that his book will have great success in the future, in spite of Scholem and his brother Benjamin." And Teddie added:

"I've finished reading *Elective Affinities* and agree with Friedel [Kracauer] on its interpretation"—and now follows a comment that will surprise you—"but definitely less so with Benjamin, who in fact reads into the text rather than extrapolates from it and essentially doesn't grasp the meaning of Goethe's existence." That's how impertinent we were!

Now, to give you another example of the combination of intellectual wit, seriousness, and concern for each other's private lives, I would like to read from a letter written by Kracauer and Teddie together, which will conclude my selection from the twenties. On December 8, 1923, Teddie wrote, on the occasion of my marriage: "I wish you and Golde [my wife] luck; at the same time [I wish] that, as a quiet bourgeois husband, you are less abducted by mail, telegraph, and train from the protected sphere of productive conversations than has been your habit thus far."

Kracauer, however, commented in the same letter on Teddie's remark: "Such pseudo-philosophical, noble rhetoric Teddie regards as naïve, and he prefers to make use of it in small talk, that is to say, in letters, seminars, and discussions with young ladies. His own literary style is, as you probably know, of such a quality as to . . . make Benjamin's . . . scurrilous language sound like . . . baby talk. However, the young philosopher wants it no other way, and I guess we will just have to let him have his way." And here Kracauer made a lovely remark: "If Teddie one day makes a real declaration of love and gives up his perfectly sinful bachelor status . . . for the equally hypocritical state of marriage, his declaration of love will undoubtedly take such a difficult form that the young lady in question will have to have read the whole of Kierkegaard . . . to understand Teddie at all; otherwise she will surely misunderstand him and reject him, because there will definitely be something about a "leap" and about "belief through the absurd," and she will believe that Teddie the philosopher considers her to be

absurd, completely the wrong thing to think." I am sorry that dear
Gretel [Adorno] cannot listen to this prophesy today, for in the end
the story had a very different outcome. And Teddie responded to
this in the same letter with extraordinary wit, alluding to Benjamin's famous last sentence in his *Elective Affinities* essay,[2] and
criticizing Kracauer thus: "You know him; for me hope remains
only for the sake of those without hope, but it is still such a long time
till then."

To conclude my account of the twenties, I'd like to mention that
this letter of congratulations arrived in Königsberg in a beautifully
calligraphed envelope—Kracauer, the architect, was very good at
these things. By the way, this reminds me of another one of those
episodes—if I may interrupt my account—very characteristic of
German Jews. My first wife was from Königsberg in Prussia. My
father, an old Frankfurt resident who, like Kracauer, Teddie, and
myself, had gone to school in Frankfurt, refused to accompany my
mother to my wedding; when I had announced my wedding plans
with a young lady from Königsberg he had told me: "You're crazy!
Königsberg, that's practically in Russia!" As early as 1923 he had
already anticipated the course of world history and so was not behind Teddie's father in his aversion to the East.

Anyway, this letter of congratulations came in an envelope deco-
rated by Kracauer and with the return address: "General Headquarters of the Welfare Bureau for the Transcendentally Homeless"; and
below, again in Teddie's handwriting: "Kracauer and Wiesengrund.
Agents of the Transcendentally Homeless. General Management at
Frankfurt Oberrad." That, of course, is an allusion to Lukács's *Theory of the Novel,* but at the same time it also anticipates what my

---

2. The phrase referred to is from the essay "Goethes *Wahlverwandtschaften"* (*Neue Deutsche Beiträge* 2, no. 2 [January 1925]: 168): "It is only for
the sake of those without hope that hope is given us."

friend Martin Jay emphasized [in his conference presentation] to-day:[3] the being-nowhere-at-home, the homelessness, the existential exile—all this was preformulated in this humorous envelope.

I now turn to the thirties, which are characterized especially by our resettlement in the United States, but also by the founding of the *Zeitschrift für Sozialforschung* and by our persistent, and ultimately successful, attempts to get Adorno to come to the United States. We stayed in contact—all of us carrying a collective responsibility for the journal, although I was, for the most part, in charge of its management—largely because of the innumerable and extremely stimulating suggestions that Adorno constantly sent to us from Oxford—some to Horkheimer, and some to me as well—about articles we should do or contributions he himself was planning to make. I will give you an interesting example; in a letter dated August 19, 1937, he wrote me concerning an essay on Karl Mannheim (to which I will soon return): "Personally, it matters a great deal to me not to function as a specialist for music, for example, but to be open to a broad range of themes; for this reason I would highly appreciate [this essay's] publication. For in principle I represent the antispecialist attitude, and in this vein I encouraged Horkheimer in his decision to write something about Raffael [the French Marxist] and about Sade, as I would like you perhaps to write something on mass culture in monopoly capitalism. . . . Specialization indeed has its dangers, particularly in the isolated situation in which we find ourselves."

He thus not only divined the specific intellectual interests of each of us with an extremely subtle sympathetic understanding, but he also encouraged us and identified with those interests. And he was ultimately successful: the essay on Sade in *Dialectic of Enlightenment* is essentially Horkheimer's work, and my book *Literature, Popular*

3. Martin Jay, "Adorno in America," in *Permanent Exiles*.

Culture, and Society was published as the first volume of my collected works.

Here I come to an important point concerning the thirties. Previously—and obviously in vain—I have tried to destroy a legend about whose background no one is better informed than I, since the other parties concerned are no longer alive: that we, using financial means, forced Walter Benjamin to comply with our editorial requests concerning his articles for the *Zeitschrift für Sozialforschung* and at times to forgo their publication. It might be news to you that Teddie's contributions were subject to the same "censorship"—but without our ever having denied him or Benjamin a penny. The essay on Mannheim he wrote of from London on August 19, 1937, was not accepted, nor was one on Husserl; and in several reviews we made major substantive changes. Thus, for example, I wrote to him on September 21, 1937: "I've had your reviews copied now, and in a form reflecting the consequences of my changes, with which, by the way, Marcuse agrees. . . . If you approve of the abridged versions I would like to ask you to submit the manuscripts . . . so that they can be prepared for typesetting." Teddie then wrote to me on October 31: "That's how it is with my scribbling; it is, fortunately or unfortunately, formed in such a way that ridiculously minor changes can, under certain circumstances, mess up the whole thing. . . . I ask you to accept my proposals in this spirit, and not as an expression of pedantic self-righteousness. I believe that they can be executed almost entirely along the lines of your suggestions for changes. Only the deletions on pages seven and nine have major implications. The essay in its current form has already, as you know, been rigorously abridged. . . . However, I understand very well the . . . considerations that have motivated you to make these deletions. Maybe you can insert a sentence containing the idea of what has been deleted without being offensive. Let me conclude by saying that God will reward you for your effort in such cases."

That's how it really was—we always negotiated our texts with one another. Two of my own essays were not published until much later either. Like everything else, they finally appeared in print via our *Flaschenpost*.[4] For example, there was a long study of naturalism that was not published because Meyer Shapiro thought that it was superficial and distorted. Well, I told myself, if that's the way it is, forget it. And another longer essay on German biographies by Emil Ludwig and others was rejected because we didn't want to offend German Jews in exile. But we offended them later anyway! Such negotiations—among other things—led, of course, to arguments and disputes; but when you don't have arguments, then you'd better get a divorce. Finally, though, what counts is not the malicious remarks people occasionally make about each other, but rather the remaining opus.

I would like to pick out one more thing from the correspondence of the thirties, because it illustrates what Teddie meant to me, and I guess also to Horkheimer, who once said to me, "One learns so much from Teddie." Whatever I now know about music, particularly modern music—which, of course, is already old music for you—I learned from him, and I was finally even praised by him as a result. Thus I wrote to him from New York in October 1937 that the Kolisch Quartet had very cleverly performed four concerts, on four consecutive nights, of the music of Beethoven—his late quartets—and of Schönberg, so that you really learned to interpret Beethoven through Schönberg and Schönberg through Beethoven. Teddie responded to this: "I am glad that you also liked the first quartet of Schönberg so much. I think that it is most useful as an

---

4. Critical Theory's efforts have often been described as a *Flaschenpost,* or a "message in a bottle," a phrase coined by Adorno in *Minima Moralia: Reflections from Damaged Life,* trans. Edmund F. N. Jephcott (London, 1974), p. 209. The full phrase is "messages in bottles on the flood of barbarism."

introduction to the mature Schönberg, along with the two major works from the same period, the chamber symphonies and the second quartet. . . . I am of the opinion (and Berg, by the way, was too) that once you have experienced the first quartet, not even the latest and strangest things of Schönberg remain totally unintelligible. I would like nothing better than to demonstrate such things to you *in concreto.*" And he meant it. Adorno was an extremely generous person concerning all these intellectual things. There was no "I don't have time for that"; when you turned to him for help, he gave you his attention.

Now a couple of words about the forties. This was when Adorno joined Horkheimer's exodus from the East Coast to the West Coast, going to live in Santa Monica, near Los Angeles. It was a time when we engaged in an extremely intense scholarly correspondence, which I don't want to go into now. It was when Horkheimer wrote *The Eclipse of Reason,* with Adorno as well as Pollock and myself contributing to its composition—it really was a kind of collective effort. The only correspondence in which changes were discussed was between Adorno and me, though, for Horkheimer and I talked about it on the phone. It was also during the forties that *Dialectic of Enlightenment* originated. Having the chance, on my frequent visits to Adorno's apartment in Southern California, to witness the two of them coin every phrase together remains an unforgettable experience for me, a singular experience—the production of a truly collective work where each sentence originated by joint effort. I, too, had the satisfaction of being able to contribute to some of the book's "Theses on Anti-Semitism." There was an atmosphere of serenity, calmness, and kindness (Gretel was also there quite often), not to mention hospitality, that felt like a bit of utopia—in any case, that's how it seems today. The collective works and discussions on various studies on anti-Semitism fall in the same period as well. I myself took part in the planning of *The Authoritarian Personality,* occasionally mediating between Teddie and his colleagues, American professors, and playing the role of the appeasing diplomat who doesn't take the quarrels of others seriously. I quieted Teddie, telling him that what the empiricists wanted wasn't so bad, we just had to be patient with them and make them familiar with what we understood as theory, then everything would come out all right.

Here is a particularly interesting personal reminiscence: Teddie wrote to me on December 6, 1942, probably remembering his former illusions about German domestic policy, "I don't want to finish without once again having stated that Hitler will be defeated!" This phrase is remarkable in that not all the core members of the Institute shared his confidence. Thank God Teddie was right.

Another correspondence was initiated the year both his parents and my father died—but I don't want to keep you much longer by going into this. I'd like to point out only one thing from this frequent epistolary exchange, since it reminds me of Teddie's generosity. I was in the process of writing a book on popular culture; I had certain ideas for this topic and wrote Teddie on February 23, 1948: "Whatever thoughts you have about how to organize something like this would help me immeasurably. Do you still remember your extemporaneous reflections"—I remember as if it were yesterday—"when we drove down Sunset Boulevard on a Sunday in thick fog and you conjectured how you would organize a lecture on the sociology of literature? That is exactly the model I have in mind for my present study." Such was the nature of our intellectual solidarity, the imprint of which was so strong that one could live from it for quite some time.

Finally, a few words about the fifties, when Adorno had returned to Frankfurt. First, some personal remarks; on August 5, 1959, he wrote to me: "In about ten days we hope to move into our own apartment, Kettenhofweg 123 [which is still Gretel's address], very close to the university and where the Institute will be located. Right now, they are removing, in a frightful din, the rubble from the lot on which the Institute will be constructed." By that time several members of the Institute, some of whom are here tonight, were still working in the basement of the destroyed building, located near the corner of what was then Victoriaallee and Bockenheimer Land-straße. I read to you from this seemingly unimportant passage be-cause it is so intimately personal and therefore expresses something of the almost symbiotic relationship we maintained, even over a great distance. A second personal document is relevant only for me; thirty years ago I was here in Frankfurt for a longer period of time, to give a talk in the Institute, and Teddie sent me a telegram on September 25, 1953: "Reservation Hessischer Hof. Most cordially. Teddie." Here I am again at the Hessischer Hof, on almost the same day thirty years later, but this time no Teddie was there waiting for me.

Teddie came back to Frankfurt for the first time in 1948, full of deep longing but also with a certain anxiety about having to teach German students again. He told me about it on January 3, 1949: "I cannot keep secret from you the fact that I was happily overwhelmed by the European experience from the first moment in Brittany [where he had spent his vacation] and that working with students excels everything you would expect—even the time be-fore 1933—in intensity and rapport. And the contention that the quality of the students has sunk, that they are ignorant or prag-matically oriented, is mere nonsense. Instead, much suggests that, in isolation and estranged from politics, they had plunged into intellectual matters with an unequaled fanaticism. The decisively negative factor that is everywhere in evidence derives from the fact that the Germans (and all Europe, in fact) are no longer political subjects, nor do they feel themselves to be; hence, a ghostlike, unreal quality pervades their spirit. My seminar is like a Talmud school—I wrote to Los Angeles that it is as if the spirits of the murdered Jewish intellectuals had descended into the German students. Quite uncanny. But for that very reason it is at the same time infinitely canny in the authentic Freudian sense." Just let this important letter take its effect on you.

In order not to exhaust your patience I will limit myself to just one more remark. This affects me particularly and expresses an opinion that I share and by which I have been moved throughout this entire conference. Teddie wrote to me on December 2, 1954— sorry to be slightly narcissistic again—regarding the essay I mentioned earlier on the genre of biography that was so popular before Hitler. It was by now perfectly acceptable to publish the essay because we no longer had to show special consideration for formerly exiled Jews, so we planned to include it in an attempted revival of the *Zeitschrift für Sozialforschung* in the fifties. This plan came to nothing, however, and instead a series of sociological studies arose, to be published by the Institute; its first volume was the festschrift for Max Horkheimer's sixtieth birthday, in which my essay finally appeared.

"Concerning the study on biography," Teddie wrote in December 1954, "I am of the firm opinion that it should be published. Not only because I think it is necessary that you make an *acte de présence* in the first issue, but also because I believe that the topic has the same relevance today as it did before. The genre is inexterminable, the love of the German people for Stefan Zweig and Emil Ludwig has undoubtedly survived the Jews, and the biographical essays that inundate illustrated magazines (often still featuring Nazi celebrities) derive in large measure from this kind of writing, the dregs of the dregs. Your arguments are so striking that we shouldn't do without it. And your work has methodological significance as well, insofar as it represents a very legitimate parody of the official practice of *content analysis*. To enumerate sentences of the sort 'Never before has a woman loved like . . .' [I had put together innumerable phrases in which each person states about everybody and everything else that he, she, it, is the greatest thing that ever happened to the world] is quantification rightly conceived." And now I turn to the passage for the sake of which I selected this letter in conclusion: "Finally," Teddie continues, "I would like to say that I fundamentally do not adhere to the conviction that our works will become outdated for external or thematic reasons a couple of years after they are written; for the emphasis of what we are doing lies, I would think, in a theory of society and not in ephemeral material." I have the same response to some of the criticisms launched during this conference, which allege that the agenda of classical Critical Theory is no longer relevant today. No, I agree with Teddie, who continues his letter: "We, at least, should not pursue the kind of modernity that consists in making abstract chronology the standard for relevance and that thus represents the exact opposite of the truly progressive." I would like to add here, with a certain hope and without aggressiveness, that I've heard as well in the critical melodies of the outstanding papers of this conference a distinctive theme that may resonate longer than our critics would like to concede.

9

In Memory of
Walter Benjamin:
The Integrity
of the Intellectual

BY LEO LOWENTHAL

Walter Benjamin ends his essay on surrealism with the image of "an alarm clock that in each minute rings for sixty seconds."[1] The essay appeared in 1929 and bore the subtitle "The Last Snapshot of the European Intelligentsia." I can hardly find a better way to express the feelings that accompanied my preparation of these remarks in memory of Benjamin. As I studied his work once again, it seemed

This essay was originally presented as a lecture in July 1982 during a colloquium on Walter Benjamin in Frankfurt, sponsored jointly by Suhrkamp Verlag and the University of Frankfurt. It was later published in part as "Die Integrität des Intellektuellen: Zum Andenken Walter Benjamins," *Merkur* 37, no. 2 (March 1983): 223–27. The first English translation of this essay appeared in *The Philosophical Forum* 15, nos. 1–2 (Fall–Winter 1983–1984): 146–57; it has been re-translated for this volume by David J. Ward.

1. Walter Benjamin, "Surrealism," in Benjamin, *Reflections,* trans. Edmund F. N. Jephcott (New York, 1978), p. 192.

indeed as if a clock were incessantly sounding an alarm: Benjamin's immediacy today set off uninterrupted shocks in my mind and demanded constant alertness.

Although I begin my lecture with similarities that link Benjamin and myself both biographically and intellectually, I am quite conscious that by drawing such parallels I may appear to be equating myself with him. This is not my intention. Being only eight years his junior, I might be tempted to overestimate the value of mere survival and thus see things with which I myself am associated as more important than they are in the context of the fate experienced by a generation of German and German-Jewish intellectuals. When I speak of the past, that is, of Benjamin's oeuvre and the memory of his person, this past becomes entirely present. Benjamin's fundamental themes—and it is not by coincidence that I mentioned his essay on surrealism first—have accompanied me throughout my life.

While the mere fact of outliving someone cannot alone legitimize a memorial address, I do not feel too uncomfortable with my task. In the relationship Benjamin and I had—direct or indirect—there was no discord. Elsewhere, I have spoken out with indignation against insinuations from some quarters concerning allegedly humiliating dependence and intellectual suppression in Benjamin's dealings with the Institute of Social Research. Gershom Scholem, who was to speak to you today, no longer lives. In his memory, I would like to read a few words from his long letter to Benjamin dated November 6 and 8, 1938. Scholem mentions a visit to our Institute in New York, and he reports: "I think the people of the institute have every reason to frame you in gold, even if only in secret. In our brief but harmless encounters, I had the impression that people like Marcuse and Lowenthal realize this as well." There could never be any doubt on that score.

The extent of my involvement with Benjamin's publications in our *Zeitschrift für Sozialforschung* is meticulously documented in the notes to his collected works. I will refer here to just one episode regarding his essay "The Paris of the Second Empire in Baudelaire," published posthumously by Rolf Tiedemann in 1969.[2] As managing editor of the journal, my main concern was to publish this essay—part of a planned book on Baudelaire belonging to the Arcades Project—as soon as possible. There were repeated delays, owing in part to Benjamin himself and in part to the complex correspondence between Adorno and Benjamin. On August 3, 1938, Gretel Adorno wrote to Benjamin from the Adornos' vacation address: "And now to the most important matter, to Baudelaire. Leo Lowenthal was visiting us here for a couple of days when your letter arrived. We thought it best to show him your letter right away. Lowenthal was beside himself [about the delay] and declared that he absolutely must have the essay for the next issue."[3]

Then, when the essay arrived, Adorno and I had an argument, which I lost. In a letter to Benjamin dated November 10, 1938, Adorno wrote: "The plan is now to print the second chapter ("The *Flâneur*") in full and the third ("Modernism") in part. Leo Lowenthal in particular supports this emphatically. I myself am unambiguously opposed to it."[4] At that point—and this played a role in the subsequent attacks on Adorno—the essay was not accepted for publication, undoubtedly through Adorno's influence.

He presented his objections bluntly, as the correspondence between him and Benjamin shows. Although Adorno's criticism up-

2. This essay can be found in Benjamin, *Charles Baudelaire: Ein Lyriker im Zeitalter des Hochkapitalismus* (Frankfurt am Main, 1969); and in English translation in *Charles Baudelaire: A Lyric Poet in the Era of High Capitalism,* trans. Harry Zohn (London, 1973).

3. Walter Benjamin, *Gesammelte Schriften,* 5 vols. (Frankfurt am Main, 1972–1982), vol. 1, pt. 3, pp. 1084–85.

4. Adorno to Benjamin, November 10, 1938; quoted in Theodor W. Adorno, *Über Walter Benjamin* (Frankfurt am Main, 1970), p. 142. Also in Benjamin, *Gesammelte Schriften,* vol. 1, pt. 3, p. 1098.

set him at first, Benjamin did put it to use very productively. On the basis of the revision suggested by Adorno, a new, independent essay emerged, "Some Motifs in Baudelaire," which we published in 1939, in the last German-language volume of the journal. In his essay, Benjamin explicitly connected his themes of the crisis of aura and the loss of experience, which he had treated separately in his "Storyteller" and "Work of Art" essays.[5] This decisive shift of emphasis in turn gives the first Baudelaire essay, whose publication I had supported, a weight of its own.

No one who is familiar with the German intelligentsia in the Weimar Republic and in exile will be surprised to learn that my circle of friends and acquaintances overlapped extensively with Benjamin's, among them Adorno, Hannah Arendt, Ernst Bloch and Kracauer, Horkheimer and Lukács, Buber and Rosenzweig. These names also signify both definite identity and confrontation, for example in early relations with the Jüdische Lehrhaus initiated by Buber and Rosenzweig. There was another almost tragicomic parallel between our two biographies: Benjamin's *Habilitation* [qualification as lecturer] for the University of Frankfurt in 1925 was rejected on the basis of objections by German philology professor Franz Schultz and could not be rescued, even by the intervention of Hans Cornelius, philosopher and teacher of Horkheimer and Adorno. A year later the same thing happened to me. In 1926 my *Habilitation* as well—it was in the philosophy department—was prevented by Schultz in his capacity as dean, although Cornelius supported it most warmly.

As far as I remember, I did not yet know Benjamin personally in 1925, although the themes of our work already overlapped at

5. All three essays can be found in English in Walter Benjamin, *Illuminations: Essays and Reflections,* ed. Hannah Arendt, trans. Harry Zohn (New York, 1968). The last two also appear in Benjamin, *Gesammelte Schriften,* vol. 1, pt. 2.

important points. Benjamin was greatly interested in Franz von Baader, whose religious philosophy of redemptive mysticism and solidarity with society's lowest classes is evident in Benjamin's "Theses on the Philosophy of History."[6] I wrote my dissertation in 1923 on Baader's philosophy of society. Today I gather from Benjamin's review of David Baumgart's biography of Baader,[7] and from his correspondence with Scholem,[8] that the vanguard position of this conservative, Catholic philosopher of religion—particularly his political morality and his affinity to those who suffer in this world, to the *Proletärs,* as he called them—had similarly attracted us both. Although at the time I was very radical politically, I did with a clear conscience write my dissertation about a conservative thinker. It strikes me as an additional confirmation that Benjamin had also been engrossed in this man's writings.

Another more important convergence of our intellectual interests lies in the unyielding critique he conducted in 1931 of the enterprise of literary history and criticism. My first essay in the first issue of the *Zeitschrift für Sozialforschung* in 1932 had borne the title "On the Social Situation of Literature." It passed judgment in its own way on the then-reigning university and literary establishment with its apolitical, *lebensphilosophischen,* and ultimately reactionary categories. It is hardly a coincidence that these same philologists whom Benjamin had taken to task were not treated gently in my essay either. I am ashamed to admit that I was not then familiar with Benjamin's essay, which had appeared in *Die literarische Welt.*[9] Otherwise I would certainly have cited it positively,

6. In Benjamin, *Illuminations,* and *Gesammelte Schriften,* vol. 1, pt. 2.
7. Benjamin, *Gesammelte Schriften,* vol. 3, pp. 304ff.
8. *Briefwechsel Walter Benjamin–Gerschom Scholem, 1933–1940* (Frankfurt am Main, 1980).
9. Walter Benjamin, "Literaturgeschichte und Literaturwissenschaft," *Die literarische Welt* 7, no. 16 (April 17, 1931); also in *Gesammelte Schriften,* vol. 3, pp. 283ff.

if not considered my own essay superfluous. Benjamin was quite familiar with my later socioliterary work. I know for example that he was at first hardly enthusiastic about my essay on Knut Hamsun, in which I analyzed Hamsun's novels as anticipations of fascist mentality. But he did appreciate my study on the reception of Dostoevsky in Germany. In these and other studies, I had essentially begun to formulate the now familiar questions of reception theory and *Wirkungsgeschichte* [the history of effects], admittedly with clear emphasis on the critique of ideology. That coincided with Benjamin's interests. He wrote to me from Denmark on July 1, 1934:

> In the few days since my arrival in Denmark, the study of your Dostoevsky essay was my first undertaking. For a variety of reasons it has been extremely productive for me, above all because after your preliminary reference to Conrad Ferdinand Meyer, I now have before me a kind of reception history that is precise and in its precision—as far as I know—entirely new. Until now such attempts have never gotten beyond a history of the literary material because a sensible formulation of the essential questions was lacking. An early and interesting venture, which admittedly has little to do with your observations, would be Julian Hirsch's "Genesis of Fame," with which you are probably familiar. In many ways, Hirsch never gets beyond the schematic. In your work one is dealing with the concrete historical situation. One is, however, surprised to learn just how contemporary the historical situation is in which the reception of Dostoevsky has taken place. This surprise gives the reader—if I may infer from myself to others—the impulse that sets his own thinking into motion. . . . A certain continuity of class history right through the world war has been made visible for Germany, as has its mythic apotheosis in the aura of cruelty. In addition, illumination came for me from a remote source, falling all the more revealingly on figures and trends from which literary history's

usual point of view was able to derive but little. I found that
the discourses on naturalism confirmed what you had inti-
mated to me in Paris; they met with my unqualified agreement. What you say about Zola is particularly interesting. . . . To what extent has this German reception of
Dostoevsky done justice to his work? Is it not possible to
imagine any other based on him, in other words, is Gorky's
the last word on this subject? For me, since I have not read
Dostoevsky for a long time, these questions are presently
more open than they seem to be for you. I could imagine that,
in the very folds of the work into which your psychoanalytical observations lead, elements can be found that the petit-
bourgeois way of thinking was unable to assimilate.

My essay on C. F. Meyer and his reception as ideologue of the
German national *grande bourgeoisie* appeared to Benjamin of some
importance in another context as well. In his efforts to have an
article about our Institute in New York published in the culturally
conservative émigré journal *Maß und Wert,* it occurred to Benjamin
to stress the aesthetic contributions as politically unthreatening and
yet secretly to point out their political significance to those who
knew how to read between the lines. As he informed Horkheimer
on December 6, 1937, he wanted to try to introduce, through the
back door so to speak, the radical critique of the present that informed the *Zeitschrift.* He wrote, "The closest we might come to it
[the sphere of actuality] would be to approach it in aesthetic disguise, i. e., by way of Lowenthal's studies on the German reception
of Dostoevsky and on the writings of C. F. Meyer."[10]

But the most profound contact between Benjamin and myself
lay in our shared fascination with the dichotomy, which has never
been resolved and indeed resists resolution, between political, secu-

10. Benjamin to Horkheimer, December 6, 1937; in Benjamin, *Gesammelte Schriften,* vol. 3, p. 682.

larized radicalism and messianic utopia—this thinking culminated in Benjamin's concept of *Jetztzeit* [now-time], which was intended to explode the homogeneous continuum of history and the notion of unending progress.[11] In this messianic-Marxist dilemma, I am wholly on Benjamin's side; even more, I am his pupil. Like him, I initially came into close contact with the idea of the complementarity of religious and social motives through Hermann Cohen's school in Marburg; but also just like Benjamin, I later realized that the way of Hermann Cohen's neo-Kantianism leads into a bad infinity.

The Jewish assimilation into the liberal philosophical tradition (with or without socialist bias) was all the more futile because intellectual liberality remained something foreign in Germany. Just as the German university and later the fascist state drove him away, Benjamin was from the outset never at peace with the institutions of the cultural establishment. Was it prophetic instinct that the school desk, the first institution he confronted, suggested to him the law that would govern his life? In the section "Winter's Morning" from his book *A Berlin Childhood Around Nineteen Hundred,* he writes: "There [in school], once I made contact with my desk, the whole tiredness, which seemed to have vanished, returned tenfold. And with it the wish to be able to sleep my fill. I must have wished that wish a thousand times, and later it was actually fulfilled. But it was a long time before I recognized that fulfillment in the fact that my every hope for a position and a steady income had been in vain."[12]

In a letter to Scholem dated June 12, 1938, Benjamin says of Kafka: "In order to do justice to the figure of Kafka in its purity and

11. For a good account of Benjamin's complicated concept of *Jetztzeit,* see Richard Wolin, *Walter Benjamin: An Aesthetic of Redemption* (New York, 1982), pp. 48ff.

12. Walter Benjamin, *Berliner Kindheit um Neunzehnhundert* (Frankfurt am Main, 1950), p. 38; also in *Gesammelte Schriften,* vol. 4, pt. 2, p. 248.

its peculiar beauty, one must never forget: it is the figure of one who has failed."[13] These words apply to Benjamin himself, not only in the tragic sense that he took his life when he was not yet fifty years old (is this his childhood wish to sleep his fill being tragically fulfilled?), but also in the more positive sense that in Benjamin's life and in his work the suffering of the species—of which he spoke in his most significant book—is constantly reproduced. It is impossible to determine—and it makes no difference today—to what extent Benjamin consciously or half-consciously brought about his failure and to what extent it was determined by the historical space in which he had to live. World War I, inflation, expulsion, exile, and internment in France—these facts outline the historical context clearly enough. But his integrity as an intellectual remains decisive in the motif of failure. He was never really able to decide on a bourgeois profession. The educated bourgeoisie, and even the less well educated, could have asked maliciously: what in fact was Benjamin's profession? Even the attempts he made in this direction are not really believable; perhaps he did not quite believe in them himself. He certainly did not follow his father's wish that he establish himself in the business world. His *Habilitation* was turned down, he never held a steady position as editor for the *Frankfurter Zeitung* or for any publisher, and finally an attempt to secure a position at the University of Jerusalem went awry. The thought of leaving, by the way, was never without ambivalence for him. And so from 1933 on, he repeatedly promised Scholem that he would move to Jerusalem, and he repeatedly put off going. He stayed in France until the last minute. In his letters to Adorno and to Horkheimer, it becomes clear that he conceived of the Arcades Project as a commitment that could be brought to completion only in Europe, in fact only in Paris. Would the only refuge he seemed once to have decided upon, the home that beckoned, namely membership in the Institute of Social Research, the emigration to the United States that had been

13. *Briefwechsel Benjamin–Scholem,* p. 273.

planned to the last detail, the move in with the rest of us in New York, would that have been a satisfactory solution for him? He did not live to see it. What a cruel allegory of failure!

Were there a Benjaminian fate, it would be that of the radical intellectuals of the Weimar Republic and that which followed. He himself was most aware, not only in terms of his own person, but also in his theoretical-political analysis of the intellectual, that there was no such thing as "free-floating" intellect—an idealized concept fashionable at the time in Karl Mannheim's coinage; no such thing as the so-called classless intellectual; no such thing as the "organic" intellectual à la Gramsci; nor even any such thing as the so-called intelligentsia (a word Benjamin thoroughly disliked). He knew that, in a bitter sense, the intellectual is homeless. As a German intellectual, he experienced that homelessness firsthand and paid tribute to France, in whose intellectualism he trusted. In a brief note in the *Literarische Welt* in 1927, he said the following about the French Association of Friends of the New Russia: "The problematic situation of the intellectual, which leads him to question his own right to exist while at the same time society denies him the means of existence, is virtually unknown in France. The artists and authors are perhaps not any better off than their German colleagues, but their prestige remains untouched. In a word, they know the condition of floating. But in Germany, soon no one will be able to last whose position [as an intellectual] is not generally visible."[14] In his programmatic essays about French intellectuals— for example, in the essay on surrealism cited above or in the article first printed in our journal, "On the Current Social Position of the French Author"[15]—Benjamin criticized attempts to restore to in-

14. Walter Benjamin, "Verein der Freunde des neuen Rußland—in Frankreich," in *Gesammelte Schriften,* vol. 4, pt. 2, p. 486.

15. Walter Benjamin, "Zur gegenwärtigen gesellschaftlichen Standort des französischen Schriftstellers," *Zeitschrift für Sozialforschung* 3, no. 1 (1934): 54–73.

tellectuals an independent status without commitment, stressing by contrast experiences of radical politicization. One must grasp the paradoxical definitions together: "untouched" and "largely visible." The latter points to the necessity of taking a political stand, the former to maintaining the integrity of the intellectual. In the crisis, the intellectual remains "untouched" in his integrity when, instead of withdrawing into the ivory tower of timeless values, he takes a stand.

"Untouched" in the sense of *noli me tangere* is a fitting word for Benjamin's social stance as an intellectual. His urbanity concealed a willfulness of commitment that used even his urbanity as a weapon. In the genteel elegance of his manner and his epistolary style, Benjamin let his readers know that lines had been drawn, lines that would not allow an infringement on his integrity. He had to pay for that. The intellectual marketplace in both Western and Eastern Europe understood Benjamin's intentions precisely. The *Frankfurter Zeitung,* in spite of its liberality and the occasional hospitality it showed the avant-garde, refused to publish the polemic essay "Left Melancholy,"[16] in which Benjamin settled accounts with pseudo-radicals. For him, their radicalism was nothing more than "leftist theater" for the consumption of the educated bourgeoisie, who used this radicalism-by-proxy to put distance between themselves and society's real political and moral problems whenever they paid their conscience-money—which committed them to nothing at all—at the box office and the book store. Benjamin received similar treatment from the other side as well: the truncation—tantamount to rejection—by the *Great Soviet Encyclopedia* of his marvelous Goethe essay,[17] the genuine radicalism of

16. Walter Benjamin, "Linke Melancholie: Zu Erich Kästners Gedichtbuch," *Die Gesellschaft* 8, no. 1 (1931): 181–84; also in *Gesammelte Schriften,* vol. 3, pp. 279ff.

17. Walter Benjamin, "Goethes *Wahlverwandtschaften,*" *Neue Deutsche Beiträge* 2, no. 2 (January 1925).

which was unbearable to the manipulative Soviet cultural policy, speaks volumes.

Was he a pariah? The ragpicker (no one wants to "touch" him), about whom Benjamin has a good bit to say, especially in the Baudelaire essay, knows no disguise, plays no roles. The ragpicker is as he is, stigmatized and yet independent. What he has given up, and what society would not allow him, is mimicry, playing up to the stronger of opposing forces, to those who dominate in society. Mimicry is, as I see it, one of the most perceptive categories for categorizing what is phony, false—false consciousness, false politics, cowardly attempts to find cover. Just think of that passage in his review of Kästner's volume of poetry, which sparked his essay "Left Melancholy," in which Benjamin in a single breath pinions both the feudal mimicry of the lieutenant in the Imperial Austrian Reserves and the "proletarian" mimicry of the disintegrating "leftist" intellectual: the reserve lieutenant of the bourgeoisie, crushed after World War I, who finds a futile resurrection in the Nazi empire; the leftist melancholic who fetches his tidy fees from the bourgeois press while trying to secure the sympathies of radicals internationally, and who ultimately disappears quite helplessly in the witch's cauldron of the 1930s—these are far removed from the failure of Benjamin with his Angelus Novus–like view of the ruins of history. Benjamin remains on the side of marginality, of negativity; he remains the figure on the fringe who refuses to take part. With his persistence in saying no—the "salt of refusal," as he called it in his essay on Stefan George[18]—he becomes what I am tempted to call the esoteric figure of the intellectual. Most of what has been said about the definition of the intellectual—sociologically, anthropologically, and in terms of cultural politics—amounts to nothing before the figure of Benjamin, who is exactly what intellect should be: independence in a self-imposed exile. Hence every attempt to

18. Walter Benjamin, "Rückblick auf Stefan George," in *Gesammelte Schriften*, vol. 3, p. 397.

reduce him to a formula in order to fit him into someone's convenient set of categories, rushing to label him messianic or Jewish or
Marxist or surrealist, was bound to fail. To use a fitting expression
of W. Martin Lüdke's, what remains is the "difference," the idiosyncratic, the endless searching; what remains is the unrelenting,
sorrowful gaze.

That can be seen precisely in his essay about Karl Kraus.[19] In less
than flattering terms, Kraus rejected the essay as a psychological
portrait of himself. In reality, though, Benjamin's essay is auto-
biographically inspired: it is testimony for marginal existence and
against mimicry; it is testimony of the relentlessness of the ever-
watchful court of judgment, of the daily Last Judgment. What a
shame Karl Kraus did not understand it.

The following words on Kraus appear in that essay: "Kraus ac-
cuses the law in its substance, not its effect. His charge is the betrayal
of justice by law."[20] The linguistic tensions between *Recht* [right]
and *Gerechtigkeit* [justice], *Recht* and *Gericht* [court], that perpetu-
ally convening "Last Judgment," are decisive for Benjamin. Perhaps I can make that clearer with two quotes. The first is Schiller's
sentence, which has been quoted to death: "World history is the
world's court of judgment." The other is by Ibsen: "Writing means
holding a day of judgment, judgment over oneself." Neither Schiller's nor Ibsen's formulations could have been acceptable to Benjamin, for they are overcome dialectically. If history is the world's
court of judgment (and Hegel agrees that it is), then the victors have
not only won the spoils, but they have also declared themselves on
the right side of the law. In Benjamin's great formulation, "History
has always been written by the victors." Schiller's bourgeois idealism, according to which the world court will have the final word,
but only as an "idea," has always been reconcilable—tragically, as

19. Walter Benjamin, "Karl Kraus," in *Reflections*.
20. Ibid., p. 255.

they say—with the continued existence of bourgeois society. And that is what Max Horkheimer and Herbert Marcuse mean with their concept of affirmative culture. Surely Ibsen's phrase about holding a day of judgment is an indictment against the ideology of the individual in individualistic, bourgeois society. But since he assigns to writing and to the writer a role in which the writer preempts truly autonomous human existence, and thereby the passive observer or reader as recipient of his guilt appears to be redeemed with him, the monadic isolation of class society is neither converted nor overcome in revolutionary form.

Burkhardt Lindner, to whom I showed a first draft of this paper, wrote me, adding:

> Benjamin's use of "court" stands in radical rejection of "right" (law). He criticizes so-called positive right as a rationalization for dominance and violence; it lays claim to justice only erroneously. Justice must be applied to the individual, to the particular. Justice is the messianic emergence or the purifying, profane power of revolutions. Correspondingly, Benjamin also rejects the notion of world history as world court. Only the revolutionary interruption of history or the messianic cessation of history can disrupt the repressive continuum and pass judgment over what has been.

In the concept of "court of judgment" of which Benjamin becomes the advocate, the motifs of political radicalism and historical materialism are combined with the messianic element of Judaism. This constellation of political radicalism, messianism, and Judaism is characteristic of Benjamin. In the volume of material on his theses "On the Concept of History,"[21] one finds passages like this: "Each moment is a moment of judgment upon certain moments that pre-

21. See *Materialien zu Benjamins Thesen "Über den Begriff der Geschichte,"* ed. Peter Bulthaup (Frankfurt am Main, 1975).

ceded it." Or this: "Without some sort of test of a classless society,
the past is nothing more than a jumbled collection of facts. To that
extent, every conception of the present participates in the conception of the Final Judgment."

At this point, I would like to return once more to the association
between Walter Benjamin and the representatives of Critical Theory. Sometimes it even extended to similarities in formulation. As
an example, in Horkheimer's programmatic article "Traditional
and Critical Theory," published in the *Zeitschrift für Sozialforschung*
in 1937, these words occur: "The intellectual is satisfied to proclaim
with reverent admiration the creative strength of the proletariat and
find satisfaction in adapting himself to it and in canonizing it. He
fails to see that such an evasion of theoretical effort (which the
passivity of his own thinking spares him) and of temporary opposition to the masses (which active theoretical effort on his part might
force upon him) only makes the masses blinder and weaker than
they need be."[22] Nearly ten years earlier, in 1929, Benjamin had
written: "The intellectual adopts a mimicry of proletarian existence
without this linking him in the least with the working class. By
doing so, he tries to reach the illusory goal of standing above the
classes, especially to be sure that he is outside the bourgeois class."
And later, in his 1938 essay about our Institute in *Maß und Wert,* he
cites that passage from Horkheimer's essay, adding: "The imperial
nimbus in which the expectants of the millennium have cloaked
themselves cannot be dissipated by the deification of the proletariat. This insight anticipates the concern of a critical theory of
society."[23]

22. Max Horkheimer, "Traditional and Critical Theory," in Horkheimer, *Critical Theory: Selected Essays,* trans. Matthew J. O'Connell et al.
(New York, 1972), p. 214.

23. Walter Benjamin, "Ein deutsches Institut freier Forschung," in
Gesammelte Schriften, vol. 3, p. 522.

Benjamin, like the rest of us, had to go through the painful process of recovering, theoretically and emotionally, from the disappointments dealt us by the history of the Soviet republic and the Communist movement from the mid-twenties on. As I formulated it once before, we felt that we had not abandoned the revolution, but rather that the revolution had abandoned us. Thus arose the disastrous situation of which Jörg Drews speaks in a review of the Benjamin-Scholem correspondence: "The cruel dilemma, namely through what categories and by means of which future-directed group the antifascist intellectual might find orientation, was the central problem for Benjamin after 1930."[24] It was the central problem for all of us.

Here it once again becomes clear why Benjamin's original confidence in Marburg neo-Kantianism, which attempted to unite Kant's moral system with a socialist conception of progress, ultimately had to be disappointed. Because I underwent a similar development myself about ten years later, I am particularly moved even today by what Benjamin says about that. There is a passage in the drafts of the theses "On the Concept of History," from which I quoted before, in which Benjamin connects the critique of neo-Kantianism with his critique of social democratic thought—linking them in the concept of endless progress, the ultimately quietist attitude of the average socialist. By contrast, Benjamin holds up his certainty of the always-waiting presence of the messianic spark:

> In the notion of the classless society, Marx secularized the notion of the messianic age. And that was good. The trouble arises in that social democratic thought raised that notion to an "ideal." That ideal was defined in the neo-Kantian teaching as an "endless task." And this teaching was the school philoso-

24. Jörg Drews, "Katastrophen Abgerungen: Zum Briefwechsel Zwischen Benjamin und Scholem," *Süddeutsche Zeitung* 194 (August 8, 1980).

phy of the Social Democratic Party. . . . Once the classless
society was defined as an endless task, then the empty and
homogeneous future was transformed, so to speak, into an
anteroom in which one could wait more or less sanguinely for
the appearance of the revolutionary age. In reality there is not
a single moment that does not carry with it *its own* revolutionary opportunity.[25]

Benjamin had already spoken of the necessity of overcoming neo-
Kantianism in his significant short review, dated 1929, called
"Books That Have Stayed Alive."[26] He cites *History and Class Con-
sciousness* by Lukács, among others, and about Franz Rosenzweig's
Star of Redemption he says: "A system of Jewish theology. As re-
markable as the work itself is its genesis in the trenches of Mac-
edonia. Victorious incursion of Hegelian dialectic into Hermann
Cohen's *Religion of Reason*."

Here we come once more to the third element I spoke of, which
joins the messianic and the political: the Jewish. Some of us long
denied its essential role in our development. In retrospect, this
must be corrected. After all, Benjamin in his time and I in mine
came into contact with positive Jewish influences as a result of our
protest against our parents—Benjamin through his encounter with
Scholem, I through the friendship of the charismatic Rabbi Nobel,
the Buber-Rosenzweig circle, and the Jüdische Lehrhaus, which
later became important for Benjamin as well.

The utopian-messianic motif, which is deeply rooted in Jewish
metaphysics and mysticism, played a significant role for Benjamin,
surely also for Ernst Bloch and Herbert Marcuse, and for myself. In
his later years, when he ventured—a bit too far for my taste—into

25. Benjamin, *Gesammelte Schriften,* vol. 1, pt. 3, p. 1231.
26. Walter Benjamin, "Bücher die lebendig geblieben sind," *Die literarische Welt* 5, no. 20 (May 17, 1929).

concrete religious symbolism, Horkheimer frequently said (and on this point I agree with him completely) that the Jewish doctrine that the name of God may not be spoken or even written should be adhered to. The name of God is not yet fulfilled, and perhaps it will never be fulfilled; nor is it for us to determine if, when, and how it will be fulfilled for those who come after us. I believe that the essential thing about practical socialism that so shocked us is the idea that one is permitted to plan for someone else. The notion of something perhaps unattainable, perhaps unnameable, but which holds the messianic hope of fulfillment—I suppose this idea is very Jewish; it is certainly a motif in my thinking, and I suppose it was for my friends as well—but quite certainly it was for Benjamin a shining example of the irrevocable commitment to hope that remains with us "just for the sake of the hopeless."

In the sixth of his "Theses on the Philosophy of History," Benjamin writes: "Only that historian will have the gift of fanning the spark of hope in the past who is firmly convinced that *even the dead* will not be safe from the enemy if he wins. And this enemy has not ceased to be victorious."[27] Now that the edition of Benjamin's collected works is completed, the publishing house and the group responsible for it can collectively regard themselves as the writers of Benjamin's history. It will remain a concern to all of us, especially the younger generation, to defend from the enemy his gift to us (and Benjamin never made that easy for us—which is a gift as well). The enemy comes in many guises, such as the paltry accusation that the appearance of a classic-type edition is a burial ceremony that puts Benjamin firmly and finally into his coffin—and we all know that, particularly in Germany, although a classic may mean hours of nostalgic leisure-reading, it also means ritual quoting and being forgotten. Yet the philosopher of a negative theology, the architect

27. Walter Benjamin, "Theses on the Philosophy of History," in *Illuminations*, p. 255.

of history as ruins in temporal and atemporal space, the thinker of the contradiction (whether intentionally or not, he himself is not free of contradictions), the traveler on Hegel's path of positive negation, is entirely safe from the fate of a German classic. This fate cannot touch Benjamin, and indeed, he has already survived the enemy.

Part III

Ongoing Conversations

10

The Utopian Motif in
Suspension: A Conversation
with Leo Lowenthal

INTERVIEW WITH W. MARTIN LÜDKE

What has not been lost is, of course, the critical approach: the
process of analysis, retaining the good and rejecting the bad,
the need to accuse, the indictment of all that exists . . . , but
without explicit hopes. What has occurred is not a retreat into
skepticism or cynicism, but sadness. The utopian motif has
been suspended.

These remarks by Leo Lowenthal may have the ring of resignation, and not surprisingly so. At the beginning of the war, according to an anecdote told by Hanns Eisler, some members of the
Institute of Social Research were standing on the shore of the Pacific
when suddenly Adorno, seized by melancholy, said: "We should
throw out a message in a bottle." Eisler remarked dryly that he
already knew how the message should read: "I feel so lousy." This

Originally published as "Das utopische Motiv ist eingeklammert:
Gespräch mit dem Literatursoziologen Leo Löwenthal," in *Frankfurter
Rundschau*, May 17, 1980. Published in English in *New German Critique* 38
(Spring–Summer 1986). Translated by Ted R. Weeks.

kind of resignation, however, is not at all characteristic of Lowenthal. His sentences are marked by sober objectivity: they aim to destroy possible illusions in order to promote political action.

To be sure, Lowenthal's thinking is deeply rooted in the framework of Critical Theory, which he helped establish and develop; however, pragmatic tendencies are also evident, as well as an inclination to redirect speculative flights of intellectual fancy back to the path of existing conditions. For him, thinking the possible has always meant thinking within the bounds of present conditions, without, of course, reducing it to that alone. Perhaps his humor also plays a role in this.

For the first issue of the *Zeitschrift für Sozialforschung,* Lowenthal wrote the programmatic essay "On the Social Situation of Literature," an essay that is now recognized as a milestone in the history of the sociology of literature. His attempt in this essay to develop a social conception of literature necessarily takes issue with the objections that were raised against a materialistic theory. "By no means," Lowenthal points out, "does every causal question demand an infinite regression." For example, he continues, "An investigation into the causes that led Goethe to Weimar hardly requires a study of the medieval origins of German cities."

In his eighties, Leo Lowenthal has lost neither his vitality nor his quickness—and certainly not his sense of humor. He remains a scholar of the old school, in the positive sense of the term, who has nonetheless retained a touch of roguishness. Herbert Marcuse had a similar disposition, though he was perhaps a bit more sarcastic. Coping with these two, who spent much time together over several decades, must have been a trying experience for humorless erudite scholarly experts.

Today Lowenthal still lives in the middle of town, close to the Berkeley campus of the University of California. He has an open house, open for both visitors and students. When one sits in the living room, gazing at the well-kept yet exuberantly lush garden, all semblance of utopia is destroyed by the constant ringing of the telephone: a German student not long in California who wants to locate a certain book, students who want to discuss their work with him, colleagues, friends, and, day in, day out, members of the families of those colleagues from the Institute who remained in the United States after the war. Now, following Marcuse's death, Lowenthal is the last survivor from the inner circle of the founders of the Frankfurt School (a designation, incidentally, that he strictly rejects).

The methodology of the critique of ideologies, that is, the determination of the "socially necessary illusion," a central motif of Critical Theory, also occupies a position of central importance for Lowenthal's work in the sociology of literature. To be sure, his studies never follow a simplistic base-superstructure schema; they never aim to reduce literature to ideology but, on the contrary, always attempt to describe the "authentic element" in "false consciousness."

Now as much as ever, Lowenthal insists on the need for ideology critique. When I brought up some contemporary objections, referring to the "obsolescence" of this technique, he demurred: "In that respect I can't agree with you at all." Especially in the examination of "mass media, mass culture," he continued, ideology critique is needed more urgently than ever before—now is not the time to take the aesthetic dimension of mass media more seriously, as is so often demanded. Of course, the mass media have changed, but the tendencies leading to the enslavement and stultification of humanity have become even stronger. In an earlier period, when mass media offered the possibility of escape from the oppressiveness of everyday life, a "certain amount of free play for the imagination" was still left, whereas "the present-day phenomenon of the mass medium really doesn't leave any freedom at all for the imagination. I would be more inclined to consider it criminal to bury ideology critique now." In this situation, that is, in competition with mass media, art has been driven into a strictly defensive position.

Speaking of the resulting dilemma, that as the critical meaning of art increases its affirmative tendencies become correspondingly stronger and art becomes increasingly integrated into "the system," Lowenthal emphasizes the difference between the historically oriented analysis of past great works of bourgeois art and the art of the present day. The great art of the past has by no means lost its significance. "However," says Lowenthal, "my suspicion is that great literary art doesn't exist today." Of course, even today art is created that is oppositional or at least intends to be oppositional, but it has "only a very slight impact."

Our conversation then turned to those tendencies that might point beyond bourgeois, late-bourgeois, or late-capitalist society. Already in the mid-thirties, Critical Theory came increasingly to doubt the existence of a historical, revolutionary subject and rejected any hope of salvation founded on historical-philosophical theories, all because of the looming threat of a relapse into barbarism. To quote Lowenthal: "I would begin first of all by saying that one of the factors that brought the fathers or forefathers of Critical Theory together was a political-revolutionary consciousness. With the possible exception of Adorno, all of these men—Horkheimer, Pollock, Marcuse, even Fromm (he, of course, was more interested in the Jewish-utopian side)—were politically active and had strongly developed activist characteristics and ideas."

In describing the later development of this circle in his conversations with Helmut Dubiel, Lowenthal used the phrase "we did not abandon the revolution; the revolution abandoned us." He remains, in his words, "a revolutionary," but "without any possibilities of revolution, and thus, if you will, politically apathetic." He is aware of the contradiction—and that the exaggerated formulation is somewhat off the mark. "I believe that today it is very difficult to imagine what a shock the disappointment over developments in the Soviet Union meant for intellectuals, much earlier in Germany than in the United States, where this realization came only after the Moscow trials. I would go almost so far as to say that the belief in the possibility of change through political action, in the direct influence of theory on politics, was destroyed. It took us some time to realize this. At first, of course, the revolution was seen as the beginning of a process whereby politics would recede behind theory and theory would, as it were, assume the place of politics. At the same time, this theory must also always be clearly differentiated from the so-called Communist reality in the Soviet Union. As Horkheimer so rightly remarked, 'One cannot criticize the Communists without simultaneously criticizing the anti-Communist critique of the anti-Communists.'" The Institute's work crystallized around this problematic of ideological criticism of bourgeois society and criticism of false revolution—still based on the hope that this work would contribute to change. This was also, Lowenthal continued, the real meaning of Adorno's 'message in a bottle': "The symbol of the message in a bottle and its esoteric message arose, after all, out of the feeling that one could contribute to change, that the message would get through to the right people, that possibilities would once again arise."

What came instead was the second great shock, namely the end of World War II, which ended not with the total, shattering destruction of fascism through the triumph of democracy by a democratic movement, but rather with a military defeat. "That was," Lowenthal asserts, "possibly the greatest tragedy of our time. Now, even in our theoretical work, trust in change increasingly has been lost. What has not been lost is the critical approach, the process of analysis, the need to accuse, to say no, the indictment of the *status quo*." No system will last forever, including this bourgeois-capitalist society, but "I can no longer believe in the transformation of this social order into a new one." One possibly decisive insight was the "realization that the ideal of a future socialist or communist society, in which man's mastery over nature is, after all, further increased, can itself exert a corrupting effect on humanity"; that is, even this ideal will not lead to a society that is more humane than the existing one.

Here Lowenthal remembers Herbert Marcuse, with whom he shared a close friendship from the early thirties until Marcuse's death in 1979: "The least pessimistic friend in our group was probably Herbert Marcuse. But if you take a look at the groups Marcuse singled out as the hopeful builders of a new society—women, the counterculture, people in the Third World—it is hard to imagine that these groups would form a politically viable synthesis. After all, these are completely heterogeneous elements. They could be used as symbols of negation, but hardly as a basis for positive political action. . . . Historical-political coherence is dwindling; yes, it is gone," says Lowenthal, summing up.

Lowenthal then explained again one central concept of Critical Theory: the unity of progress and regression. The formulation is Adorno's, who said that the path of progress leads not from savagery to humanity but from the slingshot to the H-bomb. Progress in man's control over nature, that is, manifests itself at the same time in the oppression of human nature.

I asked him whether he could see the ecological movement, the Greens in Germany, as a factor that could point the way beyond this social order. Lowenthal answered dryly, "I wish you and myself luck. But I can't believe it. I see no possibility by which the ecological movement could really ally with the decisive forces in modern society in a way that would be more than a band-aid for society's wounds. I find the Green movement extraordinarily attractive, but I fear that here it's all too easy to talk oneself into believing in illusions that are comparable to those of radical theater or even of religious cults. The ecologists aren't so very different from them; it's just like with the bike riders and vegetarians. To be sure, the ecological movement has achieved much: the protection of the environment, greater caution in the construction of nuclear power plants—all of that is very good, but it will remain at that level. I don't believe there will be a great qualitative leap. The ecological movement is, I believe, an essentially bourgeois movement—a continuation of the best characteristics of European liberalism of the second half of the nineteenth century, fundamentally a movement for enlightenment. But after all, by now we know enough to realize the illusory character of mere enlightened movements."

I asked Lowenthal about the possible influence cooperative interdisciplinary work might have on present social science; here I referred specifically to the cooperative effort that characterized the Institute, which he joined in the mid-twenties, and that was reflected so clearly in the *Zeitschrift für Sozialforschung,* which he edited for several years.

Lowenthal first explained the inappropriateness of the term "interdisciplinary" to describe what the Institute did: "Actually, that means nothing more than to leave the disciplines as they are while developing certain techniques that foster a kind of acquaintance among them without forcing them to give up their self-sufficiency or individual claims." More decisive for the Institute—its actual founding idea—was the interconnection of theory and praxis, the attempt to mediate between the two by means of work carried out according to a program dictated by the theory of social change. The list of themes researched at that time contains most significantly those that were produced by the state of social development, of history.

"In practice this had the result that nothing I witnessed being produced at the Institute in, shall we say, its 'classical' years, between 1926 and 1945, was not to a great extent a communal effort. To be sure, each of us wrote his own books and articles, but nothing was published before all the others had read it and criticized it."

Lowenthal prefers not to commit himself on the question of the influence this "attitude" has exerted; here he remains rather skeptical. Certainly there exist in the United States, especially at the better universities, many forms of interdisciplinary cooperative work, as well as institutionalized forms, that definitely aim for critical consciousness; ultimately, however, these too are little more than "band-aids." "Nonetheless," he repeats, "a band-aid is better than nothing at all."

We turned then to the Jewish-messianic element in the speculative concepts of a critical social theory. Not just representatives of Critical Theory, including Adorno, Horkheimer, Marcuse, Pollock, Fromm, and even Benjamin, but nearly all the philosophers of our century who made radical change of social relations a key element of their philosophical "program"—Ernst Bloch, Georg Lukács—came from Jewish backgrounds. To what extent, I asked Lowenthal, had this Jewish religious heritage, in a more or less secularized form, found its way into these utopian concepts?

Lowenthal's reaction made it clear that he did not take to this particular question. "I am always somewhat ill at ease concerning this problem," he said, pointing out that the alleged specifically Jewish nonconformist and radical motivations in the theories of Marx and Freud were shared by "many who were not Jews." "Still," he admitted, "there may be something to your assertion." Continuing, he alluded to Jewish messianism and its historical consciousness, according to which history is seen as a process that can lead only to something better. The fundamental idea of Christianity—that the main historical event already occurred, in the middle of the course of history, so to speak, and that thereafter there is nowhere to go but downhill—goes totally against Jewish religious or secular "theology."

"My grandfather was a pious Jew, but my father rebelled against Judaism. The fact that at one point I had a positive attitude toward Judaism, and even observed religious and dietary laws for a time, was for my father quite dreadful. Erich Fromm was the only one from the circle of Institute members who came from an orthodox background, and he also lived much longer by the rules of the

Jewish religion than the others. As for myself, I am of Jewish origin, a German Jew, who is today an American citizen. Nothing more.

"But certainly for Benjamin, and also for Bloch and Marcuse, the Jewish–messianic motif played a significant role. In his later years, when for my tastes he became a bit too involved in religious symbolism, Horkheimer once said—and I believe we were all in complete agreement with him on this—that the Jewish article of faith that one may not pronounce the name of God is very decisive. The unattainable, the unapproachable, the unnameable, which nonetheless contains a sense of longing that one may finally reach the goal, may ultimately speak its name. This conception is certainly very Jewish; it is a motif in our thought even today."

Suddenly Lowenthal turned the tables on me: "Why do you ask? It sounds to me as though you were a Jew fighting for the cause." I expressed the concern that with the death of Adorno, Horkheimer, Bloch, and Marcuse this motif could disappear from social-philosophical thought. Lowenthal dismissed the possibility: "Once something has been contributed by the Jewish element to the arsenal of progressive thought, it can no more disappear than can the concept of love, *caritas,* among Christians, even though there are many fewer practicing Christians today. If the concept were really as fragile as you suggest, then it was never really alive."

I objected that Habermas, who after all had held very consistently to the intentions of Critical Theory, had, in his own words, "uncoupled" his variant of Critical Theory precisely at the point of "unfounded hope": that is, from the speculative-utopian call for a resurrection of nature, a reconciliation between man and nature. Habermas discarded this motif as a kind of ballast.

Lowenthal responded, "Maybe he is right. Perhaps it is ballast. Possibly that is all for the best. When I speak of such things, I feel a bit old and obsolete. After all, one cannot live only on utopian hopes based in never-never land, whose realization seems scarcely within the realm of the possible. Maybe this is a cause of the sadness I spoke of at the outset. But perhaps the theoretical realism I sense in Habermas is the only means of salvaging the motifs present in Critical Theory and thereby of protecting them from a complete disintegration into an empty, melancholy pessimism."

11

The Left in
Germany Has Failed

INTERVIEW WITH PETER GLOTZ

Peter Glotz: Mr. Lowenthal, we are having this discussion for the *Neue Gesellschaft/Frankfurter Hefte,* the theoretical periodical of the Social Democratic Party (SPD) and, in a roundabout way, successor to *Neue Zeit.* I would therefore like to ask you about your experiences with the cultural politics of the SPD. I know your experiences lie in the distant past. Walter Benjamin once spoke of the bad positivism of worker-education policies, and in a conversation with Matthias Greffrath you spoke of the "cultural philistines of the movement for a *Volksbühne* [people's theater]," in which you were involved during the 1920s. What were your experiences, more than fifty years ago, concerning the Social Democratic Party's ability for self-representation? How did it deal with the cultural hegemony of the bourgeoisie, which certainly existed in the Weimar Republic?

Leo Lowenthal: I was never at the center of Social Democratic politics and was never a member of the party; I merely participated

Originally published as "Gespräch Glotz/Löwenthal: Die Linke in Deutschland hat versagt," in *Die Neue Gesellschaft/Frankfurter Hefte* 32, no. 10 (October 1985): 880–87. Translated by Benjamin Gregg.

in various assemblies and helped organize certain associations that were closely tied to the party, for example the Frankfurt group of the *Volksbühne* movement and the league for *Volksvorlesungen* [lectures for the people], and I served as the so-called cultural counsel to the chief of police, who was a Social Democrat.

Glotz: And he was supposed to be advised on cultural matters?

Lowenthal: It never happened. They gave me this handsome title and also a document stating that I was the police chief's advisor on cultural affairs. Seriously, though, my experiences with the *Volksbühne* and the *Volksvorlesungen* were a lot of fun for a cultured, leftist member of the bourgeoisie, but I didn't see anything in it that had to do with Social Democratic politics or even with the labor movement. Much of my time, outside my regular professional obligations, was spent on lectures that were financed essentially by Social Democratic circles. I very much enjoyed giving educational lectures on world literature, all the way from Shakespeare and Cervantes to the present. To what extent that contributed toward raising the political and moral consciousness of labor circles, however, I can't say. I saw Horkheimer in my audience, but not the weary face of the proletarian. It's almost a sad joke; the one time I can remember being directly involved with labor organizations was when the German publishers association invited me to give a formal address. The topic: "The German Language as Reflected by Social Developments." Even the title shows you I was pursuing a lost cultural ideal with no specific connection to the tasks of a radical political party or labor union. I felt that the top party or labor union management who would be interested in this kind of cultural activity were really acting like conformists. They simply wanted to be part of what was going on and to do exactly what the others had presumably done ever since idealism's beginnings at the turn of the nineteenth century.

One of my functions at the *Volksbühne* was to negotiate with the producers for the program we wanted for our members. There I felt I had to maneuver a bit, since the "comrades" always tended to produce Lessing, Goethe, and Schiller; Georg Kaiser or Carl Stern-heim were evidently too risky. For my part, I tried to convey to the *Volksbühne* audience a politically and morally oriented attitude through my program notes. Today as well, I fail to see any signifi-cant structural changes. I find the word *Bildungspolitik* [politics of education] very problematic.

Glotz: *Kulturpolitik* [politics of culture] has been absorbed by *Bildungspolitik.*

Lowenthal: *Kulturpolitik* is a word I can't at all recall being used in the Weimar Republic. I think we see here an aspect of the very interesting but tragic history of the SPD.

Glotz: I'd say the concept of *Kulturpolitik* came into being in the Federal Republic's first decade through the efforts of several men in the SPD—Waldemar von Knoeringen and Willi Eichler, for example. But then the concept quickly disappeared into *Schulpolitik* [politics of schools]. There was a debate on comprehensive schools, on a three-tiered system, on the system itself, but for all intents and purposes the subject of culture didn't come up again in the Federal Republic for decades.

Lowenthal: That's really quite typical. Whenever you use the word "*Kulturpolitik*"—however problematic the word "culture" may be—you establish an agenda that touches the entire social complex. The concept of *Kulturpolitik* has something slightly eso-teric about it; it means that you draw on economic elements on the one hand, and on historical and ideological elements on the other. Just look at current neoconservative movements. It's simply not possible to fight neoconservatism unless you approach the whole problem from the vantage point of *Kulturpolitik,* since in the final analysis we're talking about values, about tendencies aimed at change, about an emphasis on ethics, about notions of a new order.

None of this can be accomplished without "culture" being placed at the center as a key concept.

Glotz: We'll come back to the subject of neoconservatism. I read in connection with *Neue Zeit* that you place special emphasis on a very characteristic experience. The critiques of Hamsun in the *Neue Zeit* of the 1890s were thoroughly critical, as you yourself said. The literary critics of the SPD wrote there that one doesn't find living people portrayed in Hamsun, only atmospherics. But then after World War I there came the usual clichés about "gripping images of life and the soul." What I'd like to ask is, does this suggest an erosion in aesthetic theory, an early conformity to bourgeois cultural standards already in the years from the 1890s to the decade between 1910 and 1920? Of course, in Franz Mehring you can identify a Social Democratic position on literary criticism.[1] Even in World War I you wouldn't find that, much less today. My question then is—and I refer explicitly to the present—has the independent aesthetic position disappeared along with a socialist party that had its own worldview and class-standpoint? Has aesthetic agnosticism become necessary for a modern party?

Lowenthal: I see in the way the critical reception of Hamsun changed something closely linked to Social Democracy and to the entire left, namely an involuntary process of becoming more and more bourgeois. All these things have to do with the fact that historical development in Germany has been nonsynchronous [*ungleichzeitig*].

Glotz: You mean Bloch's concept of *Ungleichzeitigkeit?*

Lowenthal: Yes, he said that, in essence, a bourgeois revolution

---

1. Franz Mehring (1846–1919) was an orthodox Second International Marxist, the author of several histories and of a biography of Marx, and the first major Marxist literary critic. His most notable work is *Die Lessing-Legende* (1893).

never took place. I feel this stronger than ever now. I've lived for over fifty years in America, a very bourgeois country indeed; there the word "*Staat*" [the state] is, in the German sense of the word, practically untranslatable.

Glotz: "Government" is something different.

Lowenthal: Right. And one doesn't speak there of the administration [*Regierung*] in power as, for example, "the English"; it's simply "the Thatcher administration." But in Germany people say to me, "you" Americans—and I really don't know why I should be held responsible for Reagan's domestic and international policies. This situation is also reflected in the sad history of the SPD's relationship to literature and art. The uncertainty of judgment about what is bourgeois and what transcends the bourgeoisie stems not from the Enlightenment but from a version of German idealism. Much more than the historical Enlightenment, it is the schoolmaster, with his talk of great cultural values, great ideas, Kantian ethics, and so on, who lurks behind Social Democratic cultural imagery.

Glotz: The influence of Schiller on the bourgeoisie . . .

Lowenthal: Yes, it is Schiller's influence on the bourgeoisie more than Lessing's. If you look at developments in England and France, you see quite clearly the extent to which aesthetic valuations have been assumed by politicians and political theorists as well. There, literature mirrors not only progressive or regressive developments but a country's evolution as well. It's different in Germany—and this lack of the aesthetic in political culture is almost unique for a civilized nation.

Glotz: You have often represented the problematic of art and mass culture as a fictive dialogue between Montaigne and Pascal. Montaigne was capable of appreciating that man wants to escape social pressure and that he needs diversions, whereas Pascal gives us the famous saying "All strong diversions are a danger for Christian life!" If I may begin by asking a general question, isn't it logical that the left would of course assume Montaigne's position in this dialogue?

Lowenthal: I have great sympathy for Montaigne, and Montaigne had great sympathy for people who need diversion because the pressure of circumstances, the pressure of labor, the pressure within relationships is so frightfully great. Sometimes people have to—how shall I put it—grasp for soporific measures in order to go on facing the enormous strains of everyday existence. Yet this fundamental sympathy for the humane, realistic, wise position of Montaigne (who knowingly withdrew from his world) does not justify contemporary commercialization—of which neither Pascal nor Montaigne, of course, could have had any knowledge; it doesn't justify the complete and total planning of a person's entire leisure time through the "leisure industry," all the way from the printed word to television.

No, what I wanted to point out were two tendencies moving counter to each other, tendencies that have been around as long as civilization. I have always tried to think historically. And I'd like to add: this is one of the great dangers in the present situation, especially in the Federal Republic—that historical consciousness is taking on frightfully revisionist characteristics.

Glotz: Then isn't your position quite different from that presented in *Dialectic of Enlightenment,* by your friends Adorno and Horkheimer, or from some positions of the second generation, say of Jürgen Habermas in his book *Structural Change of the Public Sphere*? For Adorno at least, mass culture can be nothing other than a degeneration of art.

Lowenthal: You've maneuvered me into a curious position. But so be it—I find it stimulating. In no way do I differ radically from my colleagues and friends in the critique of mass culture. However, I do believe that we have to distinguish between mass culture and technologies *used by* mass culture. I think that's something that Adorno and Horkheimer, in their programmatic research, placed less value on than I do. There is in my opinion a radical difference between art and mass culture, a difference we shouldn't want to eliminate. Art is not mere subjectivity. An artist communicates something that cannot be represented through other intellectual means. Art expands our experience, it expands our knowledge, it adds something to our quality of life that other intellectual methods—whether organized science or philosophy—cannot. Furthermore, what we've been calling mass culture, or as Adorno and Horkheimer more appropriately dubbed it, the culture industry, is a business. Whether the business is run by parties or warehouses or chemical concerns is irrelevant. It is not the advancing of new knowledge that counts, but the introduction of products into the market. This difference between art and mass culture must be maintained—especially in the current situation, which tends to a relativization of all values, to a nihilism of an unbelievable kind, where people like myself are maneuvered into positions in which they seem completely reactionary because they stubbornly maintain a notion of autonomous art and criticize mass culture as an ever greater enslavement of all people.

Glotz: All right, let's retain the concept of autonomous art. But might I suggest a more differentiated analysis of mass culture? I'd propose the following thesis: mass culture makes possible a wider reception of cultural products than ever before.

Lowenthal: What do you mean by that?

Glotz: Thanks to paperback books, and inexpensive books in general, thanks in part too to book clubs, works of world literature as well as new theoretical works have become inexpensively available for the first time. Today you can buy for a relatively small amount of money a tape of Mozart, Mahler, Wagner, or Alban Berg, in the finest imaginable performance, and play it at home. Yet at one time in history, Mozart was court music. Isn't there a positive element in spreading the possibility of participating in the cultural process?

Lowenthal: You're making it a bit too easy for yourself. Certainly it's a good thing when important works of literature are made more accessible. Certainly it's a good thing that there are fine recordings. (Adorno disputed that playing records and listening to live music are equivalent, but I don't want to get into that now.) It's a good thing when records or tapes are accessible. But the question is, what's really taking place? If Mozart and Beethoven are played over and over again for a listener who isn't able to appreciate the music, or if they're played as background music in cafés, department stores, restaurants, at the hairdresser's or dentist's, then I fail to see anything particularly valuable in it. That's really nothing but the desire to be part of the action.

Glotz: Sure, but you can't say that people buy records solely to distract themselves from the dentist's drilling. It's now possible for someone to experience the music of, say, Mahler at home, whereas earlier, before the technical capacity to reproduce artwork was developed, this wasn't possible.

Lowenthal: I'd like to become your ally. But give me a minute. If you look more closely at the phenomenon we've provisionally been calling the culture industry or mass culture, it's not decisive that people are buying pocket books of Kant and Merleau-Ponty or tapes of Mozart, Beethoven, and Schönberg. Rather, the phenomenon is characterized by "Dallas" and "Dynasty" and God knows how many other shows—I mean that ninety percent of the output of so-called mass culture are products of this kind. Back to my original comment: I'd like to become your ally, but I don't know if you'll have me. I place value on the following factors. I'm of the opinion—and here I part from Adorno and Horkheimer—that you shouldn't make the media as such, the technology of the media, responsible. On the contrary, as a consequence of the capital structure within which these media are used, as a consequence of the political-economic *form,* the entire technological arsenal has been appropriated. The aesthetic and cognitive potential of film, radio, and television hardly gets a chance. Of course, there are the art films and the radio and television plays, but even then, in terms of their diffusion, they're only peripheral phenomena. People have abandoned the field to the enemy. The last thing I'd advise a Social Democratic *Kulturpolitiker* to do would be to continue abandoning the field. Of course, one should be concerned about this threat, but what really matters is how to *avoid* it. My feeling is that two things should be linked: first, continued advancement of the technical and aesthetic possibilities of the media, which in the case of film wouldn't be all that hard and would also foster a good newspaper and magazine press; and second, a consistent effort analytically to grasp that which is being cheaply propagandized and which ultimately harms us all. There must be *both:* the appropriate utilization of the new media and a radical critique of a mass culture that just stultifies our intelligence.

Glotz: I'd like to talk about a concept I sometimes think could become—and probably should have long ago—a central concept of Social Democratic *Kulturpolitik:* popularization. I know there's the old-fashioned schoolmaster (you mentioned this earlier) who popularizes in the wrong way, and I also know there's autonomous art that doesn't allow popularization, or not very easily. Nevertheless, I wonder whether the German resignation vis-à-vis popularization, which I find quite different from the Anglo-Saxon tendency, isn't somehow wrong. Is there a reasonable, thoughtful form of popularization?

Lowenthal: What is popularization? What do you mean by that?

Glotz: To provide more people access to a serious experience of autonomous art.

Lowenthal: Mr. Glotz, every word in that sentence is burdened. Popularization has a positive connotation only when it broadens the experiential base of those for whom something is being popularized. Let me give you an example. Last night I suggested you have a look at the Thyssen-Bornemisza Collection. You'll go there, and since you're a man of great learning, you'll continuously make intellectual associations. But if you take someone to the collection who lacks this background, it won't lead to anything. I can't provide any recipes; I only know that if you don't want to teach a person how to experience aesthetic products, then all this information—mere popularization—backfires and only strengthens the tendency toward cheap, passively enjoyable amusement. Hence, without a genuine—if you'll excuse the word—*education* of people to aesthetic experience, then a kind of popularization that would be at all meaningful is impossible.

In my studies on political agitation I've tried to formulate it like this: the essence of the agitator, in principle the essence of the fascist leader, is to try to perpetuate himself and not to become superfluous. "I'm the only one in possession of the truth"—that's the attitude. But if we turn this around, we can say that the essence of the legitimate elite consists in a pedagogical ideal, which is ultimately to make yourself superfluous as a teacher. But at the beginning you must act as a teacher, and if you don't have the courage to acknowledge this elitist concept of the instructor who expands experience and transmits knowledge and demonstrates models, then you're abandoning the field to those who are seeking to fill a vacuum.

Glotz: I agree with your thesis. But consider two examples. For decades, even centuries, there have been museums in Germany that offer no help at all to those who visit them; instead, these museums presuppose that as a child you had exposure to a bourgeois library in your parent's house. But in many cases no such library exists, for example in the working-class family. Today, however, we have modern museum didactics seeking to lead people without a high school or college background into new realities. A second example: there are enormously successful book associations that make millions, Bertelsmann for example. I wouldn't describe that as an example of Social Democratic *Bildungspolitik,* but I think it's catastrophic that, time and again, the labor movement almost let the Gutenberg Book Guild [a progressive, SPD-sponsored book club] fall apart. I consider it a failure of the labor movement that Bertelsmann [one of the largest publishing companies in Germany] is so large and the Gutenberg Book Guild so small. Wouldn't you concur on these two examples?

Lowenthal: I agree completely. But then, why don't enterprises like the Gutenberg Book Guild succeed? They don't succeed in part simply because there is not enough interest among those to whom your political efforts are dedicated. Such success is possible only by means of a major educational effort, but how that could be realized I don't know. I know only that Germans today recoil even from the word "education."

Glotz: Particularly the left . . .

Lowenthal: The left, Mr. Glotz, especially the leftist intelligentsia in Germany, has failed; indeed, it is also failing, more and more, in the United States and France. Those in Germany who identify as leftist intelligentsia or seek to do so—a movement that is widely documented in journals—much too often celebrate a nihilistic departure from everything that could lead them in the right direction. A lot of things, indeed too many things, are problematized, but the wrong things are problematized: the concepts of enlightenment, of reason, of the individual; the concepts of history, of morality, of an independent art. All of these things are being problematized, all lumped together; completely arbitrary topics are being conceived; the modern age is being sold out. You have written, quite rightly, that the project of the modern age is far from being completed, but that fact is continually denied.

Today many "postmodern" architects want to construct buildings and living spaces that seem to have more of a mythological than a functional significance. Objective reality seems to have evaporated. This tendency, which I find most disturbing, is equally striking in postmodern literature. Its seeming concreteness is phony—we are confronted with distorting mirrors, or picture puzzles that whirl and swirl the dead about. To me this represents an unreflected revelry abounding in irrationalist concepts, an ever-present flirtation with mythology.

Unfortunately, this "mythology" characterizes a certain so-called leftist intelligentsia much more than a rightist one. The right, the neoconservatives, are in fact quite positivistic, oriented toward the practical; the left, however, loses itself in intellectual meanderings that can only make the situation worse. If it's not possible to form a really *new* leftist intelligentsia, one that continues to grow theoretically, as Critical Theory tried to do, then I expect only the worst for Western Europe's future—not so much its industrial future, but its cultural, moral, and political one.

Glotz: I don't know to what extent you follow what this "leftist" intelligentsia in the Federal Republic has been producing in new literature. I'll mention four important names, two from the younger, two from the older generation: Botho Strauß, Peter Handke, Heinrich Böll, Günter Grass. You once wrote, "Art is the great reservoir of the creative protest against social misery which allows the prospect of social happiness to shine dimly through." Or again: "The voice of the loser in the world process articulates itself in the work of art." That refers to the marvelous sentence of Walter Benjamin, that history is always written from the perspective of the victor. But you say that literature should be written from the perspective of the loser. These two sentences contain an implicit aesthetic; if you apply them to the contemporary literary production, what's your impression of German literature in the 1980s?

Lowenthal: I don't want to treat all of it as the same thing. I have a strong aversion to the kind of literature that loses itself in the private sphere to such an extent that it no longer has any connection to the public, social sphere—and no longer wants any such connection. That's not at all true of Böll and Grass, but I think it is true of Strauß and the later Handke. I don't mean that these authors possess no literary qualities; in fact, they are highly talented and describe a certain contemporary situation quite accurately. But unfortunately, I feel compelled to see this literature in a context of other currents, more diffuse, obscure, and underground in nature. These are currents of irrationalization and privatization, the significance of which the leading political parties don't seem to have grasped yet. Good examples of such currents are certain German literary journals with such titles as *Konkursbuch* [Bankruptcy Book] and *Tumult*. They're essentially saying: not only do we have to place everything in doubt, we've got to throw everything overboard, we've got to start over.

But *what* we're supposed to start over with is never determined. And this element of arbitrariness is also present in the literature of inwardness, the so-called New Subjectivity. What took place in the Federal Republic in connection with the fortieth anniversary of the end of World War II, on May 8, 1985, illustrates what I mean: a terrible orgy, an attempt to rewrite history from point zero, a kind of history of negative salvation. Once again thoughts are being formulated that you would think were no longer thinkable—for example, a mythological neonationalism. And formulations of this kind have once again achieved a level of public exposure that would have been impossible just a couple of years ago. Take the *Frankfurter Allgemeine Zeitung,* in which leading articles appear about a people that persecutes others "unto the seventh generation." Unbelievable! Or a mass-circulation, illustrated magazine such as *Quick,* which can so arrange the title page that on the bottom right, next to the picture of a half-naked woman, the title of an article appears— "The Power of the Jews"—an article that shamelessly distorts the so-called Jewish influence in the United States and hence the world. There you can read the usual anti-Semitic clichés, including: "Four million Jews—Jewish sources speak of six—perished." These, Mr. Glotz, are things that contribute to a corruption of historical consciousness. Here I'll restrain myself lest I find myself in the grotesque situation of making a connection between *Konkursbuch* or Botho Strauß and such vulgar political tendencies. That would be sheer nonsense. However, I must say that the current atmosphere in the Federal Republic is confusing. I regret that there appears to be no clearly defined movement opposed not only to those I mentioned but also to the so-called *Wende* [turnabout].[2] It is with some bitterness that I add: I'm afraid the intellectual left has failed thus far.

2. The term *Wende* derives from a 1983 Christian Democratic Union slogan promising a "moral and intellectual turnabout" in Germany under the administration of Helmut Kohl.

12

Against Postmodernism

INTERVIEW WITH EMILIO GALLI ZUGARO

Zugaro: Professor Lowenthal, you spent three months in Berlin as a fellow of the Wissenschaftskolleg [Institute for Advanced Studies]. Did you pursue a defined research project during this period?

Lowenthal: "Research project" is perhaps too large a word. What currently interests me are certain literary, philosophical, intellectual currents condensed in the not entirely transparent word "postmodernism." Since my interests have always been in literature and the sociology of literature, I wanted to study the extent to which deconstructionist theory, which is very influential in the United States today, has made inroads in the Federal Republic as well. I wanted to draw parallels.

Zugaro: Do these tendencies exist in Germany, too?

Lowenthal: To my surprise I found that this particular approach to literary texts is almost unknown in the Federal Republic; in any case, it hasn't had any resonance. Rather, I found a different kind of critical stance toward modernity, one that is spreading. Although it is much less interesting theoretically than what is tak-

This unpublished interview, conducted in Berlin in May 1985, was translated by Benjamin Gregg.

ing place in literary theory in the United States, politically, morally, culturally, it may be even more significant—if only in a negative sense. As an intellectual from the Critical Theory tradition, as someone interested in problems that do not come up arbitrarily within institutionalized scholarship but that possess a topical, directly relevant meaning, this discovery was something of a godsend, so to speak. I began to study this movement—if it is one—in written works as well as through conversations with its proponents and opponents. I didn't arrive at any final conclusions, of course—the time was too short for that. But if I live long enough I'll try to write something on this.

Zugaro: Did I understand you to mean that these currents, although they have no solid theoretical foundation in Germany, are nonetheless influential politically?

Lowenthal: I don't think they're politically influential at this time; in fact, I think they're completely impotent politically. I'm of the opinion, however, that these tendencies—which to some extent are reflected in journals and which correspond to similar movements in architecture, film, and theater—could potentially exercise a direct or indirect political influence. Of course, that's not at all the case right now, but we've learned to be vigilant.

To get to the point: the spread of irrational and neomythological concepts, or "nonconcepts"—this thoughtless and irresponsible choice of thoroughly arbitrary topics that are not rooted in any rational and moral tradition—is something I think deserves attention.

Zugaro: What kind of statements are you referring to specifically?

Lowenthal: The statement that the age of enlightenment has come to an end, that we're in the age of *post-histoire*. I can't imagine what that's supposed to mean; history continues with every new day! Sometimes you have the feeling that this new irrationalism has completely lost all faculty for common sense, that the concepts of history, progress, autonomous art—which, perhaps, have become untenable—no longer have *any* meaning at all. People are satisfied with a loosely conceived concept of "subjectivity," where whatever happens to be going through your head at the moment is considered meaningful. People write about and discuss—if they discuss at all—controversial topics such as terror, horror, deterioration, passion, intimacy, and God knows what else without committing themselves to any position at all. I sometimes describe this manner of writing, which is found in such journals as *Konkursbuch* and *Tumult,* as a trite version of *écriture automatique.* The difference is, the surrealists tied it to a very definite—I'd almost say moral, if not revolutionary—concept, whereas this contemporary orientation is fundamentally apolitical and wants to be.

Zugaro: In the 1930s you caused an uproar with a study on Knut Hamsun. At that time you maintained that in Hamsun, nature represents a flight from any kind of socially critical position. Could one say that there are art movements today that, for the same reason, seek refuge in themselves without recourse to psychoanalysis or to any historical, critical position?

Lowenthal: I think that's a very important topic. What you say is quite correct. This so-called postmodernity is a pseudo-philosophical orientation that would base itself—I think without justification—on Nietzsche, who was much more a moralist than an immoralist. It sees itself connected to or having points in common with the literature of new interiority.

This cult of the purely subjective—and it really doesn't matter whether it's a cult of the hedonistic or of the tragic, since neither one has any connection to the social—feeds orgiastically on the raptures, ecstasies, derangements, or ensnarements of pure subjectivity. You referred to Hamsun, probably because you know I predicted fifty years ago that he was a fascist, at a time when no one was willing to believe it. I certainly don't want to make such claims about the personalities involved in postmodernism, who, as persons, are quite harmless. That would be downright absurd. But I am concerned that certain tones are being heard again. For me it's a kind of *déjà vu* phenomenon, as if the *bohème* of the first half of the twentieth century was forming itself anew. Of course, some of their representatives, in their irrational, pseudo-romantic stance, have become harbingers of fascist or National Socialist ideologies. But it's certainly not true that we're living today in a situation where fascism is just around the corner. Nonetheless as a *gebranntes Kind* [literally: a "burned child"; i.e., once burned, twice shy]—please excuse the harsh metaphor—one has to be more alert than ever vis-à-vis movements that add yet another burden to an already diseased and, in the negative sense of the word, materialistic atmosphere. Perhaps I reveal an exaggerated self-confidence because, as a surviving representative of Critical Theory, I can go somewhat further back in time, and so by means of my historical conscious-ness I can call attention to a phenomenon deserving attention. Per-haps some of the representatives of this new irrationalism, this new mythology, could be persuaded to rethink their position, given the responsibility that a theory propagating irresponsibility must assume.

Zugaro: Could one say that the postmoderns filled a vacuum resulting from the transformation of Critical Theory into a culture industry after the student revolts, or, as you termed it, the "re-bellion of the sons"?

Lowenthal: That's a thoroughly legitimate hypothesis. I be-lieve such tendencies always arise where a vacuum occurs, espe-cially a political vacuum. It's the third time in this century, after all. First came the period when people realized that the dreams of bour-geois moralism simply cannot be realized. Here you have the reac-tionary schools of France in the first decades of the twentieth cen-tury, you have the mythological tendencies à la Moeller van den Bruck and others, and you have parts of the youth movement—

these all became established in Germany before and immediately after World War I.

Then you find a second period: the deep disappointment, especially among the younger motivated intellectual circles in Germany—the insight that the Soviet Union most certainly can't be the avant-garde of revolutionary social change. It was a time of sobering up. This took place in Germany much earlier than, for example, in the United States, where it was twenty years before people finally realized what was what. In this situation of disappointment in the revolution, new and exceedingly nihilistic movements started to spread again. Or else something quite unique developed: a stance, as represented by Critical Theory, that insisted that the whole problem of social change and of the intellectual's perspective had to be completely rethought.

Now we're so to speak in the third phase. This can be substantiated with historical details, for I believe that many of the movements we're discussing are directly or indirectly connected with the collapse of the student movement in the sixties and early seventies. Here, too, the imagination once existed to forge a new political will, an alliance of the so-called proletariat (which no longer existed in the strict sense) and the intellectuals, the students. But after the complete internal and external psychological collapse of this idea, there arose a colossal need for the vacuum to be filled. Since other credible tools and ideologies were not available, a large part of the intelligentsia slowly sank into this irrational and mythological behavior, into this dangerous swamp.

Of course, one shouldn't moralize. These aren't evil people. But in my opinion they're victims of a desperate situation in which the impatience, the expectation that something has to happen—even if that means that nothing at all should happen—overwhelms the rationally advisable attitude of waiting, of critical thought.

Zugaro: You think, then, there's no hope at all?

Lowenthal: Here I would agree with Walter Benjamin, whose words at the end of his analysis of Goethe's *Elective Affinities* have been quoted a thousand times, namely, that we're given hope solely for the sake of those who are without hope. This is the source of my irritation, not to say my obstinacy, regarding these postmodernist movements. You simply cannot abandon the critical thoughtfulness of a nay-sayer if you want to remain a yea-sayer. As a human being, you don't have the right to teach almost systematically that the end of humanity in history has already occurred and that human energies capable of changing what Georg Lukács calls the "infamy of the status quo" can no longer be developed. As Ernst Bloch would say, you must remain true to this "utopian spark"; the situation may well call for sorrow, melancholy, and doubt, but never despair.

Zugaro: During this time in Berlin, what was your impression about the Germans' relationship to their past? I'm referring to the period of Reagan's latest visit [in 1985], when these topics were raised once again.

Lowenthal: First of all, I'm not so sure that you can observe things better at the scene itself than from a distance. My situation was privileged only insofar as more press information was available to me than would have been possible in the United States. I was quite shocked by everything that took place in connection with May 8 [the fortieth anniversary of the official end of World War II]. But it wouldn't be honest to say that it completely surprised me. It was merely further documentation of the fact that the Germans, at least in the Federal Republic, want to finish with their history by subjugating and raping it rather than confronting it. I am tempted to say that they practice *post-histoire* by saying: "We've heard enough of that," or: "We'll simply leap over these twelve years." At the same time, things come to light again, things that have not been repressed, I think, but simply swept under the carpet. I mean these very suggestive anti-Semitic voices and sentiments, which were expressed particularly in the press.

Zugaro: Which newspapers are you referring to?

Lowenthal: All the way up to the *Frankfurter Allgemeine Zeitung,* not to mention such mass publications as *Quick.* They demonstrated to me that no process of genuine moral rehabilitation took place following the National Socialist period. On the contrary, these voices still contribute to a covering-up, and thus they terrify the wounded. Reagan's visit to Germany and the scene at the military cemetery resulted from conniving manipulations by governments and media. The irony is that Reagan, who himself makes superb use of the media for the purpose of political manipulation, was the one taken in. In essence, he became the one manipulated, and he in turn was unable to manipulate public opinion in his own country—this was confirmed by large portions of the American public, not only Jews, but also, for instance, most conservative senators.

Zugaro: Professor Lowenthal, thank you for this interview.

Index

Abendroth, Wolfgang, 39, 41
Ackermann, Nathan, 136
Addison, Joseph, 127
Adler, Mortimer, 72
Adorno, Gretel, 207, 211, 212, 218
Adorno, Theodor W., 4–5, 9, 11, 25, 46n.8, 58, 69, 72, 75, 81, 124, 125, 129, 139, 140, 156, 224, 240, 244, 245, 253, 254; on art, 121, 123, 128, 168, 171, 186–87, 196–97, 252; and Benjamin, 67, 68, 183–84, 204, 206, 218–19; on Critical Theory, 215; on cult of personality, 188, 189; on culture industry, 185–88, 189, 195–96; and emigration from Germany, 204, 208; and Flaschenpost metaphor, 63, 66, 148, 210n.4, 237, 241; on Hegel's system, 184; and Kracauer, 184, 203, 204, 205, 206, 207; on Lowenthal's study of popular biography, 188, 214–15; and postwar Germany, 2, 189–90, 195, 212–14; on progress, 242; on Schönberg, 210–11; on Sibelius, 72–73, 130, 185; as specialist in music, 71, 72, 120, 183, 192, 197–98, 208, 210–11; on Wagner, 167, 183
—Works: "Culture and Administration," 194; "Culture Industry Reconsidered," 193, 195–96; *Dialectic of Enlightenment,* 77, 109, 183, 185, 186, 195, 208, 211, 252–53; "The Fetish-Character in Music and the Regression of Hearing," 122; "Fragments on Richard Wagner," 183; *Introduction to the Sociology of Music,* 197; "Reflections from Damaged Life," 190. See also *Authoritarian Personality, The*
Advisory Board for Jewish Refugees from Eastern Europe (Beratungsstelle für Ostjüdische Flüchtlinge), 20, 22–23, 203
Africa, U.S. policy toward, 91, 92
Alcan Press (Paris), 56, 57, 74
Alternative, 68
American Jewish Committee, 89, 135, 137
American Jewish Labor Committee, 82
American Journal of Sociology, 135
Americans for Democratic Action, 158
Anti-Semitism, 78, 102–3, 185, 186; in America, 30–31, 32, 89, 97–98, 136; in Eastern Europe, 22; in Germany, 27–29, 30, 31–32, 45, 259–60, 267; history of, 32; and stereotypes of Jews, 23, 32–33, 37, 102; studies